THE RICHARD & JUDY
BOOK CLUB READER

To my book group: Ann, Cherilyn, Jenny,
Margaret, Pauline, Sue, Sylvia – H.C.

To Scotty Ramone, with love and gratitude
for your role as informal research assistant – J.R.

The Richard & Judy Book Club Reader
Popular Texts and the Practices of Reading

JENNI RAMONE
Newman University College, UK

and

HELEN COUSINS
Newman University College, UK

ASHGATE

Published by
Ashgate Publishing Limited
Wey Court East
Union Road
Farnham
Surrey, GU9 7PT
England

Ashgate Publishing Company
Suite 420
101 Cherry Street
Burlington
VT 05401-4405
USA

www.ashgate.com

British Library Cataloguing in Publication Data
The Richard & Judy book club reader: popular texts and the practices of reading.
  1. Book clubs (Discussion groups) – Great Britain. 2. Richardandjudybookclub.com.
  3. Books and reading – Great Britain. 4. Madeley, Richard, 1957– – Books and reading.
  5. Finnigan, Judy, 1948– – Books and reading. 6. Booksellers and bookselling – Great
  Britain. 7. Best sellers – Great Britain. I. Ramone, Jenni. II. Cousins, Helen.
  070.5'0941-dc22

Library of Congress Cataloging-in-Publication Data
  The Richard & Judy book club reader: popular texts and the practices of reading / edited
      by Jenni Ramone and Helen Cousins.
      p. cm.
  Includes bibliographical references and index.
  ISBN 978-1-4094-0133-9 (alk. paper)
  1. Book clubs (Discussion groups)—Great Britain. 2.Richardandjudybookclub.com
3. Books and reading—Great Britain. 4. Madeley, Richard, 1957– —Books and reading.
5. Finnigan, Judy, 1948– —Books and reading. 6. Booksellers and bookselling—Great
Britain. 7. Best sellers—Great Britain. I. Ramone, Jenni. II. Cousins, Helen. III. Title:
Richard and Judy book club reader.
  LC6656.G7R53 2011
  070.50941—dc23

2011014975

ISBN: 9781409401339 (hbk)
ISBN: 9781409438137 (ebk)

Printed and bound in Great Britain by the
MPG Books Group, UK

Contents

Part 3   After The Richard & Judy Book Club

Notes on Contributors

Helen Cousins completed her PhD on African women's writing and gendered violence at the University of Birmingham in 2001. Her current research focuses on Black identity in literature of the African diaspora in Britain, and the definitions of Black literature through a study of genre and the popular postcolonial. Collaborative projects include work on African literature online and exploring popular reading practices online. Helen has been a Senior Lecturer in English at Newman University College, Birmingham since 1996.

Beth Driscoll is a freelance writer and researcher at the University of Melbourne. Her doctoral thesis investigates aspects of the contemporary literary economy. As well as publishing widely in print and online news and opinion media, Beth has published articles on book clubs, prize lists and bestsellers, including a recent article for *Popular Narrative Media* titled "How Oprah's Book Club reinvented the woman reader," and "The Politics of Prizes" for *Meanjin*, 2009.

Danielle Fuller is Director, Regional Centre for Canadian Studies, and Senior Lecturer in the Department of American and Canadian Studies at the University of Birmingham. She has published research on various aspects of American and Canadian literary cultures and cultural production, and is committed to investigations that combine textual and empirical methodologies. Her book, *Writing the Everyday: Women's Textual Communities in Atlantic Canada* (2004) won the Gabrielle Roy Prize (English-language) in 2005. Danielle is on the editorial board of *Studies in Canadian Literature* and *Essays on Canadian Writing*. She is currently the Director of the AHRC-funded Beyond the Book research project, and serves on the Board of Directors for the Birmingham Book Festival. She has made over 20 presentations on Beyond the Book research to date, including plenary and keynote lectures to both academic and non-academic audiences in Finland, Canada and the UK, as well as running workshops for public librarians and graduate students.

Jenny Hartley is Professor of English Literature at Roehampton University. She is the author of *The Reading Groups Book*, published by Oxford University Press in 2001 and subsequently reprinted. This is the only full-length survey of reading groups in the UK. Her most recent book, *Charles Dickens and the House of Fallen Women*, is published by Methuen.

Alex Kendall is Associate Dean for Research and Business Development at Birmingham City University. Her research and writing focus on reading and identity in relation to young people's literacy practices, literacy in post-compulsory education and issues related to professional identity. She is co-editor of *Insights from Research and Practice: A Handbook for Literacy, ESOL and Numeracy Teachers*.

Julian McDougall is Reader in Media and Education at Newman University College, Birmingham. He is the author of *The Media Teacher's Book* (Hodder), *Studying Videogames* (Auteur) and a range of Media Studies student textbooks. His research into media literacy, media education and young people's engagement with multiple reading practices is published in a range of journals.

Nickianne Moody is head of Media and Cultural Studies at Liverpool John Moores University. She also acts as the convenor for the Association for Research in Popular Fictions and edits *Popular Narrative Media* both of which exist to promote the study of popular fiction. Relevant publications include editing *Gendering Library History* (2000), *Spanish Popular Fiction* (2004) and *Judging a Book by Its Cover* (2007).

Kerry Myler is currently completing PhD research at the University of Southampton on Psychics and Psychotics: The Matter of the Body in Doris Lessing and R.D. Laing. Some of her recent conference papers have addressed Constructing Intelligible Bodies in Lessing and Laing, Mary Barnes's Journey into the Womb of the World and The Sexual Politics of Madness: Women's Bodies and Anti-Psychiatry in David Reed's *Anna* and R. D. Laing's *The Politics of Experience*.

Lorna Piatti-Farnell is a Senior Lecturer in English at Auckland University of Technology. Her research interests focus mainly on critical readings of Twentieth and Twenty-first Century literature and culture. She specializes in culinary scholarship and has published on several areas of literary studies, including food and horror fantasies in American Cold War poetry, sugar politics in American literature, gender issues in contemporary comics, food and domestic politics in Postcolonial writing and food, gender and monstrosity in American literature. Lorna is currently working on her first monograph, entitled *Food and Culture in Contemporary American Fiction* (Routledge), which focuses on literary negotiations of food, eating, class, ethnicity, gender and memory. Other research interests include Gothic literature, film studies and graphic novels.

Jenni Ramone is a Senior Lecturer in English at Newman University College, Birmingham, having worked at Newman since completing her PhD on Salman Rushdie and translation at Loughborough University in 2007. She is the author of *Postcolonial Theories* (Palgrave Macmillan). Her research interests include South Asian and Middle-Eastern postcolonial and diaspora literature, postcolonial life-writing, and recent work includes reading the literature of Beirut in the context of the city's hosting of the World Book Capital City event in 2009.

DeNel Rehberg Sedo is an Associate Professor in the Department of Public Relations and within the Cultural Studies program at Mount Saint Vincent University (Halifax, Canada). A communications scholar by training, she is the Co-Director of the interdisciplinary collaborative project, Beyond the Book: Mass

Reading Events and Contemporary Cultures of Reading in the UK, USA and Canada. DeNel's published and on-going research includes work on contemporary women's book groups, on-line reading communities and pedagogy within Second Life. DeNel is editor of and a multiple contributor to *From Salons to Cyberspace: Readings of Reading Communities*, which is undergoing final revisions for University of Toronto Press. She has presented Beyond the Book research on more than 15 occasions in the past 3 years, including plenary and keynote invitations to speak in Mexico and Canada to both scholars and practitioners.

Acknowledgements

With thanks to Andrew Smith for his time and his enthusiasm for the project. With thanks to Andrew Martin, photographer, and to Claire Dyer, model, for helping to create a beautiful book cover.

Introduction:
On Readers and Reading

Jenni Ramone and Helen Cousins

The Richard & Judy Book Club only lasted for four years (2004–2008) in its most recognizable format as a 10-minute segment on the couple's Channel 4 show, and then for a further year as an extended program on a less popular cable television channel. But in that short time, the club instigated much debate in the media as well as in libraries and bookshops across the UK; now those debates are taking a firmer place in academia, in relation to literature, culture, media, and education. The Richard & Judy Book Club phenomenon launched face to face reading groups all over the country as well as fostering a more transient online book club community. It dominated the work of public libraries, particularly at the announcement of each new list, requiring libraries to stock multiple copies of the books, all placed on short loan with a strict no-renewal policy in many libraries in an effort to meet demand. Frenzied borrowers rushed to complete reading the whole list, and then eagerly shared their views on the merits and shortcomings of the selection. In the media, more was made of the club's impact on book sales and the authors' careers, though, as the interview article forming Chapter 10 of this book shows, immediate fame and fortune was not a given for the chosen authors. Not all of the selected texts were accessible genre fiction, and the club's more challenging selections gave the book club a greater level of complexity than some commentators liked to admit. The broadsheet press had much to say about the readers targeted by the Richard & Judy Book Club. The televised discussions were criticized for failing to challenge readers, or for assuming readers are stupid. Conversely, the club was castigated for promoting dross to readers deemed unable to discern the difference between these "reads" and "good writing."[1] As will become clear, our general position is that it is important to acknowledge the range and depth of the recommended books; the "reads" are an eclectic mix of literary fiction, non-fiction, genre fiction – the commonality they share seems merely that they are contemporary works. Because of this, the Richard & Judy Book Club does not only hold interest for research into book clubs, reading practices and pleasures, and the book trade. It is also of keen interest to those working in popular fictions, in online interactions and communities, and in media. Richard & Judy's

---

[1]   For example in Senay Boztas's article in The Observer, Sunday, August 17, 2008 entitled "Richard and Judy 'treat their readers as stupid'" while Janet Street-Porter's "Booker prize snobs have lost the plot" in The Independent (15 October 2008), which suggests that literary critics are out of touch with "real public" reading interests.

broadcast book club offers a compelling comparison with its predecessor, Oprah's Book Club, and with the various later incarnations, both official and unofficial, as the closing chapter of this book explores in more detail.

The Richard & Judy Book Club Reader engages with the book club as an element within a variety of communal reading practices, and as part of the literary economy. At the same time, it offers theorized readings of specific book club books to indicate the breadth of the selected texts and some of the questions they raise for literary and cultural studies. The essays in this collection situate this specific book club phenomenon within the contexts of publishing, reading practices, and popular fiction. While this particular book club will have a limited life span, and while Richard and Judy's personal presence as the public face of the club has been subject to change, the debates raised by their original broadcast book club continue to shape the publishing industry, the public's perception of reading and of talking about what they read, and the way that university departments debate popular, contemporary fiction, bestsellers, and prize books.

Richard Madeley and Judy Finnigan are recognized and experienced daytime television presenters known for their ordinariness, their willingness to represent the everyday, the average person, and had not until recently been associated with literature or publishing. In this familiar capacity, Richard and Judy launched their Book Club as a 10-minute slot on their teatime entertainment and chat show in January 2004, and with this began challenging the way that people in Britain, from the general reader to publishers to the literati, thought about books and reading. Initially, the Richard & Judy Book Club discussed 10 books, short-listed from a much longer list of what have been called "breakthrough" novels, not necessarily first novels, but the first of the author's to be determinedly promoted or celebrated. This format quickly lent itself to variation, and as well as admitting biographies and other non-fiction on to the lists, a second reading list of Summer Reads was created, functioning very much along the lines of the initial book club, but catering specifically for holiday or summer reading, implying that these books should somehow reflect the feeling of holiday: they should be lighter, more exuberant, more emotional, and must in this way replicate the escapism of being far away from home in the summer.

Book clubs and reading groups are nothing new. Jenny Hartley in her book *Reading Groups* notes that: "Reading in groups has been around for as long as there has been reading. … The Romans did it, emigrants on board ship to Australia did it … in fifteenth-century France a group of women who gathered to spin during the long winter evenings took turns to read aloud to each other" (Hartley 2001, 1). In recent incarnations, reading groups rejected certain genres, such as crime, romance, and courtroom drama as too lightweight, and Hartley's research published in 2001 (before the Richard & Judy Book Club launched) suggests that bestseller lists and reading group choices don't cross over, a position that is well supported by her abundant data collated to compare reading group selections with bestsellers for concurrent periods. The Richard & Judy Book Club has changed this, of course, as, even excluding the Richard & Judy Book Club itself from the category into which a conventional book club might be placed, it is difficult to ignore the many new reading groups that have emerged in response to the Book Club's reading selections, and who meet to discuss those texts. Equally, there had been celebrity book clubs previously, such as Edwina Currie's book club hosted at Nightingale House, a Jewish residential home for the elderly (Hartley 2001, 32), and broadcast book clubs like the Radio 4 Bookclub program hosted by James Naughtie, which operated as a prestigious yet largely traditional reading group concept, where "the author usually attends, fielding questions, comments, and sometimes criticism from an audience of twenty-five, drawn from reading groups around the country" (Hartley 2001, 5). However, the Richard & Judy Book Club was the first televised book club in Britain and, of course, it took the original televised book club – Oprah's Book Club in America – as a guide.

It appears that one factor in the tremendous explosion of interest from Oprah's televised, celebrity-endorsed book club was a perception of it as a non-threatening and a democratic phenomenon: a factor summarized by a book shop owner, Linda Bubon, who claims that Winfrey "has made [reading] seem like something that you should really do without castigating you for not having done it in 10 years" (Rooney 2005, 119). And this was a sentiment shared by thousands: according to Rachel Jacobsohn, who runs a national information exchange service for book club members, "there are around 500,000 book clubs in America today, twice as many as in 1994. They have between five million and 10 million members. She attributes the growth to Winfrey" (Rooney 2005, 14–5). However, even though Winfrey was their natural model, Oprah's first book club differed from the Richard & Judy Book Club in many ways.

Winfrey has described her purpose in hosting the book club as a way to fulfill the wider mission of her show: to "uplift, enlighten, encourage and entertain," to "transform people's lives" by getting "people to take charge," and ultimately "to bring a happiness and a sense of fulfillment into every home" (Rooney 2005, 13, 137). This isn't something that the readers can do on their own with the books – they require Winfrey's guidance to lead their reading. For Kathleen Rooney, whose work on Oprah's Book Club provides an interesting dialogue with this one on Richard and Judy's, Winfrey is: "an intellectual force" who is, "like any good intellectual ... a demonstrably intelligent, erudite, and well-spoken person" (Rooney 2005, 13). Control of the book club is her own: "Winfrey's literary taste ... is, by all appearances, fairly autonomous: she does her best to be a thoughtful, discriminating, and independent selector of literature" (Rooney 2005, 20). Discussing Eckhart Tolle's *A New Earth*, for example, Winfrey sets herself up as this kind of expert reader, reassuring her audience that the book is "the best in its genre" that she has ever read, and claiming that it has the power to "change your life" so that you'll "stop wasting time" and "focus on your Being ... on Earth."[2] Not only is she an authority over the books she selects, and which she

---

[2]   This discussion is recorded immediately after an Oprah show and is held on Oprah's official YouTube channel at the following location: www.youtube.com/oprah (accessed 6 October 2008).

places convincingly in the context of her wider reading, but she also performs the role of mediator between the authors of those texts and her audience: Winfrey explains that she interviews some of her chosen authors for a radio program (in addition to the interviews on television) where she is free to pursue more obscure – or literary – conversation and to engage with more quirky individuals than a television audience could "handle," like Eckhart Tolle who she claims would be "too much for TV." So she assumes a more sophisticated and practiced literary presence than both her studio audience and the television audience.

Conversely, Richard and Judy's engagement with the texts means that they perform the role of book club facilitators more than leaders, and in the main they defer their opinions of the book under discussion in order to allow their invited guests to talk about the books in detail. Richard and Judy become participants in what Naughtie (in relation to his radio book discussions) describes as "a readers' conversation" (Hartley 2001, 5) rather than gatekeepers to the literary texts. This makes for a many-voiced response to each book, allowing multiple reviewers to reinforce or debate the book's value. Unlike Winfrey, who chooses books that she is passionate about from her own voracious reading, Richard and Judy are actually "front men for the Amanda lists" (Appleyard 2008); that is Amanda Ross, MD of Cactus TV, who relaunched the Richard & Judy Show on Channel 4 with great success. The book club was her idea and she is responsible for making the final choices of books for the Book Club lists, a role that she continues to perform in the new TV Book Club launched in 2010, which has emerged to replace the Richard & Judy Book Club. She is not a part of Richard and Judy's new book club, a more commercial and wholly online operation, sponsored by high street stationer and bookseller WHSmith and Galaxy chocolate. The process used by Amanda Ross is a far cry from Winfrey's personal endorsements. Ross allows publishers to submit up to six books to be considered for the lists: "with a small team, Ross reads at least a couple of chapters and the synopsis of every book to get down to a shortlist … it is all down to her. She makes the final choice" (Appleyard 2008). Winfrey's discussion is implicitly underscored by her own position, which is recommendation enough for her audience. However, it appears from book sales that even Madeley and Finnigan's reading of and enthusiasm for the books is sufficient, supporting many of Hartley's survey respondents who claimed that a celebrity endorsement was the initial encouragement needed to begin a reading group (Hartley 2001, 42, 62).

Winfrey shows an ability to work across the popular and the literary spheres, but this has led to criticism that she doesn't do enough to bring the text to the audience. Kathleen Rooney claims that, as an intellectual in the unique position of being able to discuss literature with her audience, she could have done much more:

> Winfrey sadly underestimated her audience's ability and willingness to comprehend and to engage in discourse about the significance of their participation in such a revolutionary club, resorting more often than not to what amounted to little more than Reading is Fundamental – And Fun!–style sloganeering. This in turn was tied to Winfrey's tendency to underestimate her audience's ability to appreciate intelligent discussion of [Oprah's Book Club]-

selected books themselves, and to resort instead to the imposition of various competing narratives – including those of her show, herself, and her readers – upon the novels. (Rooney 2005, 22)

But even Richard and Judy, positioned as more general readers in line with their audience, have been attacked for the very same omission: Andrew O'Hagan, speaking at the Edinburgh International Book Festival accused the book club of being:

> a wasted opportunity ... [it has] a massive captive audience of people who aren't completely undiscerning; they aren't stupid. Why are they treating them as if they are stupid? There is an opportunity to use that connection to turn a generation on to good writing. (Boztas 2008)

The debates generated by that phrase "good writing" are outlined below – here, we want to consider what might be the "proper work" of Richard and Judy's (and Oprah's) Book Club. It is apparent through the format of the book club slot on Richard & Judy's show, that readers' responses are very personal. The invited guests discuss how the issues in the books link to their own experiences and explore their emotional responses to the text. To illustrate this, we can consider in detail the discussion of one of the 2006 Summer Read choices, Dorothy Koomson's *My Best Friend's Girl*, broadcast on July 26, 2006, which epitomizes non-competitive, non-academic, encouraging book talk.

Before introducing the celebrity who will present the book in more detail, Madeley confesses that though this is a novel firmly in the category "chick-lit," he enjoyed it so much that he cried, and this is a position that he and many other reviewers repeat throughout the Book Club slot, strong emotion being a necessary factor in selecting a good Summer Read to take on holiday. After a general endorsement of the book, a film is presented of the celebrity guest, Donna Air, an actress and presenter, talking about the book while on an Italian holiday; the plot summary is gradually delivered amid idealized holiday images: boats and cocktails, cliffs and harbors, sea and sunshine. While viewers watch Donna Air shopping in the market, walking through picturesque streets, and relaxing in cafes, she is all the time pausing to read the book; reading the novel is figured as the ideal activity for a holiday and not a distraction from it. By idealizing the notion of reading on holiday, reluctant readers are encouraged to take a book with them, and seasoned beach readers are persuaded that this is the selection for them. Air's presentation is predominantly a summary of the book's plot. She describes a woman struggling to come to terms with her new guardianship of her best friend's daughter, after the death of her best friend. The little girl had been born after the best friend's adulterous affair with the heroine's ex-partner. Air claims that she identified with the book because she is a mother herself, and that the book made her laugh and made her cry while she watched the character grow.

Following on from the video review, the Book Club moves to the studio where further invited celebrities – actress Sian Reeves and presenter Lowri Turner – discuss the book with occasional prompts from Richard and Judy. Both of these celebrities focus on comparing their own personal experiences with the book's subject matter, something that Hartley has observed is a key feature of a number of traditional (non-televised, or, non-celebrity) reading groups, though certainly not a consistent feature, because there are as many groups who avoid reducing the text to a general reference to their own life as there are groups who function primarily to build a sense of personal community around the books that they discuss by sharing their own experiences. Hartley found that some groups do digress from the text under discussion, and "where groups 'digress' to can be anywhere between 'the very personal and the wildly universal'. For some, the personal is what they come for" (Hartley 2001, 90). The sense of community and a free and open space for sharing opinion and experience, which often defines the book club discussion, is sometimes countered by more rigorous rules and codes about what can and cannot be discussed, including rules stating that "we never mention domestic circumstances," that "mention of children's activities [is] banned, now extended to grandchildren," and some clubs have a more general "no-gossip rule" (Hartley 2001, 91). A further level of review of *My Best Friend's Girl* is presented in the form of a group of women on a yoga holiday. This group is the equivalent of an audience, but they form a carefully chosen group. Each of these readers provides a brief comment in reaction to the novel, and most of the readers describe the ability to identify with the character, the emotional involvement, and the book's appropriateness for holiday reading, being an easy read, a "real page-turner." Again, after the more objective atmosphere of the studio, these final reviewers are seen among cacti and flowers and evocative scenery, and they discuss the book while wearing swimsuits to reinforce the notion that the book complements the holiday experience.

As well as being considered ideal holiday reading, the novel is praised for its potential for adaptation to TV drama or film, a likely response from those involved in television, perhaps. But it is possible that it is all part of the televised book club process that brings the reading experience and television together. Readers might well enjoy engaging with these narratives through textual and visual mediums that maintain the practice of sharing that is characteristic of book club reading; and of course, a television series or drama can generate further income and create greater awareness of both the book club and its authors among the general public. Reviewers note this novel's generosity towards male characters, and they insist that because of this it isn't a novel with a specific or restricted audience: Madeley affirms that even though he doesn't normally read "chick-lit," the novel doesn't have an exclusively female audience, noting that like him, Winston Churchill was famously a "blubberer." He notes that it is a strength, not just of the book, but of their book club, that he has found and enjoyed this novel, thus restating a common purpose of reading groups: to find and enjoy books that you might never otherwise have read. He concludes the discussion by responding to the final comment that the ideal reader is a single girl on holiday looking for beach reading with a reaffirmation of the wide potential audience for the novel: "or," he says, "a fifty-year-old man who cries easily."

It is precisely the over-emphasis on reading the novel through the personal that has led many to criticize Oprah's Book Club:

> Winfrey's use of television encourages the imposition of competing narratives – specifically the life stories of her audience members and her own mythologized biography – on the narratives of the books themselves, thereby running the risk of applying texts capable of multiple interpretations and uses to a single-minded, socially controlled, and largely therapeutic end. (Rooney 2005, xiii)

This criticism, which applies equally to the Richard & Judy Book Club, misses the point that what happens on the television is not the act of reading itself: readers might not see book club reviewers engaging critically with the texts, but they do more than listen to such "competing narratives" when they read the books themselves. It is also worth noting that implicitly, even in the Richard & Judy reviews, experience is separated from reading: none of the holiday reviews – neither Donna Air's review nor the further report from the group of women on a yoga holiday – actually include the family that makes this book relevant to the reviewers' experiences. All of the women are pictured alone or with other adult women on holiday, as if, although the context of parenthood is valuable to fully emotionally engage with the novel, it's just as important that this engagement is produced away from the family and not surrounded by it.

In the studio, Lowri Turner and Sian Reeves discuss in detail their own clear parallels with the kinds of choices faced by the character in the novel who has died and had to appoint a friend as her child's guardian: one of the guests discusses provision made in her own will to determine that her friends will perform these duties while the other speaker notes that she was consciously aware that her friends couldn't have performed this role if she needed them to when she had her first child, because of their immaturity. The kind of adoption of the book performed by these readers is what Michel de Certeau has called "poaching," where the reader "invests in texts something different from what [their authors] 'intended' … [the reader] combines their fragments and creates something un-known" (de Certeau 1984, 169–70). Yet, when the discussion strays too far from the book (to observations that the child in the book is better behaved than the participants' real children, for example), Richard and Judy are on hand to turn back to the book itself, reminding the others that the child's good behavior was dependent on the plot, and then moving on to place the text in its literary genre: "chick-lit."

Genre is a key feature of the discussion: perhaps because Madeley opens the book club with a reference to the book as an example of "unashamed" chick-lit, the guests build on this definition, and in praising the book, describe it as an example of chick-lit at its best, not "just" chick-lit, but chick-lit at its height, and even perhaps a text that is going beyond the glamour and tension of the standard contemporary romance to "branch into other genres," as Lowri Turner suggests, by dealing with more "grown-up" issues and deeper questions of identity, though the discussion doesn't conclude which other genres this novel might reach. Richard and Judy are well aware of the genre of this text, and of their own engagement with the genre. This is evident in the way that reviewers' reports on the novel take place on location, mid-holiday: the Summer Read is as much a part of the holiday experience as the cocktail, the pool, or the beach view. Whether the Richard & Judy Book Club cannily latched on to the popular holiday activity of reading by the pool, or influenced a whole new group of holidaymakers to take a book with them is more difficult to deduce. In effect, the Richard & Judy Book Club is promoting literature in a different way to suggest that many of the novels offer more depth than the fiction ordinarily placed in that genre, making the choices more appropriate for their "discerning" readers. This separates them from Oprah's Book Club: where Richard and Judy mediate the discussion of their choices through a negotiation of popular genre categories, Winfrey locates her choices predominantly within a "middle-brow" category relabeled as "accessible literary fiction" by Marty Asher, editor in chief at Vintage books (Rooney 2005, 16).

It is unclear at present whether Richard & Judy's Book Club has created more readers or only shifted the reading choices and practices of current readers, but what is apparent is the club's profound effect on book sales. The Book Club discussion of *My Best Friend's Girl* begins with Madeley's brief introduction, not so much to the book, but to the purpose of discussing the book at all: only the fourth book to be reviewed this particular summer, Madeley claims that the three previous summer titles were so popular that they were jostling for the number one bestselling slot, adding: "the publishing world has never seen anything like it." He insists, though, this is acclaim that is "richly deserved" by the authors, and not simply an effect of advertising. Elizabeth Long describes how, likewise, "Oprah's Book Club selections skyrocketed to the top of the bestseller list, generating hundreds of thousands of dollars for their publishers, giving fiction a new cultural clout, and bringing stardom to even obscure literary novelists" (Long, in Farr 2005, ix). The publisher of Toni Morrison's *Song of Solomon* had released 360,000 copies of the book between its release in 1987 and October 1996 when the book was discussed on Oprah's Book Club: at this point, correctly anticipating a jump in sales, the publishers immediately printed 730,000 new copies, and Barnes & Noble sold 16,070 copies the day the book was discussed on the program. Thus, "Winfrey provided a bigger boost for Morrison's commercial clout than the 1993 Nobel Prize for Literature" (Gray, cited in Rooney 2005, 123). In the bestseller lists for the UK in 2006 and 2007, five Richard and Judy recommended reads appear in the top 20 titles; in 2006 *Labyrinth* was listed second with 865,402 sales and in 2007 *The Interpretation of Murder* with 797,081 sales was only outperformed by the final installment of the Harry Potter series. Yet Richard and Judy's and Oprah's Book Clubs have been both justified and demonized on the basis of their book sales. The popularity of the books meant that they were considered outside the interest of academics, or serious readers of literature. Richard Madeley's comments regarding their book club selections' quality *and* popularity offer the briefest of engagements with the debate between consumer and academic reading.

Recent studies in reading and publishing suggest that it is naïve to maintain a rigid distinction between popularity and quality, or to assume that such factors have only very recently impacted on reading; Ross, McKechnie, and Rothbauer insist that "the book industry has developed sales strategies that work by focusing readers' attention on a select number of books: the best-seller list, the prize book, the book club" (2006, 189). Oprah's Book Club choices range from "pleasure reading" to "capital-L-Literature" (Farr 2005, 12). The first to discuss serious literature through the medium of television, the Oprah Book Club was, for Rooney, "a crucible for the heated clash between high and low literary taste" (Rooney 2005, 2). Though many with serious literary tastes avoided Oprah's Book Club and the novels selected (and this it seems is also true of the Richard & Judy Book Club), this was based more on the attitude of those readers to bestselling books than on the quality of the texts themselves: as Oprah critic Cecilia Konchar Farr has suggested: "I think we have moved beyond the opposing ridiculous point, that popularity ... inevitably breeds mediocrity" (Farr 2005, 93). This is something that is increasingly of interest to literary studies as much as it is of interest to publishers and librarians, because some bestselling books go on to achieve "canonical status" when they are placed on "college syllabi" (Ross, McKechnie, and Rothbauer 2006, 190). Sometimes this is in the context of studies in popular literature, but increasingly, the boundaries are blurring between the conventional categories of low-, middle-, and high-brow literature, to the extent that such categorization becomes redundant, where celebrity-endorsed, high-volume broadcast book clubs promote literary fiction, and books that have become bestsellers through such promotion and that would previously have been ignored in literary circles because of their genre or their emotive style and subject matter, are now read critically alongside canonical texts. As a result, as Rooney maintains, Oprah's Book Club "with its sometimes surprising heterogeneity and eclecticism – stands to prove that there exists a far greater fluidity among the traditional categories of artistic classification than may initially meet the eye; that we needn't shove every text we encounter into a prefabricated box labeled 'high,' 'low,' or 'middle'" (Rooney 2005, 5).

Richard & Judy endorsements have rarely included high-brow, literary texts but only a narrow perspective would dismiss their choices as genre fiction. O'Hagan's comment above claimed that the club could have been used to encourage people to read "good writing," which clearly implies that the lists exclude this. It is true that there is genre fiction and many of the books could be labeled "popular." However, also included, for example, have been Julian Barnes's *Arthur and George*, *This Book Will Save Your Life* by the feted American author, A.M. Homes, *Cloud Atlas* by David Mitchell, as well as demanding historical non-fiction such as *White Mughals* by William Dalrymple and *Perdita: The Life of Mary Robinson* by Paula Byrne, plus a swathe of what has been termed middle-brow fiction or accessible literary fiction. Journalist John Walsh, writing in *The Independent* about literature and the digital age describes the future of fiction:

> big on plot and incident, short on interior monologue – the sort of titles that the Richard & Judy Book Club strenuously promotes ... Can this, then, be the future of reading: an increasing number of low-brow, plot-driven works will flood the market, consigning works of literary merit to a watery grave. (Walsh 2008)

Using the Richard & Judy Book Club in this way as a short-hand for inferior fiction is clearly reductive. While they do not have the same agenda as Winfrey – who did want to engage her audience with more challenging literary texts, using the more low-brow titles as a way to entice readers in – the Richard & Judy Book Club does understand that its audience is discerning; they are willing and able to engage with a range of reading. In fact, unlike Winfrey, they include non-fiction such as travel writing, historical biography, and have even used the club to generate new writing through the show's "How to get published" competition, which offered a prize of a publishing contract with Pan Macmillan and an advance of £50,000 (this was won by Christine Aziz's novel *The Olive Readers* and also secured publishing contracts for the four runners-up).

In fact, the predominant feature of the books is often not that they are "plot-driven" but that they offer readers opportunities to engage emotionally with social issues and this can be a way into the most literary of texts. Farr notes this as a valid and important additional way to read texts alongside more aesthetic practices (2005, 42), particularly for readers who are not (yet) trained in academic reading practices. The argument is that an interpretation based on personal response also and equally produces meaningful engagement; it can lead into consideration of the aesthetic effects of the text but this might possibly be viewed as a specialist response more appropriate to "professional" readers of literature. It is unhelpful to consider the Richard & Judy and Oprah Book Club discussions as inferior, or as only a precursor to "better" practices; rather, these interpretations can be seen as appropriate and equally as meaningful in the context of a book club where there is more emphasis on sharing the reading experience. Perhaps in encouraging personal and social responses to texts, these book clubs are recreating the meaning of middle-brow fiction, which becomes less of a category of books than a different way of engaging with all sorts of literature where reading has moved further into the social arena, and away from being a solitary activity. To validate this way of reading, it is important that the book club lends a kind of authority to the texts chosen and it is undeniable that the Richard & Judy Book Club does this even if this is not based on the hosts' claims to literary authority. Rather it seems that the volume of positive reviews presented in quick succession through the format of the TV slot lends this authority to the overall support for the novel: in the case of *My Best Friend's Girl*, if the first celebrity report hadn't convinced you, and the studio debate with further celebrities wasn't enough, then 10 "real" people should certainly secure a solid readership. And it is important that all of the books do attract a huge readership, or at least huge sales, to maintain the reputation of the book club and its presenters as recommenders of good (readable) books. Once the bestselling precedent is set, any book that does not achieve this status would cast doubt on the whole project.

It is important to note that neither Madeley nor Finnigan, nor indeed Ross, profit directly from the sales of the books. Farr notes that "Oprah has never had any financial stake in the sales of the books she chooses" (Farr 2005, 20) and similarly, Ross "keep[s] herself pure …[s]he doesn't make money out of the club"

(Appleyard 2008). However, Appleyard also makes the point that the celebrity reviewer of *The Conjuror's Bird*, Tony Robinson, unexpectedly "trashed" the book in the studio interview: "His negativity took Richard and Judy aback, and it seriously damaged sales" (Appleyard 2008). So, clearly, one aim of the Book Club is to promote and sell the books. It can be mentioned again that the Book Club section focused on *My Best Friend's Girl* opened with the statement that each of the previous selections had become bestsellers: the book club seems to need to justify its airtime by its sales, as much as it needs to justify (and sell) the book under discussion. The televised book club is just one factor in what some commentators have described as a vast commercialization of publishing and reading in general: Ross, McKechnie, and Rothbauer insist that

> we need to recognize that best-sellerdom takes place within a communications circuit that also includes authors, publishers, booksellers / libraries, and readers', and while some insist that the power to produce a bestseller is firmly in the hands of the reader, others claim that readers are 'powerless before the manipulations of commercial forces that have reshaped publishing, turning it from a gentleman's literary club to a business that treats books just like any other commodity.' (Ross, McKechnie, and Rothbauer 2006, 191)

Instead of demonizing the Richard & Judy Book Club because of its power to sell books, this volume seeks to address more specifically which books are promoted by Richard & Judy, and to consider the impact of such promotion of books and reading on reading habits, preferences, and on book talk.

Even very successful new authors like Paul Torday, whose *Salmon Fishing in the Yemen* was a bestseller in 2007, listed at position 86 for the year and selling over 160,000 copies, is marketed as "author of the Richard & Judy bestseller" when interviewed about his new book.[3] This marks one of the ways in which the Richard & Judy Book Club (perhaps even more than Oprah's Book Club, because of the relaxed and non-threatening format that they adopt) has displaced the conventional assumption that the reading group is "associated with coercion, snobbery, and the closed mind" (Hartley 2001, 137). This might have something to do with the kind of reader who makes their selections based on recommendations from daytime television, a reader very much like the "general reader" that Janice Radway observes is targeted by the Book-of-the-Month Club (Radway 1997, 10), a general reader that has been absent from reader-response theory, where "implied readers, intended readers, mock readers, narratees, competent readers,

---

[3] YouTube video, "Paul Torday, author of the Richard & Judy bestseller SALMON FISHING IN THE YEMEN talks about his new paperback THE IRRESISTIBLE INHERITANCE OF WILBERFORCE," available at http://uk.youtube.com/ watch?v=rmH4jN0v9L4 (accessed 6 October 2008). Bestsellers 2007 list in the Guardian, available at http://image.guardian.co.uk/sys-files/Guardian/documents/2007/12/28/lrv_16_ gdn_071229_01__.pdf (accessed 22 October 2008).

superreaders, and readers who are members of implied audiences or interpretive communities" dominate (Ross, McKechnie, and Rothbauer 2006, 50).

After Richard Madeley and Judy Finnigan left Channel 4, the Richard & Judy Book Club continued for a season on digital channel Watch, and it has in 2010 been replaced by The TV Book Club on More4, with a new group of hosts and a new format, which is discussed at length in the final chapter of this book. Then in winter 2010, Richard and Judy launched their separate, new, online-only Richard & Judy Book Club. Both this and the TV Book Club have had further opportunity to thrive due to their significant online presence: the online book club is potentially as multi-vocal and it is more far-reaching than a slot on a TV show could hope to be. Where reading groups belie the notion that reading is a solitary activity by putting into action what Hartley calls an "impulse to share" reading (2001, 2), the online book club bridges these two states: online, readers may interact and feel a part of a community, while they don't necessarily have to log on synchronously or to reveal too much about their identity, retaining some of that prized reading solitude. Here again, Winfrey came first, also having an online presence:

> On the Oprah web page (www.oprah.com), the dates of the Book Club shows were advertised weeks in advance, and an animated online discussion, often including live chats with the author, preceded and followed the shows. Readers who visited the site were invited to consider some in-depth discussion questions, posted as soon as the new book title was divulged, a practice that has since become common in publishing, as Reader's Guides with discussion questions for book groups are increasingly appended to many contemporary novels. (Farr 2005, 11)

As well as an online book club site that is connected with the broadcast show, there are many other forms of online book clubs, ranging from reviews and lists posted on Amazon, to sites like Bookcrossing.com, where the objective is to discuss and share books by leaving the books, labeled, for a new reader to find, so the individual copies of the books themselves have a life that is recorded on the site, and this can be either an international or a very local journey involving multiple readers who each post comments about the book if they choose to, as well as recording the dates at which they found the book, and released it for a new reader to find. Such book sharing has attracted criticism from publishers who have insisted that sharing books restricts book purchasing, signaling the commercialism integrated in new modes of reading including broadcast book clubs. It is interesting to note that, in a recent interview discussing the new TV Book Club, Ross spoke several times about safeguarding readers' £6.99, the average price of a paperback book included in the book club selection (*You and Yours* 2010), a reiteration of a comment made to Danielle Fuller, cited in the essay by Fuller and Sedo in this volume. In response, the organizers of the Not the TV Book Group, a group of book bloggers, make the explicit point that they will be "encourag[ing] people to borrow from libraries if they can" (Flood 2010).

The Bookcrossing organizers claim that the reviews, the online and public interaction, and the impulse to release books all encourage its members to purchase more books in general. However, many forms of book sharing, such as those encountered in libraries, have continued to play an important role as locations for mediating between recommendation and reading in Richard & Judy's Book Club as it has had in the lives of previous reading groups: "public libraries facilitate groups by ordering sets of books, providing venues, and perhaps a member of staff to coordinate (some have courses on how to set up a group)" (Hartley 2001, 9). In Leicestershire libraries, for example, multiple paperback copies of the books were displayed on specially designed racks and made available to borrowers for one week only. These books were constantly in use, and readers would demand to know when those they hadn't yet read would be returned, sometimes out of frustration vowing to buy the books when a waiting list for a particular title was particularly long, just so that they could complete all of Richard & Judy's summer selections before the end of the season. Other readers would try the books faithfully and then return them, expressing disappointment that they "never enjoyed" Richard & Judy's choices, a predicament that the wide variety of books chosen for the list surely intended to avoid.

Formerly, the Richard & Judy Book Club website held full lists of all books featured in the book club since it began in 2004, as well as full lists for the Summer Reads. All of these were available to buy if in stock. The site also included a book club in an online form where readers could discuss the books. In this way, the site functioned as an online alternative to the real world reading group, meaning that many more participants could read together at their own pace and with a less regulated sense of involvement. This was purged from an updated version of the site, perhaps because, inevitably, online forums attract off-topic discussion (and potentially, remarks that might discourage book sales). However, a number of interactive elements reminiscent of the reading group, or intended to be used by real world reading groups remained, such as a (moderated and edited) reader review process, and reading notes on all of the books still listed on the site, produced in attractive documents and including a summary of the text, a brief author autobiography, and a number of questions intended for use by reading groups. In recent years, reading notes or guides have often been produced for groups by librarians, publishers, and other mass reading groups. For her work on reading groups, Hartley gathered data on such guides and notes, and found that though "a few have experimented" with externally produced notes, the response from traditional book club members was often negative, and most groups refused to use them. Members prefer to provide their own "rich framework for their discussion through reference to other books, films, and social and political issues" (Hartley 2001, 99) rather than sticking closely to the text, which is what the tone of such guides invariably encourages, with questions like "What significance do you think 'The May Fly Story' (pages 165–167) holds for Mr Watts, and why?," or "Why does Matilda write Pip's name in the sand next to those of her relatives? How do you think this makes her mother feel?," in the Richard & Judy Book Club reading notes to Lloyd Jones's *Mister Pip*. Even though the prototype for such reading guides emerged from within reading groups, where "an early 'how to' literature sprang up, with publications like L.M. Griffiths's *Evenings with Shakspere [sic], a Handbook containing special help for Shakspere Societies dedicated to lady-members of the Clifton Shakspere Society*" (Hartley 2001, 49), the reluctance to use reading guides seems to be caused by the feeling that such restrictive discussion topics go against the spirit of the reading group, which is an independent group, distinct from the classroom or seminar room. This issue is taken up by Kendall and McDougall in Chapter 3, who argue that the reading lists replicate restrictive reading practices found in schools.

The Richard & Judy Book Club was part of a long-running Channel 4 daytime program that came to an end in August 2008. When they were preparing for their flagship part in the launch of a new TV channel Watch, with a show called Richard & Judy's New Position every weeknight at the more desirable hour of 8pm, Richard and Judy claimed that their very successful book club would continue despite the show where it was originally launched coming to an end. Their new program lasted for one season in 2009, and has in 2010 been replaced, somewhat seamlessly, with The TV Book Club (including a replacement of the website). It remains to be seen how the new book club will develop, and how far the formula can be replicated, reshaped, and reinvigorated in response to both viewer demand and the influence of the new hosting team. The Richard & Judy Book Club has played an important part in changing reading practices in the UK, but it has not achieved this singlehandedly. This book demonstrates the club's role in a global network of broadcast and digital reading groups. In particular, contributors make detailed comparisons between the Richard & Judy Book Club and Oprah's Book Club, the new TV Book Club, and to the extension of reading groups into new locations, including online spaces.

Chapter Summary

In the first section of this collection, The Richard & Judy Book Club Readers, contributors explore the changing book market, and the impact that changes in the way that books are sold has had on readers, and on the meaning of reading. This is connected with notions of reading as an elite activity but the chapters in this section also show how the Richard & Judy Book Club has been instrumental in questioning the divisions between what has been recognized as high and low culture. By considering the readers who both reject and embrace this method of marketing and recommendation, the section explores some of the different modes of interpretation – both traditional and established – and those newer models being developed by the rise of reading as a popular leisure activity.

In Chapter 1, Danielle Fuller and DeNel Rehberg Sedo start by considering how commercialization within the field of print media has often been met with a suspicion that reading experiences within that paradigm cannot be properly pleasurable, insightful, or independent. Through their research with focus groups (as part of their Beyond the Book project) they discuss the misgivings of the traditional reading classes about new reading phenomena such as the Richard &

Judy Book Club, which appear to challenge their views about reading and good taste. An interview with Amanda Ross (who devised the Richard & Judy Book Club and selected the books for each series) and an analysis of the format of this section of the Richard and Judy magazine show are used to explore the disruption of such elitist notions of reading, including the use of the husband-and-wife team of Richard Madeley and Judy Finnigan as ordinary readers, the inclusion of celebrity discussants in the studio, and the profiling of authors who provide a context for the books being discussed. Fuller and Sedo suggest that the Richard & Judy Book Club has promoted a non-elitist model of reading but that, further, it has been instrumental in blurring the boundaries of what might be considered high and low culture.

Nickianne Moody, in Chapter 2, looks more closely at the effects of the Richard & Judy Book Club (and other book promotions such as The Big Read) on the book industry. She suggests that despite the potential of such marketing tools to generate large book sales, these initiatives have also encouraged supermarkets to sell books, who can access the recommending power of "the sticker" to sell heavily discounted books. Moody explores elitist notions of reading, which mark adult reading experiences as having to be intellectual, as opposed to childhood reading, which is described by adults as more affective and often more pleasurable. By analyzing the comments on the Richard & Judy Book Club website forum, she identifies the valued aspects for readers of the books recommended by this club: the notion of "truth" or realism; the focus on characterization; and the importance of learning or personal development through reading.

The distinction between adult and childhood reading is also explored in Chapter 3 by Alex Kendall and Julian McDougall. Taking as a starting point those models of reading and literacy developed as part of the English of the school curriculum as opposed to the literacies associated with Media 2.0, this chapter draws on research carried out with young people about their attitudes to reading. By considering the recommended reading questions that usually accompany Richard & Judy Book Club reads, and paying particular attention to *A Thousand Splendid Suns*, Kendall and McDougall suggest that they replicate a model of interpretation still embedded in a school-type understanding of literature. It is interesting to note that Fuller and Sedo in their chapter suggest that reading groups tend not to use such questions: Kendall and McDougall's chapter might go some way to explain why this might be.

In Chapter 4, Jenny Hartley provides an insight into how the texts have been received by prison reading groups. Hartley runs a reading group in a women's prison, and another in a men's prison, where *The Time Traveller's Wife* was chosen as the top read. Hartley discusses the importance of the location of a reading experience identifying the themes of this book with the situation of those reading it.

Part 2, Reading the Richard & Judy Book Club Selections, offers readings of the books themselves. The chapters in this section focus on a selection of books from the Richard & Judy Book Club lists. This collection cannot hope to address all of the titles discussed by the Richard & Judy Book Club, but it does offer an indication of the kinds of scholarship that can be based on the books themselves.

The chapters here go some way towards showing the range of books on the lists, while offering specific theoretical readings of different categories of books.

In Chapter 5, Kerry Myler shifts attention to the author, noting that for the purposes of the television book club, the author cannot be dead (as Roland Barthes famously declared) but must be alive, present, and visible to promote and discuss their work. The chapter explores why an embodied author (and the return to authorial authority) is so necessary to the type of reading promoted by the Richard & Judy Book Club. Through a study of Lori Lansens's *The Girls*, which is narrated by conjoined twins, she explores how that imperfect body is mediated by the appropriately feminine and able body of the author. In addition, she considers the impact of sharing a body on the narrative voice, which cannot claim to be a single "I" in this circumstance.

Beth Driscoll continues with a consideration of the feminine and of the domestic theme in Chapter 6. She suggests that the Richard & Judy Book Club stages a mode of reading associated with women and with middle-brow literary culture. Her chapter examines the presentation and discussion of Dorothy Koomson's *My Best Friend's Girl* and Lori Lansens's *The Girls* showing how the producers, hosts, authors, and guest reviewers privilege emotion, personal connection to characters, social issues, and domesticity. While such ways of reading have historically been disparaged as feminine and middle brow, Driscoll suggests that the Richard & Judy Book Club's deployment of mass media and consequent cultural and commercial impact unsettle this subordinate positioning.

Jenni Ramone's Chapter 7 considers how the Richard & Judy Book Club has reinstated and reconfigured the storyteller figure in society. She discusses the notion of retelling in relation to academic (and less apparently academic) interpretations of literature. She suggests that the storyteller figure remains in the marginal space of storytelling cafés, but also emerges more robustly as a figure in the digital space represented by the Richard & Judy Book Club. She considers Karen Joy Fowler's *The Jane Austen Book Club* and its retelling of Austen's novels and Austen the author, to consider why a book that seems so perfectly suited to a reading group (a book about a reading group) was received negatively by readers on the Richard & Judy Book Club website forum.

In Chapter 8, Helen Cousins looks at two of the postcolonial novels that appeared on the Richard & Judy Book Club lists: *Half of a Yellow Sun* by Chimamanda Ngozie Adichie and Khalid Hosseini's *A Thousand Splendid Suns*. By also considering readers' forum comments, and the reception of another Richard and Judy recommendation, *The Bookseller of Kabul* by Anse Seierstad, she notices the importance of authenticity of authorship for readers who, as also suggested in Nickianne Moody's chapter, value some of these books as educative and informative. Cousins considers how the "postcolonial exotic" operates in relation to this notion of authenticity, which is expressed in terms of the novels' characters and settings as distinctly other to an English experience.

The final chapter of this section (Chapter 9) considers the role of food books in the Richard & Judy Book Club by paying particular attention to one of the non-fiction selections, the autobiographical food book *Toast* by Nigel Slater. Lorna Piatti-Farnell looks at issues of cultural identity, memory, and interpersonal relationships through the concepts of recipes, food products, and branding, noting that "food books" have become very popular in the last 15 years. She specifically explores how Slater's childhood is evoked through his memories of food, its smell as well as its taste, and its relation to culture and community.

Part 3, After The Richard & Judy Book Club, comprises an interview article with Andrew Smith whose *Moondust* was chosen for the Book Club in 2006, and a chapter on the new TV Book Club, which replaced the Richard & Judy Book Club. Chapter 10 offers a reading of *Moondust*, one of the few non-fiction titles selected by the book club. This reading extends Smith's discussion of his experience of being one of the Richard & Judy Book Club authors, how he feels it has impacted on the reception of his book, and his career as well as talking in detail about the process of researching and writing a book like *Moondust*. Chapter 11 suggests that The TV Book Club is essentially a continuation of the Richard & Judy Book Club but it also explores the differences in the format of this program: The TV Book Club is a distinct program, whereas previously Richard and Judy hosted the book club as a small segment of their show, and the new program is hosted by a larger, permanent group of celebrities. The chapter considers a range of reactions to the new book club, including Amanda Ross's description of the new format, and considers the books included in the new series, such as Sarah Waters's *The Little Stranger*, the first of the new book club's selections.

Reference List

Appleyard, Bryan. 2008. How the Richard & Judy Book Club has shaken publishing. *The Times*. 15 June, http://entertainment.timesonline.co.uk/tol/arts_and_entertainment/books/article4120189.ece (accessed 29 October 2008).

Bestsellers 2007 List. 2007. *The Guardian*. 28 December, http://image.guardian.co.uk/sys-files/Guardian/documents/2007/12/28/lrv_16_gdn_071229_01__.pdf (accessed 22 October 2008).

Boztas, Senay. 2008. Richard and Judy 'treat their readers as stupid'. *The Guardian*. 17 August, http://www.guardian.co.uk/books/2008/aug/17/edinburghbookfestival.fiction?gusrc=rss&feed=books (accessed 29 October 2008).

Certeau, Michel de. 1984. *The Practice of Everyday Life*. Trans. Steven Rendall. Berkeley: University of California Press.

Farr, Cecilia Konchar. 2005. *Reading Oprah: How Oprah's Book Club Changed the Way America Reads*. Albany: State University of New York Press.

Flood, Alison. 2010. Forget Richard and Judy, join the Not the TV Book club. *The Guardian Books Blog*, 5 February, http://www.guardian.co.uk/books/booksblog/2010/feb/05/richard-judy-not-tv-book-club (accessed 5 March 2010).

Hartley, Jenny. 2001. *Reading Groups*. Oxford: Oxford University Press.

Radway, Janice. 1997. A Feeling for Books: The Book-of-the-Month Club, Literary Taste, and Middle-Class Desire. Chapel Hill: University of North Carolina Press.

Richard & Judy Book Club. 2008. http://www.richardandjudybookclub.co.uk (accessed 29 October 2008).

Rooney, Kathleen. 2005. *Reading with Oprah: The Book Club that Changed America*. Fayetteville: The University of Arkansas Press.

Ross, Catherine Sheldrick, Lynne McKechnie, and Paulette M. Rothbauer. 2006. *Reading Matters: What the Research Reveals about Reading, Libraries, and Community*. Westport, Connecticut: Libraries Unlimited.

Torday, Paul, author of the Richard & Judy bestseller SALMON FISHING IN THE YEMEN talks about his new paperback THE IRRESISTIBLE INHERITANCE OF WILBERFORCE. 2008. http://uk.youtube.com/watch?v=rmH4jN0v9L4 (accessed 6 October 2008).

Walsh, John. 2008. Can intelligent literature survive in the digital age? *The Independent*. 14 September, http://www.independent.co.uk/arts-entertainment/ books/features/books-special-can-intelligent-literature-survive-in-the-digital-age-926545.html (accessed 29 October 2008).

You and Yours. 2010. BBC Radio 4, 17 February.

PART 1
The Richard & Judy
Book Club Readers

Chapter 1
Suspicious Minds:
Richard & Judy's Book Club and Its
Resistant Readers

Danielle Fuller and DeNel Rehberg Sedo

It is a lifestyle show, but these books oversell a reduced, unimaginative notion of what people's literary enjoyment might be.

—Andrew O'Hagan quoted in Boztas 2008)

They're not very deep in what they say about [the books], are they? I think it's sort of a bit surface, 'this is fabulous, you must go out and read it, and here's our celebrity who really, really liked it too, so if you like them then you must enjoy it'.

—Lauren, Focus Group participant, Birmingham 2007

Dismissal, condescension and suspicion are not responses that were widely represented within British media coverage of the Richard & Judy Book Club. If anything, journalists appeared to be in a state of jaw-dropping awe of their brand power and its capacity to make bestsellers of every title selected for either the general book club lists or the Summer Reads. However, as O'Hagan's telling remarks indicate, any notion of blatant commercialization is suspect for those who associate book reading with the liberal humanist notion of a free, unfettered imagination. Combine the hard-sell with the unquestionably popular genre of the daytime magazine show, and you inevitably promote a limited version of reading pleasure, lacking in reflection and literary sophistication – so the logic of O'Hagan's comments would seem to suggest. Made in the context of the high-profile and high-culture environment of the Edinburgh Book Festival, O'Hagan's response to Richard & Judy's Book Club also speaks to the media hierarchies that still structure dominant notions about cultural consumption and taste in Britain. Within this hierarchy, watching television is below reading, going to the cinema, a play or a concert, and "lifestyle" television is a low-brow genre bereft of intellectual content.

In fact, book reading is not popular when compared with the time that British people spend pursuing other leisure activities (Bennett et al. 2009, 95), but the reading of books still carries with it considerable prestige. Readers of books also constitute a niche audience, but they have disproportionate spending power. Various studies demonstrate that an intensification of the market for books took place in the late twentieth century, so that although more books were being produced than ever before, they were being read by fewer people (Finkelstein and McCleery 2005, 127). This "reading class," as cultural sociologist Wendy Griswold has nominated those with sufficient education, income and cultural capital to engage with wider book cultures (festivals, author readings, building a personal library, belonging to book groups), is not a majority group within either the USA nor the UK (2008). But they do possess cultural and economic power and, as Lauren's comment quoted above suggests, they are deeply invested in, and often tenacious and defensive about, their own interpretative practices of book reading. Into this arena of literary-cultural consumption came the Richard & Judy Book Club bringing with it, courtesy of its hosts Richard Madeley and Judy Finnigan, cheery enthusiasm and a touch of celebrity glitz, along with a slate of marketing partnerships. As we explore below, it was a wildly successful combination in financial and televisual terms, but the process and products of its success aroused the suspicion of many committed readers.

In this essay we argue that the Richard & Judy Book Club threatened readers' ideological investment in reading as a "high culture" activity. We begin with a consideration of the Book Club's actual and intended audience on- and off-screen, drawing upon our own empirical investigations with readers, some of whom participated in the Club, and others who did not.[1] We then interrogate readers' articulations of resistance to the Richard & Judy Book Club. In the third section, we turn to the content and format of the 2007 edition. Our analysis demonstrates how the television show successfully used a number of strategies that disrupted elitist notions of reading and who can be a reader. By examining the messages that the Book Club intentionally and implicitly constructed about books, reading and readers, in relation to the perceptions and attitudes held by actual readers about the show, we move towards an understanding of how the Richard & Judy Book Club phenomenon provoked a decidedly twenty-first-century version of the dance of distinction.

In Search of the Book Club's Audience

Amanda Ross, the joint managing director of Cactus TV, was the initiator of the Book Club. Her company produced Richard & Judy for eight years, a period that included the entire tenure of the televised Book Club (2004–2009). In an interview in June 2006, Ross spoke about the popularity of the Book Club segment:

---

[1]   Our study of Richard & Judy's Book Club forms part of a wider investigation into contemporary cultures of reading, more specifically into shared reading as a social practice (www.beyondthebookproject.org). We are interested in why people come together to share reading, especially through large-scale public reading events that mimic aspects of book groups through the selection of one or more books. Our primary research for "Beyond the Book" was funded by AHRC grant no. 112166. Other key team members were Dr Anouk Lang (Postdoctoral Research Fellow) and Anna Burrells (Administrative Assistant).

Fuller: Do your ratings alter at all when you've got the Book Club or the Summer Read…?

Ross: Yes they do … that segment of the show's always the highest rated of the show. It does go up, it's incredible. In year two we experimented with moving it around to different parts of the show, to see if the audience followed, and they did.

By contrast, only 16 per cent of the 1,549 respondents in our survey of UK readers actually watched the Book Club on television. At first sight, this statistic appears nonsensical when considered in relation to audience ratings for the show, which, during its heyday on the UK's terrestrial Channel 4, regularly garnered 1.5 million viewers and was sometimes viewed by nearly three million people according to media reports (Jeffries 2009; Tivnan 2008). More accurately, the low frequency of television viewers for the Richard & Judy Book Club within our study suggests that the majority of readers who participated in our online questionnaire during January and February 2007 were not the target demographic for the show.

Ross was hesitant about articulating the actual constitution of Richard & Judy's audience to us, indicating perhaps, that she was anxious not to under-estimate the potential reach of the show, but also suggesting that she took pride in what she termed as Richard & Judy's "inclusive," "broad appeal":

Fuller: What actually is your audience demographic?

Ross: That's a very good question. We have no idea!

Fuller: Really?

Ross: It changes all the time. I'm told it's 46 percent ABC1, so we are the most intelligent daytime show, supposedly. We have a lot of students watching us, and we have a lot of people over 55 watching us, we have a lot of mums in between, it really is something for everyone.

Fuller: And that's a big range actually isn't it?

Ross: It is. And it's very – yeah, it's very challenging. And when I think of our 55-year-old-plus audience, I don't think of them as people who're gonna be interested in Stena Stairlifts, I think of them as people who think that they're Mick Jagger. They're sort of young at heart and will try things, and are very adventurous. (Fuller 2006)

Notable here is Ross's lively characterization of the older sector of the audience, the generation born during the Second World War, who became adults in the 1960s and are now retirement age. If this was a key age group for the show, the information that the majority of the audience is "ABC1," suggests that the audience was rather more heterogeneous in class terms. "ABC1" is often used by market researchers and statisticians to refer to a "middle class" demographic but, rather ambiguously, combines upper- (A), middle-(B), and lower-middle, white-collar workers (C1).

What Ross did not say was that the show was watched primarily by women. Yet the magazine format of the television show, which positions it within the genre of lifestyle broadcasting, suggests that it was aimed at female viewers (Bell and Hollows 2005, 9–14). The content of the afternoon television program, however, did not necessarily adhere rigidly to topics that might be deemed interesting only to women. The eclectic features could range from strife in the Middle East, to a case of stolen undergarments showing up in public places, with an interview with a famous actor sandwiched in-between (Richard & Judy 2007a). The Book Club segment always occurred during the Wednesday broadcast of Richard & Judy, the day particularly associated by UK television industry insiders with "lifestyle" programming aimed primarily at female viewers (Vernall 2007). Audiences can also be inferred to some extent from the types of products promoted during the advertisement breaks (Meehan 2002). During the 2007 Winter series of the Book Club, cleaning solutions, prepared foods and nappies, were among the products frequently featured, implying that many of the viewers were likely to be home-makers or part-time workers with young children. In twenty-first-century Britain, these roles are still predominantly undertaken by women (Office for National Statistics 2009). The scheduling of the series, on weekdays between 5pm and 6pm, on the cusp of afternoon and evening programming, also meant that many potential viewers of both sexes under the age of 65 would still be at work or commuting during the live broadcasts – an inference that was confirmed by many participants in our Richard & Judy focus groups.

In sum, the on-screen Book Club may have been framed through the genre and schedule positioning of Richard & Judy as primarily "for women," but, as we argue in the last section of this essay, considerable effort was made by the producers and by the hosts themselves to recode the segment as gender neutral. An important incentive for doing so was the commercial and cultural power of the hosts' brand, and the extension of their audience into other media. As our own research demonstrates, viewers of the televised Book Club and/or watchers of Richard & Judy's regular show, do not account for or necessarily coincide with the wider off-screen users of the Book Club.

The profile of our self-declared Book Club participants differs in terms of gender and age distribution from the expected demographic for the television show, or, at least, from the producer's understanding of who was watching it. Among our questionnaire respondents who identified as participants of the Book Club (81 per cent), the overwhelming majority were female (90 per cent) and just over a third of them (34 per cent) were aged 45–64. Only 12 per cent of respondents were in the 18–24 age range (the student demographic) and a mere 1 per cent aged 65 or over (the age group most likely to contain a high proportion of retired people) defined themselves as participants, that is, as a viewer of the Book Club, or reader of the selected titles, or visitor to the Book Club's website or online forum. In other words, our questionnaire reached readers who were not directly aligned with the television audience for the Book Club but who were nevertheless familiar with it via other media. Since we used judgment, or convenience, sampling to recruit participants for this survey, advertising through our social and professional networks and Google advertising, not all readers in the UK had equal access to our questionnaire. Our data thus suggest or indicate conclusions about reading habits and attitudes to popular culture, rather than providing definitive statistical evidence of them and we cannot generalize our findings to apply to all readers in the UK.

Among the Richard & Judy participants who responded to our online survey, visiting the website and reading the selected titles were the top two activities (21 and 24 per cent, respectively). This result suggests that readers were using the Book Club brand, or more pragmatically, the stickers, clearly signposted in many high street bookstores and public libraries through posters and book bins, as a recognizable, trusted and reliable "badge" to help them select books to read. As Viv, a 63-year-old retired teacher and participant in one of our focus groups, commented,

> I was told about [Richard & Judy's Book Club] by a friend and I thought 'what a good idea'. I've never managed to watch it very often, because of the time it is and maybe not wanting to watch it enough to record it, … having said that, when I go into Waterstone's I look for the Richard & Judy recommendations and I've read *Arthur and George*, which I thoroughly enjoyed, … So, yes I'm aware of it but haven't seen the programme very much, but am always aware of the books. (FG Participants, 30 January 2007, Birmingham)[2]

As we have argued elsewhere, some readers used the Book Club area of the Richard & Judy show's website in a similar fashion to Viv's bookstore practice, that is, as a resource to assist them in their selection of books to read (Rehberg Sedo 2008). Among the readers in our questionnaire who identified as visitors to the Book Club website, for example, 49 per cent selected "to learn about the books" as their main aim. Significantly, Ross's model for the Book Club was influenced not only by her own identity as an enthusiastic and committed reader, "I've always been really passionate about books myself," she told us, but also by her experience of feeling disoriented by the overwhelming choice on offer in large bookstores and online:

> We've taken the hard work out of choosing books for people in that, when you get to the end of that book, hopefully you won't come up to me and say 'I've wasted my £6.99,' that you'll see that there was something in it for you, and there was a point for us saying, 'You might as well read that book,' because, some of the genres, I find it difficult as well, in that I wouldn't naturally choose that [Robbie Williams's autobiography] if I was just choosing for myself or just going into a book shop, I wouldn't naturally pick up that book and say, 'Oh I'm going to read that.' (Fuller 2006)

---

[2]   In this essay we use the following format to label our focus groups: FG = focus group; "participants" or "non-participants" indicates whether the group consisted of those who did or did not participate in the Book Club; date on which the focus group took place; location. First names of respondents and selected demographic details are used with the participants' permission, but in some cases details have been edited to prevent identification. Eight focus groups focusing on "Richard & Judy's Book Club" were undertaken in Birmingham, UK, but the Book Club was also discussed within focus groups held in other UK locations as part of our wider investigations into mass reading events and contemporary reading cultures.

Ross's commentary demonstrates an awareness of the time and money pressures influencing the reader's selection practices, as well as individual genre preferences. She also implicitly articulates here her position as a powerful player in the field of "symbolic creativity" (Hesmondhalgh 2007, 5). While Ross is not a primary producer of a cultural product in the same sense as a writer or visual artist, she is, nevertheless, an image-maker working in the most symbolically influential of the culture industries – the media (Couldry 2003; Hesmondhalgh and Baker 2008, 102). Moreover, she is also an agent within the re-configured literary-cultural field of twenty-first-century English-language book publishing, a field within which, as David Wright has demonstrated, television has adopted some of the roles of cultural production and literary consecration that Bourdieu originally accorded to editors, publishers and professional literary reviewers (Wright 2007). As the producer of a successful daytime TV show, Ross had the skills, agency, authority – and the staff – to influence not only which books and authors would benefit from their exposure to a huge audience of potential readers, but also the messages that the show would construct and disseminate about those particular books, and, thus, about the meanings of reading more generally. Employing her economic, cultural and symbolic capital, Ross was a taste-maker as well as a money-maker for book publishers whose marketing budgets could never buy the type of exposure that the Book Club represented.

In fact, Ross became something of a celebrity within the UK print media precisely because she was responsible for a show, a brand and a series of canny marketing partnerships that produced a British equivalent to "the Oprah Effect" (Striphas 2009, 211–2; Wu 2008, 76). In early 2009, the British bookseller industry publication *The Bookseller.com* reported that the "value" of Richard & Judy's Book was "more than a quarter of a billion pounds. Since its launch, 100 books have been selected, with 30.3 million copies sold for a total value of £180.4m. If the books were sold at full price, the value would be £255.6m" (Allen 2009). But commercial success, measured in terms of staggering book sales, was not the sole reason why Ross was repeatedly described as the "Most Powerful Woman in Publishing" (Langley 2007) and featured in both the business and culture sections of broadsheet newspapers (McQueen 2006; Wagner 2006). Her colleagues in the media industries were also keenly aware of the symbolic power she wielded as the creator of the Book Club. One media commentator went as far as to declare that, "Amanda Ross has created a revolution in the nation's reading habits, democratising the world of books so that readers with non-literary backgrounds can enjoy literature without feeling intimidated" (Farndale 2007). However, as we shall see, this was not a revolution desired by readers who were already heavily invested in the cultural capital that has traditionally adhered to book reading in Britain.

Suspicious Minds: The Resisting Readers

Why did many committed readers spurn Richard & Judy's Book Club? According to several readers in our eight Birmingham-based focus groups, it was because the Book Club epitomized the unsophisticated tenor of popular daytime television.

For them, the book talk on the show was rudimentary, uncritical and undeveloped. Even readers who praised the "accessibility" of the Book Club book talk, often contrasted it to other shows on TV and radio, such as BBC 2's Late Night Review, which, as Wendy, a 60-year-old retiree told us, "tend to go into things very deeply and talk about sub-plots...more of a criticism of the writing" (FG Participants, 31 March 2007, Birmingham). Among readers who were more overtly resistant to the celebratory style of the Book Club discussions, there were clear signs that the show did not meet their needs as critical readers accustomed to sharing their opinions about books. Although they belong to different generations, Helen, a 43-year-old marketing executive, and Lauren, a 23-year-old sales and marketing assistant, reached agreement about this:

> Helen: It's all a bit gushing yeah, I mean, one of things I like about the book group I go to is that people will say 'this was a load of rubbish, I only got halfway through because of this, this, this' and it doesn't really tell you a lot, like you said about Richard, if he's just saying 'oh, it's a great book, I couldn't put it down.' I want to hear a bit more than that really.
> Lauren: I would agree. They're always full of praise for the book – I haven't seen much criticism ... rather than sort of honest opinions. Even if I've really enjoyed a book I can sometimes think oh, 'I didn't like that bit about it.' [FG non-participants, 23 January 2007, Birmingham]

Helen and Lauren, along with 32 per cent of our survey respondents, are experienced participants in sustained, collaborative interpretations of books within face-to-face or online groups where dissent is usual (e.g., Hartley 2001, Long 2003, Rehberg Sedo 2003).

As Sarah commented about book talk on UK radio and television more generally, "I think real-life conversations in which you're participating tend to be more interesting. Nobody swears or argues [on-air], it's not real, because people get very, very passionate talking about books in real life" (FG non-participants, 23 January 2007, Birmingham).

Clearly, the mediation of book talk through television is troublesome for many keen readers whether they wish to hear "deep" criticism about literary aesthetics, or "what the book's actually about" (Wendy). There is more at stake here, however, than readers' frustration with broadcast formats that demand fast-paced discussion and short segments, or an irritation at the mis-match between book group talk and its on-screen version. Lauren's dismissal of the Book Club's engagement with aspects of celebrity culture ("here's our celebrity ... if you like them you must enjoy it") offers an important insight into a process that many of the readers in our focus groups were either consciously or unconsciously involved in, namely, the dance of distinction. According to Bourdieu's classic formulation, taste "unites all those who are the product of similar conditions while distinguishing them from all others" (1984, 56). However, in twenty-first-century Britain, the popularization of cultural formations and practices that were once recognizably signifiers of "good taste," and, when associated with book reading, of an informed and educated mind, has complicated the process of distinction. As Jim Collins has argued, "good taste" or "how to get it" has become "a manifestation of consumer culture" but also "a complex phenomenon which complicates many of the basic assumptions about how 'taste,'" whether it be popular or elite, is recognized as such in contemporary cultures" (2002, 1).

The Book Club threatened readers' ideological investment in reading as a "high culture" activity, not only by making book reading seem accessible and attractive to those outside the "reading class" (Griswold 2008) and thus less of a "niche" pursuit, but also by blurring the markers of "good taste." As a "high-pop" cultural formation, it mixed elements of celebrity culture such as celebrity guest readers and Richard's & Judy's own profile as media personalities, with an eclectic selection of books, which included a handful of titles that had been nominated for prestigious prizes such as the Man Booker. As if to confuse those in search of "good taste" even further, this brow-blurring mix took place within a popular, daytime magazine format television show. Readers in our focus groups were often unsettled by this high-pop blend, and their anxiety about the commodification and popularization of book reading often emerged through their resistance to the branding and marketing of the Club. Several readers talked about "avoiding" the stickered books when visiting book shops and libraries, while others admitted that they were furtive and secretive about including Richard & Judy books within their reading. As Manjit, a reader in one of our Bristol focus groups tellingly expressed it, "I am ashamed to say I am a bit swayed by Richard & Judy, if their sticker is there." (17 February 2006). Meanwhile, another Bristol-based reader, Barry, suggested that even if a reader was intrigued by the books chosen for the Book Club, it was best not to admit it among fellow readers because,

> … it might cause you to be taken as less than you are if you follow them, because I think a lot of people, if Richard & Judy told you to read the telephone directory then you would. Not that you would, but you wouldn't want to be thought like that. You're not one of the lemmings or the sheep. (17 February 2006)

Barry's comment foregrounds a deft maneuver of distinction: by actually rejecting or appearing to reject the Richard & Judy selections, a reader can create the perception that they are independently minded, and do not need the guidance of the Book Club. This implicitly classed response was echoed by others participating in the dance of distinction around the Book Club and its book lists. Aware of the social etiquette that it is good manners not to reveal one's claims to cultural distinction too overtly (an etiquette "rule" that is, of course, culturally specific and coded within the normative behaviors of "middle class" British people, especially those who are "white" and "anglo-saxon"), a significant number of participants in focus groups from our different UK field sites employed qualifying phrases or mock self-deprecating remarks before offering an opinion about the Richard & Judy Book Club. These took various forms such as, "I know I'm going to seem like a snotty middle-class person now, but …" (FG participants, 31 March 2007, Birmingham), and "I'm not gonna be snobbish about them" (17 February 2007, Liverpool). These comments depend on a perceived link between class and taste in relation to the Book Club: demonstrating "snobbishness" (even while disavowing it) was a means for some of our focus group readers to simultaneously articulate their social status and "good" taste.

Our questionnaire data indicated that there were indeed significant relationships between class and participation in the Richard & Judy Book Club. When asked to select their class identification, 41 per cent of people participating in Richard & Judy's Book Club described themselves as working class, 38 per cent as middle class, 16 per cent as lower-middle and only 1 per cent perceived themselves to be upper class. There was also a significant positive relationship between participation and education, indicating that those who participated in the Book Club tended to be well-educated. However, our quantitative data actually confirm that Richard & Judy participants were less educated than other readers in our wider study, and that those who identified themselves as working- to middle- class were more likely to participate, while those who identified as upper class were less likely to participate in the Book Club.

Perhaps it was not so surprising then that the Club's book lists were the stumbling block of many a middle-class or aspirant middle-class reader. Sarah, in common with Barry who was quoted above, pinpointed the tricky nature of recognizing and establishing distinction within a literary-cultural field that has been complicated by the blatant commercialization and high-level visibility of the Book Club. She declared: "I'm not gonna be snobbish about them 'cos I think the fact that they picked *Cloud Atlas*, which was another great book, means that they have got some taste there in terms of what they're choosing" (17 February 2007, Liverpool). In addition to the store-front displays, first in Waterstone's bookstores and then in WHSmith's, and promotional posters and leaflets in public libraries, the sponsorship deal with Galaxy chocolate was also highly visible during advertisement breaks and its logo was reproduced on the back covers of some editions of featured books. Since the British media were consistently interested in how many books the show was helping to sell (Dugdale 2006; Farndale 2007; Hattersley 2006; Jeffries 2009; McCrum 2006), and a scandal about the "You Say, We Pay" phone-in quiz show feature in February 2007 brought both the hosts and Amanda Ross additional coverage, the general public was relatively well-informed about the show's production and its partnership deals. Within this cultural milieu, some readers believed (incorrectly as far as we have been able to surmise) that the producers were receiving money from book publishers and that this shaped the Book Club selections. Ann found that her suspicions about well-publicized book lists dissuaded her from reading some titles that interested her:

> I don't actually look for the Booker because I'm slightly suspicious of the prize stuff and I'm suspicious of Richard & Judy as well, I have to say. Let's be honest. I was tempted to read a couple of their books, but I think they may have another agenda. (FG Participants, 6 February 2007, Birmingham)

Disavowing Book Club selections may secure a reader's claim to good "literary" taste. Here, Ann seems to feel that commercialization has tainted the literary value of the lists.

Unlike many of our focus group participants, Ann was able to identify several Richard & Judy books. A number of readers expressed surprise when shown the selections for Winter and Summer 2006 and 2007. They had assumed that the lists focused on genre fiction or "chick lit" and had not expected to see some of their own "literary" choices, such as Julian Barnes's *Arthur and George* (especially popular among Birmingham readers because it is partly set in the city), Chimamanda Ngozi Adichie's *Half of a Yellow Sun* and William Boyd's *Restless*. A few readers were even noticeably upset, perhaps because their surprise about the Club lists revealed their own adherence to a hierarchy of genres, and thus to class-affiliated notions of literary taste. Janet, a middle-aged woman who belonged to a book group, was particularly bothered by Richard & Judy's sponsorship of Ngozi Adichie's novel, and felt that the book was "demeaned" by its popularization, "Because it's now got this great publicity thing behind it and I don't think it lets other authors have a fair crack of the whip." (FG participants, 31 March 2007). When her friend and fellow book club member Miriam asked, "But aren't you happy that through Richard & Judy they're introducing one of your favourite authors to other people?" Janet replied, "Well, I hope she won't be demeaned, I hope she won't be upset." Janet's shift from an apparent concern with the capacity of the show to produce a bestselling book at the expense of overlooking other work, to her imagination of the author's feelings about being featured on Richard & Judy's Book Club, suggests her anxiety about the disruption that the Club poses to her perception of the literary field. Her inference is that being selected for the Book Club is not a sign of aesthetic merit or literary value but of mass appeal.

Janet's assessment coincides with Bourdieu's original conceptualization of the literary field in which the autonomous work of art held high symbolic value but generated little economic return, unlike its mass-produced popular opposite (Bourdieu 1993). Yet, as we noted above, changes in the publishing industry have restructured the economics of book production and new players such as television producers and media production companies have become agents within the literary-cultural field. For readers such as Janet, the Book Club's hosts and producers were not agents of literary consecration whom they wished to recognize. However, even though our suspicious readers rejected the economic might and media machinery of Richard & Judy's Book Club, the Club's book choices left them feeling unsettled because the terms and terrain of distinction seemed to have altered. Below, we consider how the producers of the show used its medium and format to construct an entertaining piece of television that was capable of disrupting elite notions of literary taste by re-framing books as accessible to a majority of readers.

Producing the Book Club: Making New Meanings of Reading

Like all television shows in the UK, making Richard & Judy was a collaborative and creative affair for Cactus TV, involving a range of technically skilled professionals, junior researchers and office support staff. The production team for the Richard & Judy show typically numbered 70 people, and the Book Club segment was the most expensive and time-consuming feature to produce (Fuller 2006). It involved two VTs (video-taped location shoots) per book: one with the book's author and one with an actual book group somewhere in the UK whose brief opinions about the text would be edited into the last two minutes of the Book Club broadcast. Book publishers sent over 700 books to Ross for consideration for either the Winter or Summer Book Club. Each book was accompanied by a synopsis and sometimes additional material about the author such as press cuttings, which Ross, an anonymous book industry insider and two researchers used to determine which books they would read in part or in full. Through a series of selections involving several months of reading and discussion, the lists were reduced to 300 then 100 then 50 titles, at which point the selection team would, according to Ross, aim for a balance across the final 10 (Winter Book Club) or six (Summer Read) books. The criteria the selection team employed included involving "50 percent British authors" in each list, length of books ("I'm making the viewers read 10 books in a row so they can't all be as thick as *Labyrinth*"), gendered appeal ("you can't have too many that just appeal to women, not too many that just appeal to men,"), genre (always skewed towards fiction but often including one work of non-fiction), theme and content ("you can't have more than one book where the last chapter revolves around a dying dog"). To some extent Ross was also aiming to reproduce her own reading pleasures and tastes for the show's viewers: "the main thing I think about when I'm reading a book is, 'Do I want to keep turning the pages?', and "some books, you think, 'Oh yes I really enjoyed it, yes it was escapism, but actually, if I was going to have a conversation with my friend about it, what would I be saying?'" This concern with the "discussability" of a book resonates strongly with book group discourse about the types of texts that are suitable for shared reading (Long 2003, 22, 123; Rehberg Sedo 2004, 204; Taylor 2007, 26–31). Well aware of the popularity of book groups, Ross's experience as a reader was also mediated by her professional knowledge of entertainment television, which must engage and hold the viewer's attention without becoming too serious for too long. Thus, as she read potential Book Club books, she was considering whether or not they would suit the format of the show, in particular the in-studio book discussion between Richard, Judy and two guest celebrities: "What is the sofa chat going to be? Is there an issue in it, or is there something about it, … 'What are Richard and Judy gonna be talking about?'" (Fuller 2006).

Ross was also under some pressure from her commissioning editor at Channel 4 to make her idea of the Book Club work more effectively than previous British programs about books. In fact, it was the establishment of a relationship with the "Nibbies" (the Book Awards) as an event-based culmination for the Winter Book Club, combined with Ross's track record as the producer of several large-scale television specials (including award shows) that convinced Channel 4. Media exposure for the Awards, and the spectacle of the award ceremony itself would help to "sex up" (in Ross's words) the Book Club: "if a book is entertaining to read, it's going to make entertaining TV, and vice versa, so, that is the key – the key is to make sure the book's entertaining in the first place and then you're home and dry. It's gonna work" (Fuller 2006). It was this convergence of media (television, journalism, books) and the spectacle effect produced through marketing and the engagement with celebrity culture (Kellner 2003) that, as we noted above, caused some readers to be suspicious of the Book Club.

In a sense our skeptical readers were correct: on-screen, the Richard & Judy Book Club was very successful at making books less "special" and less distinct from other forms of leisure culture. Ross herself was aware of this, commenting that "book programming in the past has categorized people too much…. it's decided who its viewers are, and decided who would be interested in hearing about books, rather than thinking, 'This book could be interesting to anyone'"(Fuller 2006). In attempting to achieve this "universal appeal," the television show used a number of strategies that disrupted elitist notions of reading and who can be a reader. A key aspect of this process was the self-presentation of Richard Madeley and Judy Finnigan as "everyday, ordinary people" rather than "upper, or over-class people that are really up themselves," as Una, a participant in one of our Birmingham focus groups expressed it (FG participants, 31 March 2007). In other words, the appearance or performance of a non-threatening middle-class (white) identity was, at least for some viewers, an attractive aspect of the show. The relaxed and good-humored presentation style of Madeley and Finnigan, their joking familiarity with each other, and their media profile as both a husband-and-wife team and minor celebrities, played into this projected identity very effectively. Their light-hearted banter while sitting on a sofa in a set that resembled a living room represented their on-screen relationship as comfortably domestic. Their frequent addresses direct to camera enhanced the perception of intimacy between presenters and viewers, enabling the formation of para-social relationships, which are fundamental to the successful operation of contemporary day-time television talk shows as well as a long-standing feature of celebrity culture (Burnett and Beto 2000; Giles 2000, 2002, 2003; Greenwood and Long 2009; Rubin and McHugh 1987).

Additionally, Madeley and Finnigan represented themselves as "regular" readers rather than as professional reader-critics who possessed specialized knowledge of narrative strategies and literary aesthetics. While for some readers this was off-putting, "Let's face it, they're not literary geniuses are they?" commented Harvey (FG participants, 30 January 2007, Birmingham), for others it differentiated Richard & Judy's approach to book talk from other television book shows, as Una explained:

> they bring something to it so that there is no sort of middle class angst about it, it's there because it appeals to – if they can read it I can read it. Sometimes you get these programmes where they're professors or somebody and they're really very much, 'I thought this and I thought that,' and it's a turn-off. (FG participants, 31 March 2007, Birmingham)

Una's articulation of Madeley's and Finnigan's skill at modeling themselves as non-expert readers with whom a viewer like herself can identify, again underlines the show's deft handling of the dance of distinction and the producers' sense of its audience: readers like Harvey will look elsewhere for the guidance of "literary geniuses," the Book Club was about making reading accessible, fun and entertaining for less culturally confident viewers.

In order to construct these messages about reading, the show employed the medium of television and the genre of the magazine show with its mix of serious and light-hearted items, and its short feature segment format to good effect. Each Book Club segment began with Richard or Judy introducing the book and its author. In less than three minutes, the host typically provided a personal judgment of the book, which set the tone for the upcoming discussion. In introducing the 2007 edition of the Book Club, Richard Madeley opened the first Wednesday afternoon show with a trailer statement, declaring Jed Rubenfeld's *The Interpretation of Murder* to be a "sexy, gripping murder mystery" (Richard & Judy 2007a). Not only did this comment whet the viewer's appetite for the Book Club segment coming up in the second half of the program, but it also coincided appropriately with Madeley's on-screen role as the energetic, sometimes over-exuberant member of the host partnership, who occasionally pushed at the limits of pre-watershed live television by making risqué jokes and using double-entendres. Enthusiastic personal response and endorsement was, however, employed by both presenters. "One of my favourite authors," Madeley claimed as he introduced William Boyd's novel in a later show (Richard & Judy 2007c), while about *Half of a Yellow Sun* he enthused, "It's everything that a good book should be; exquisitely written, easy to read, utterly absorbing and profoundly moving" (Richard & Judy 2007d). Meanwhile, Judy introduced *The Girls* as "one of the most wonderful books I have ever read" (Richard & Judy 2007b). Whether the selection was framed in terms of its engagement with popular book genres – *Restless* was described as "an historical spy novel," for example – or trumpeted as a prize-winner or critically acclaimed text (as in the case of Ngozi Adichie's book), all the selections for 2007 were introduced in this upbeat manner as worthwhile stories and thus trustworthy reads.

After these endorsements, the Book Club segment formula continued with audio-visual strategies that connected viewers more directly to the book's content and its author. Playing into a notion of the celebrity writer whose domestic and personal life secures the value or meaning of their written work, viewers would be taken, via the author film, to the author's home, workplace or homeland. In a four- to seven-minute personal account of the book's characters, setting, or plot, which usually included a nod to the author's writing process, the featured writer had the opportunity to create relationships with readers and, perhaps most importantly for the inclusive appeal of the Book Club, with viewers who had not yet read their book. Wendy, a middle-aged reader who enjoyed watching the Book Club on television, found the author films both entertaining and informative because they added vivid visual detail to verbal description: "I do like the fact that they do little re-enactments you know with some of the books and I think that helps to kind of like visualize things when they're presenting them" (FG participants, 31 March 2007, Birmingham).

Not all of the author films in the 2007 edition included dramatizations of events from the narrative, but they all took the viewer on a tour of the book's setting.

During the show that featured Jed Rubenfeld's *The Interpretation of Murder*, for example, the author is seen on location in various parts of New York City (2007a). The author is shot as a talking head commentating upon the historical and geographical setting and plot of the novel, inter-cut with or sometimes back-grounded by quick takes of archived film footage and still photographs of early-twentieth-century New York. The aesthetic style and tone used was reminiscent of popular documentary television with relatively fast-paced editing, plenty of visual cues and period-appropriate music helping the viewer to quickly comprehend the voice-over. Meanwhile, the "serious" aspects of the book – its imagining of Freud's relationship with Jung, Rubenfeld's engagement with the early history of psychoanalysis – is signified by a shot of the author captured with his head down in large tomes of important-looking historical books. Such imagery also suggests that Rubenfeld has already read the "difficult" books during his research for the novel so that you, the viewer, need not worry either about the "authenticity" of the setting, nor about the potentially intimidating subject matter. In fact, this is confirmed by the author's voice-over, which states that he "dug through thousands of newspaper articles" in order to make New York City in 1909 "as real as possible." At this point, the author film for *The Interpretation of Murder* ends and the program returns to the studio for the live book discussion.

Most of the interpretive book talk portion of the Book Club segments lasted no longer than six minutes. The brief book discussions may not have offered opportunities to discuss a book as thoroughly as is possible in the more sustained discussions pursued on other broadcast book programs, or in "real" face-to-face or online book clubs, but viewers were provided with further insights into the plot, characters and settings of the featured books. Nevertheless, the four reader-reviewers – Richard, Judy and two guests – looked like a small book group as they sat on the studio sofas. Instead of describing the two invited celebrities as "book club members," Richard and Judy referred to them as "guest reviewers." In this way, the celebrity guests were lent cultural capital, while also maintaining the status of "regular readers." Of the two celebrity readers featured in each episode of the 2007 Book Club, at least one had usually acquired cultural authority in a different area of the media. News broadcaster John Humphries joined actor Olivia Williams for the discussion of *Restless*, for example, while actor Brian Cox and television journalist Rageh Omaar were paired for *Half of a Yellow Sun*; and writer-critic Bonnie Greer and comedian Richard Herring for *The Interpretation of Murder*. Stars of soap operas such as former *Eastenders* actor Michelle Collins (for *Love in the Present Tense)* and popular television actors like Alan Davies and Fay Ripley (*This Book Will Save Your Life*), who are both associated primarily with the genre of comedy-drama, were also invited to discuss 2007 selections. In this way, the Book Club mobilized the symbolic capital and popular appeal of the celebrity readers, and, in doing so, simultaneously blurred the taste-markers of "high" and "popular" culture, thereby positioning reading as a fun, yet worthwhile, non-elitist activity.

The "live" studio conversations with celebrity guests were usually enthusiastic and grounded by descriptions of their reading experiences with conversation often incorporating articulations of emotional responses to the books. These responses were discussed and valued on air, and become part of up-beat introductions to the Book Club books. Almost every discussion began with one of the hosts asking one of the guests, "What about it did you particularly like?" Judy posed this question to soap opera actor Amanda Holden about Lansen's *The Girls*, for example (2007b). To bring in the other guest reviewer, actor Colin Salmon, Judy asked him if, while reading the book, he had to remind himself that it was fiction. Salmon responded positively and continued by commenting upon his childhood reading experience. He suggested that *The Girls* was a book that he would give to his own children to read because it is "really responsible, honest storytelling." As explored elsewhere in this collection, and as our analysis of the author films above suggest, storytelling was a central concern for and an overt on-screen practice of the Book Club. The reference to personal histories and the celebrity's stories about their experiences as readers also resembles that of talk show guests more generally (and generically) (Grindstaff 2002, 228–9). Television producers of day-time programs typically use this strategy in an attempt to validate the knowledge of the viewers, and "to questio[n] the deference traditionally paid to experts, and [to] assert instead the worth of common opinion" (Grindstaff 2002, 228).

The composition and talk of the Book Club also deliberately countered "common opinion" on occasion and in particular, tended to disrupt the gendered, feminized perceptions of reading and book clubs (Harker 2008; Humble 2001; Radway 1997). By including one male and one female guest reviewer in almost every segment, the producers re-positioned common assumptions about the gender composition of book clubs. The on-screen presentation of *The Girls* and *Love in the Present Tense* also involved a direct confrontation of assumptions that potential readers might make about these books based on their titles and cover illustrations. Both books are framed by their paratexts, in particular by their cover illustrations, not as "Chick Lit" exactly, but certainly as appealing to a primarily female audience. The talk about these books, and *The Girls* in particular, followed normative gendered expectations with the men speaking about the craft of the author's storytelling and the women speaking to the novel's connections to and representations of mothering, womanhood and sexuality. Still, in discussing the quality of the storytelling, Salmon exposed the gendered aspects of the discussion and of the book's marketing by appealing directly to male viewers: "the title, unfortunately, 'The Girls,' does exclude me. I wouldn't take it off the shelf, but we're going to change that this afternoon. Boys, buy the book. It's great!" (2007b).

There were other instances in the 2007 book discussions where the talk disrupted the assumptions that some audience members might have held about mixed-gender-group book talk. For *The Interpretation of Murder*, for example, it was the women who carried the intellectual interpretive task of exploring the novel's core ideas. Invited by Richard Madeley to begin the discussion, playwright and cultural commentator Bonnie Greer focused upon the writer's technique, the book's use of the thriller genre, the pace of the story, and, the style of writing. She classified the book as a "really brilliant" interpretation of *Hamlet* and claimed that Rubenfeld's story keeps the reader "enthralled." Lest the viewer should be intimidated by references to Shakespeare's play or by the book's main characters Sigmund Freud and Carl Jung and their theories of psychoanalysis, Greer was quick to qualify the impact of Rubenfeld's narrative skill upon the plot: he "makes it accessible and you can understand these big ideas," she claimed. Madeley, on the other hand, tried to disrupt the intellectual tenor of the conversation by asking the other guest reviewer, comedian and writer Richard Herring, if he found the book "sexy." Herring, shifting his position on the sofa as if he was taken by surprise or discomforted by such a question, responded with, "it is sexy in a perverse sort of way" (2007a). He continued by offering an interpretation of the women in the novel as sexually objectified. Greer disagreed and gave an alternative interpretation of the female characters as catalysts for change within the novel's narrative action.

In this Book Club segment, then, it was the women readers who sustained a more scholarly sounding but explanatory discussion about Freud, Jung and psychoanalysis. They deconstructed Freud's theory about the interpretation of dreams and outlined his theory of the Oedipus complex, both of which feature as themes and ideas throughout Rubenfeld's historical novel. It was also Greer and Finnigan who identified interesting issues about the class system in New York at the turn of the twentieth century within *The Interpretation of Murder*. Richard Madeley, however, playing up to his role as the risqué presenter, often interrupted them and most of his commentary reduced the book talk to "sex" and titillation. Perhaps indicating his continuing discomfort with this approach, comedian Richard Herring ended his interpretation of the book with an ambiguous comment about the novel's genre, which contrasted to both Greer's intelligently articulated enthusiasm and Madeley's sexual innuendo. Herring concluded that while he thought the novel was a "page turner," it "falls between two stools." Although the viewer does not find out which genre Herring prefers, we can assume it is not historical mystery, since he claims he wanted either "more about Freud" or more "adventure." Herring's articulated reading preference points to a perpetuation of gendered reading choices for genre fiction, but his refusal to collude with Richard Madeley's "laddish" sense of humor complicates the gender politics of the book talk and the group dynamic. Thus, while this particular book talk segment is certainly not gender neutral, there are moments when aspects of an onscreen reader's commentary or behavior disrupts widely assumed ideas about genre and gender, and about gender and interpretative practices. Greer and Finnigan are particularly effective at dispelling any ideas that the viewers may have of book group talk as frivolous women's gossip.

As with all the 2007 Book Club segments, the final two minutes consisted of the second VT, an edited mini-film of a "real" book group, the BookCase Book Club, "from Central London" who had read *The Interpretation of Murder*. The establishing shot showed this mixed-gender and ethnically diverse group around a table at a café in the midst of their book discussion. Slow-paced, unobtrusive music faded out to enable the viewer to hear just one tantalizing comment from their conversation ("there's plenty of twists and turns") before the film cut to a fast-paced series of individual talking-heads offering sound-bites of opinion about the novel. A still image of a pile of books – the selections for the 2007 Book Club – were super-imposed on the right-hand side of the screen during the sequence of rapid-fire reader's comments. It was a slightly disjunctive visual cue in terms of production values, because it marred the moody aesthetic created by the subtly lit carefully framed shots of the book club in the café and the well-balanced colors of the talking heads sequence – all of which contributed to the otherwise fluent editing of the book club VT. However, the static image indicated to viewers, especially those who may only have joined the show at that moment, that these readers were part of a regular feature about books, while also referring the audience to the branding of the Richard & Judy Book Club, which was so visible off-screen in chain bookstores, the advertisement pages of newspapers and in public libraries. In this way, the Book Club was signposted within the Richard & Judy show in a similar way to other repeated segments, such as the infamous "You Say, We Pay" quiz game, which had a vibrantly colored typographical logo that took up virtually the whole screen each time it was used.

In common with the enthusiastic tone of the studio discussion, the opinions offered in all the book group films tended to be positive, focusing on sections of books, themes or characters that had engaged the reader's attention. Two members of the BookCase book club, for example, commented on how the research underpinning *The Interpretation of Murder* made Rubenfeld's representation of New York City very "evocative." A female member praised the character of Littlemore as "well drawn," and a male reader admitted that some of the "twists and turns" of plot were predictable, while others caught him out. Finally, three people explicitly recommended the novel, "as a light read with an academic edge" (male reader), with a middle-aged female group member declaring, "it's fantastic! Any reading group would have a good time reading it"... "and discussing it" added Judy Finnigan almost *sotto voce* as the VT ended and the segment returned to the studio.

Finnigan's quick-witted reaction to the final taped reader's comment not only provided a seamless word bridge back to the live broadcast, it also foregrounded the producers' declared purpose of including "real book club" footage within the Book Club feature. Amanda Ross told us enthusiastically, "I think – that's the thing that inspires [viewers] most, at the end of the article you think, 'Well, they look like me, I could be like them, I will go out and try this book.'" Following on from the studio book discussion that employed celebrities to pique the interest of viewers, the "real book club" readers were meant to secure the audience's confidence that they too could be a reader capable of engaging with the selected books and, perhaps, of sharing their responses with friends. By modeling the social practice of book group talk on-screen (and twice over), the Book Club formula conveyed the message that reading was fun and a pleasure that could be shared.

Promoting the pleasures of reading in ways that might encourage more people to read books was an aspect of the Book Club that met with the approval of many readers in our study: unsurprisingly, given the dominant discourse around book reading as a morally and educationally worthwhile activity. Even so, their responses often contained elements of distinction as they differentiated themselves from those whom they perceived to be the intended audience for the show, and attempted to mitigate any class "snobbishness" that their comments might infer. Hence, Una, who watched the show, told us, "Richard & Judy have suddenly made reading cool. You know, across the generations which *I find fascinating*, you know, *being a reader anyway*, and that's great. *Raised the awareness hasn't it*, and the interest in some of the authors and the books?" (FG participants, 31 March 2007, Birmingham) (emphasis added). In another focus group, two women from different generations, Sam (32) and Ann (59), carefully negotiated their way around the taste hierarchies and classed associations of popular leisure pursuits:

> Sam: I think it's great because they're not appealing to people that are widely read, they're people that are watching television – otherwise they'd be reading a book. So, if you're capturing a new audience…
> Ann: Yes, but you can do that, because we all watch it don't we, and read books as well. *We don't read books instead of watching Richard and Judy, we do both, don't we…*
> Sam: But *we're a certain kind of audience.*
> Ann: We're a certain kind of audience?
> Sam: Yeah. There are people that don't read and if a single one of them then turns to a Richard and Judy book then I think that's fantastic. (FG Participants, 6 February 2007, Birmingham) (emphasis added)

Ann questions Sam's assumptions about book reading and television-watching as mutually exclusive activities, but Sam marks out their membership of the "reading class" by taking up Ann's use of the plural pronoun and her direct appeal to Sam: "we do both, don't we?" and interpreting their common ground as membership of a "certain kind of audience." Despite Ann's questioning of this distinction, Sam then confirms her own difference from an imagined Richard & Judy audience by praising the show's ability to convert non-readers to books. Sam deftly side-steps Ann's implied accusation of snobbery and cultural superiority by referring to a socially acceptable idea about reading as a worthwhile pursuit that everyone should be encouraged to undertake.

Although not overtly suspicious of the Book Club, Sam, like other keen readers, found a way to register her resistance to its troubling of normative messages about reading as a distinctive practice. The final minute of the Book Club segment combined many of the elements that irritated the more explicitly resistant readers in our study. In the last part of the Book Club focused on Rubenfeld's novel, for instance, Richard Madeley and Bonnie Greer conversed briefly about how the novel cleverly explored "the unstoppable rise of America." However, if this comment was intended as a type of strap-line meant to secure the validity of the novel's selection for the Book Club, the next snatch of sofa conversation about Richard Herring's upcoming stand-up comedy tour, reminded the audience that they were watching a magazine show, one that unapologetically incorporates plugs for other media products. The shift of tone to a more blatantly commercial "sell" was then continued by Judy's introduction and emotional endorsement of the following week's Book Club selection, *The Girls* by Lori Lansen, as "my absolute favourite of this year's books...I cried." The celebratory and personal tenor of Finnigan's recommendation was, as noted above, one of the aspects of the Book Club that aroused some of our readers' suspicion about its "agenda" and the show's relationship to book publishing and marketing. As if to confirm these fears, a light-hearted piece of banter between Richard and Judy about author photographs is followed by information about how to obtain free sets of reading notes, a verbal and on-screen reminder of the Book Club's web address (which included a section where books could be purchased) and, on some 2007 Book Club shows, by an invitation to join the discussion forum and "live" online chats with the week's featured author. While these elements all increased the opportunity for viewers to participate interactively with the Book Club, they also signaled the multi-platform environment that has become part of the twenty-first-century media experience – an environment chosen by just 21 per cent of the readers in our survey who visited the Richard & Judy website and the merely 4 per cent who registered and thus gained access to the forum and the "live" web chats. Perhaps, for our resistant readers, these interactive elements appeared to interpellate them as consumers and producers (of opinion and discussion) in ways that did not fit comfortably with their identity as the readers of printed books who value the cultural capital they have acquired through that activity. For such readers, the Richard & Judy Book Club is for other people who do not yet share their knowledge and skills.

The producers of Richard & Judy's Book Club successfully employed the medium of television and the celebrity persona of the husband-and-wife team and their guests to make books accessible, fun and entertaining. In 13 minutes of adeptly produced television, Richard & Judy's Book Club celebrated reading as both an interactive and interpersonal experience. The eclectic and wide-ranging choice of genres featured reinforced the show's framing of reading as a non-elitist and, even, on occasion, as a gender-neutral activity. The Book Club segment thus promoted books as non-threatening cultural artifacts that connect to the viewer's interests and can be readily incorporated into their everyday lives. Ironically, it was the very success of this process of popularization, combined with the commodification of the Book Club selections and the branding of the Book Club, that devalued books and reading for the readers in our study. As we have demonstrated, their suspicion of the commercial aspects of the Book Club indicates an investment in a dance of distinction that, for committed book readers, has become more complicated from the late twentieth-century onwards as the production and marketing of books has changed (Squires 2007; see Moody in this collection). The reconfiguration of the literary-cultural field to which these industry changes, and the rise of the mass media conglomerates have contributed, blurs the lines of low and high culture and confuses the markers of "good taste."

As distinction becomes a more complicated practice, some readers seem to create new taste markers and hierarchies in order to take up a position that disassociates them from readers who "need" or use popular culture to influence their book choices. Media commentators predicting the possible outcome of the show's migration from terrestrial television to cable channel UKTV believed that the visibility of the Book Club through partnerships with retailers such as WH Smith and Tesco would ensure the longevity of its brand power (Tivnan 2008). Whether or not it can survive the final demise of their onscreen partnership remains to be seen.

Reference List

Allen, Katie. 2009. Ross confident of Book Club future. *The Bookseller.com.* 17 May. http://www.thebookseller.com/news/85678-ross-confident-of-book-club-future.html (accessed 11 October 2009).

Bell, David and Joanne Hollows, eds. 2005. *Ordinary Lifestyles: Popular Media, Consumption and Taste.* Maidenhead: Open University Press.

Bennett, Tony, Mike Savage, Elizabeth Silva, Alan Warde, Modesto Gayo-Cal, and David Wright. 2009. *Culture, Class, Distinction.* London: Routledge.

Bourdieu, Pierre. 1984. *Distinction: A Social Critique of the Judgement of Taste.* Trans. Richard Nice. Cambridge, MA: Harvard University Press.

Bourdieu, Pierre. 1993. *The Field of Cultural Production: Essays on Art and Literature.* Ed. Randal Johnston. London: Polity Press.

Boztas, Senay. 2008. Richard and Judy treat their readers as stupid. *The Observer.* 17 August. http://www.guardian.co.uk/books/2008/aug/17/edinburghbookfestival.fiction (accessed 18 August 2008).

Burnett, Ann and Rhea Rheinhardt Beto. 2000. Reading romance novels: An application of parasocial relationship theory. *North Dakota Journal of Speech & Theatre* 13: 28–39.

Collins, Jim. 2002. High-pop: An Introduction. In *High-pop: Making Culture into Popular Entertainment*, ed. Jim Collins, 1–31. Oxford: Blackwell Publishers.

Couldry, Nick. 2003. *Media Rituals: A Critical Approach.* London: Routledge.

Dugdale, John. 2006. Sofa, so good: Many of this year's top selling authors owe their fortunes to Richard and Judy. *The Guardian.* 30 December. http://www.guardian.co.uk/books/2006/dec/30/bestbooksoftheyear.bestbooks2 (accessed 12 August 2009).

Farndale, Nigel. 2007. The best seller. *Daily Telegraph.* 25 March. http://www.telegraph.co.uk/culture/3664052/The-best-seller.html (accessed 17 November 2009).

Farr, Cecilia Konchar. 2005. *Reading Oprah: How Oprah's Book Club Changed the Way America Reads.* Albany: State University of New York Press.

Finkelstein, David and Alistair McCleery. 2005. *An Introduction to Book History.* London: Routledge.

Fuller, Danielle. 2006. Interview with Amanda Ross. London. 26 June.

Giles, David. 2000. *Illusions of Immortality: A Psychology of Fame and Celebrity.* New York: St. Martin's Press.

Giles, David. 2002. Parasocial Interaction: A review of the literature and a model for future research. *Media Psychology* 4.3: 279–305.

Giles, David. 2003. *Media Psychology*. Mahwah, N.J.: Lawrence Erlbaum Associates.

Greenwood, Dara, and Christopher Long. 2009. Psychological predictors of media involvement: Solitude experiences and the need to belong. *Communication Research* 36.5: 637–54.

Grindstaff, Laura. 2002. *The Money Shot: Trash, Class and the Making of TV Talk Shows*. Chicago: The University of Chicago Press.

Griswold, Wendy. 2008. *Regionalism and the Reading Class*. Chicago: University of Chicago Press.

Harker, Jaime. 2008. Afterward: Oprah, James Frey, and the problem of the Literary. In *The Oprah Effect: Critical Essays on Oprah's Book Club*, eds Cecilia Konchar Farr and Jaime Harker, 321–33. Albany: State University of New York Press.

Hartley, Jenny. 2001. *Reading Groups*. Oxford: Oxford University Press.

Hattersley, Giles. 2006. She's choosing your books. *The Sunday Times*. 13 August. http://www.timesonline.co.uk/tol/news/article607041.ece (accessed 12 August 2009).

Hesmondhalgh, David. 2007. *The Cultural Industries*. 2nd ed. London: Sage.

Hesmondhalgh, David, and Sarah Baker. 2008. Creative work and emotional labour in the television industry. *Theory, culture and society* 25.7: 97–118.

Humble, Nicola. 2001. *The Feminine Middlebrow Novel 1920s to 1950s: Class, Domesticity, Bohemianism*. Oxford: Oxford University Press.

Jeffries, Stuart. 2009. Richard & Judy: Where did it all go wrong? *The Guardian*. 9 February. http://www.guardian.co.uk/culture/2009/feb/09/richard-judy-show-bookclub (accessed 10 August 2009).

Kellner, Douglas. 2003. *Media Spectacle*. London: Routledge.

Langley, William. 2007. Profile of the bookmaker: Amanda Ross. *The Daily Telegraph*. 30 December. http://www.telegraph.co.uk/comment/3645031/Profile-of-the-bookmaker-Amanda-Ross.html (accessed 17 November 2009).

Long, Elizabeth. 2003. *Book Clubs: Women and the Uses of Reading in Everyday Life*. Chicago: Chicago University Press.

McCrum, Robert. 2006. Our top 50 players in the world of books. *The Observer*. 5 March. http://www.guardian.co.uk/books/2006/mar/05/features.review (accessed 12 August 2009).

McQueen, Craig. 2006. How the Richard & Judy 'Effect' is worth £50m to book trade. *Daily Record*. 20 June. http://www.dailyrecord.co.uk/news/2006/06/20/how-the-richard-and-judy-effect-is-worth-50m-to-book-trade-86908-17258117/ (accessed 17 November 2009).

Meehan, Eileen. 2002. Gendering the commodity audience: Critical media research, feminism and political economy. In *Sex and Money: Feminism and Political Economy in the Media*, eds Eileen Meehan and Ellen Riordan, 209–222. Minneapolis/London: University of Minnesota Press.

Office for National Statistics. 2009. Labour Market Information. http://www. statistics.gov.uk/cci/nugget.asp?id=1838 (accessed 17 November 2009).

Radway, Janice. 1997. *A Feeling for Books: The Book-of-the-Month Club, Literary Taste, and Middle-Class Desire.* Chapel Hill: University of North Carolina Press.

Rehberg Sedo, DeNel. 2004. Badges of Wisdom, Spaces for Being: A Study of Contemporary Women's Book Clubs. PhD diss., Simon Fraser University.

Rehberg Sedo, DeNel. 2003. Readers In Reading Groups: An On-Line Survey Of Face-To-Face And Virtual Book Clubs. *Convergence: The Journal of Research into New Media Technologies* 9: 66–90.

Rehberg Sedo, DeNel. 2008. Richard & Judy's Book Club and Canada Reads: Readers, books and cultural programming in a digital era. *Information, Communication and Society* 11(2): 188–206.

Richard & Judy. 2007a. Channel 4. 31 January.

Richard & Judy. 2007b. Channel 4. 7 February.

Richard & Judy. 2007c. Channel 4. 14 February.

Richard & Judy. 2007d. Channel 4. 14 March.

Rubin, Rebecca, and Michael P. McHugh. 1987. Development of parasocial interaction relationships. *Journal of Broadcasting & Electronic Media* 31.3: 279–92.

Squires, Claire. 2007. *Marketing Literature: The Making of Contemporary Writing in Britain.* London: Palgrave Macmillan.

Striphas, Ted. 2009. *The Late Age of Print: Everyday Book Culture from Consumerism to Control.* New York: Columbia University Press.

Taylor, Joan Bessman. 2007. Good for What? Non-Appeal, Discussibility, and Book Groups (Part 2). *Reference & User Services Quarterly* 47(1): 26–31.

Tivnan, Tom. 2008. Last hurrah or new beginning? 15 August. *Bookseller.com.* http://www.thebookseller.com/in-depth/feature/65076-last-hurrah-or-new-beginning.html (accessed 11 November 2009).

Vernall, Lucy. 2007. Presentation about Ideas Lab™, University of Birmingham. 9 December.

Wagner, Erica. 2006. Richard & Judy & Amanda. *The Times Online.* 17 June. http://entertainment.timesonline.co.uk/tol/arts_and_entertainment/books/article675261.ece (accessed 17 November 2009).

Wright, David. 2007. Watching The Big Read with Pierre Bourdieu: Forms of heteronomy in the contemporary literary field. *Working Paper No. 45.* Centre for Research on Socio-Cultural Change, Open University. http://www.cresc. ac.uk/publications/documents/wp45.pdf (accessed 10 August 2008).

Wu, Yung-Hsing. 2008. The romance of reading like Oprah. In *The Oprah Affect,* eds Cecilia Konchar Farr and Jaime Harker, 73–88. Albany: State University of New York Press.

Chapter 2

Entertainment Media, Risk and the Experience Commodity

Nickianne Moody

This chapter argues that the establishment, growth and development of the Richard and Judy Book Club (RJBC) as a trusted brand can be best understood through positioning books as an experience commodity that require consumers to negotiate risk to be rewarded with the pleasure of consumption. The chapter outlines the shifting industrial and social contexts in which RJBC was uniquely placed to assume cultural authority and arbitrate amongst changing cultural attitudes to book buying and book reading. Presenting an analysis of readers' comments on the RJBC website, it demonstrates how this arbitration manifested into a structure of book recommendation based on non-hierarchical authority. The chapter also posits that instrumental in building this structure was readers' understanding of reading as a shared social experience.

The concluding section of the chapter considers the lasting impact of the democratization of cultural authority that RJBC consolidated. It analyses the growth of Amazon.com and its canny appropriation of the newly developed democratized structure within an online environment that could mimic offline bookshop browsing and replicate the book group experience. Although Amazon used books as loss leaders, the online retailer still managed to capitalize upon the parallel cultural shift the RJBC had effected. It did so by attracting middle class consumers with discounted books and keeping them with a business model that resolved the problems of traditional, independent and mall booksellers. Thus the chapter concludes by acknowledging that while RJBC's approach may have exacerbated the closure of independent bookshops, it is still missed by the book trade as a tool to promote bookselling in offline environs.

Industrial Context

The British book trade has regularly perceived itself to be in a state of crisis and the early twenty-first century was no exception to this. The industrial context of crisis at the time of the launch of the RJBC in 2004 comprised a dual concern about declining standards of literacy and the discounting of books by supermarket chains and online retailers. Therefore *The Bookseller*, as a publication indicative of professional opinion, at first welcomed an intervention by popular television in the promotion of popular reading but responded with alarm to the way that the

RJBC facilitated broader book sales by non-specialist retailers. This was because originally RJBC was regarded as similar to the BBC's community outreach project The Big Read (2003), which was a government initiative aimed at promoting reading as a pleasurable past time.

Fronted by the BBC, The Big Read worked with government sponsored groups such as The Booktrust, The National Reading Campaign, The Campaign for Learning, The Reading Agency and the National Literacy Trust. The agenda for the initiative was set by an initial readers' poll to find the nation's 100 favorite books and create a list reflecting the popular endorsement of a range of established and contemporary classics. The industry viewed the list as data that could support the selections made by reading groups and that would guarantee sales for the named authors, which might extend to their backlist. The BBC's involvement guaranteed high profile television coverage to run alongside other media platforms used to promote the initiative. The general public participated at a variety of external events throughout the year hosted by schools, libraries and workplaces, and through activities such as the Reader in Residence at the Cheshire show and book trade promotions (Holman 2003; Kean 2003b). Widespread public familiarity with the list led to it being distributed and promoted by non-book retailers who had previously lacked a means to recommend books. However because the initiative aimed at encouraging reading this crossover was not considered detrimental to traditional trade and so the Big Read was enthusiastically taken up by members of the Bookseller Association (Kean 2003b).

The crossover of The Big Read list into discounted non-specialist retailers aptly illustrated a duality of feeling expressed by readers towards reading in the changing book market. A 2002 survey had found that recommendation from a friend or colleague rather than industry endorsement was the main influence on book reading. The Big Read amplified this with the message that celebrities and ordinary people were passionate about reading and confident about the pleasures of popular books. Thus while readers expressed a concern that discounted prices in larger chain bookshops devalued books, they appreciated that it allowed them to consider experimenting with unknown authors. The survey also found that once a reader identified an author who met their interest they would then remain loyal to that author, however they were distrustful of cover shoutlines and promotions that attempted to connect their favorite authors with other writers. Research indicated that while book reviews may have an impact on some readers, both library and industry promotions had limited influence on persuading readers to try new authors or books (Hartley 2003). Research for the Orange Prize for fiction also confirmed the importance of borrowing books in order to reduce the risk of disappointment both in time investment and cost (Hartley 2003).

In January of 2003 *The Bookseller* was of the opinion that supermarket discounts might encourage more sales and more reading, but not visits to bookshops in pursuit of future novels (Kean 2003c). At this time *The Bookseller* raised concerns about the dramatic price reductions supermarkets were able to offer because they could demand discounts from publishers of up to 65 per cent. However research showed that supermarkets served millions of customers per week, but only

2 per cent bought books. This was largely because non-specialist booksellers still lacked a mechanism through which to encourage people to take advantage of the price being offered for new books. However this problem would be resolved in 2004 as the RJBC sticker became the trusted friend and colleague that endorsed the unknown product and encouraged readers to seek books according to convenience, in quantity and by competitive pricing.

Reappraising the issue of supermarket incursion in January 2005 a *Bookseller* survey assessed the potential damage supermarket sales of books could have upon traditional booksellers. The survey revealed that the bookshop and the book itself were perceived by the public as "elitist and inaccessible." Prospective readers felt that they were being confronted by a vast array of books that they could not evaluate and therefore refused entirely to engage in the selection process (Anon 2005a). Advertisements and promotions for books had little effect unless they coincided with recommendations from trusted sources such as friends and family. Recognizing that the industry needed to explore what could be learnt about non-book buyers in order to expand the market, in February the *Bookseller* reported that HarperCollins UK had launched a global initiative to bring readers closer to books and connect readers with authors. To do this they had identified reading groups and other communities as gatekeepers, or gatewatchers, who could communicate more freely with the elusive broader reading market and with greater authority. In this way HarperCollins UK aimed to lead the profession in understanding behavioral trends that they believed would be essential to developing the book trade (Barnsley 2005).

For other commentators developing the market meant reaching out to the third of people in the UK that the *Bookseller* survey in 2005 had shown never read books. The research had discovered that readers were polarized between being non-readers (34 per cent) and heavy readers who read on average over half an hour a day and bought between 30 to 40 books a year (Dean 2005). The survey found that readers compared price and value with other media entertainment (Bury 2005). Comparisons with the immediacy of other narrative media feature in the explanations of why the people interviewed said that they did not read books:

> I am not sure how I can say it is any better for you. I do not find that I enjoy waiting for things to happen in a book. You sit there, and all the words you have to take in – it just isn't all that interesting. (Jones 2005)

Ultimately booksellers needed to find ways to resolve the outright difficulty in choosing books that had been reported by 41 per cent of people in the survey, which these respondents claimed prevented them from reading more books (Holman 2005b).

Within this cultural context leading industry figures like Joanna Prior at Penguin recognized the importance of RJBC stating, "R&J and other collaborative approaches to books show reading as an attractive, communal thing to do. The more we can turn reading into a social activity, the better chance we have of expanding the market" (Holman 2005b). Indeed as Kaufman noted, the similarity between the success of Oprah's Book Club (OBC) and RJBC lay not in their use of media, chat show style or book selection but in their common conceptualization that the reader they addressed had stopped reading (Kaufman 2004, 241) and needed a stimulus to take up a book again. However, the traditional handselling of independent booksellers appeared to aggravate rather than resolve the problem. The survey found that the image of the bookshop was an obstacle to non-buyers as they found bookshops daunting, and 42 per cent of respondents stated that they would not be comfortable asking booksellers for advice (Holman 2005a). The range of choice intimidated non-buyers and the majority of readers surveyed continued to rely on personal endorsement and familiarity with authors (Holman 2005b).

Reflecting the massive success of the RJBC sticker as a guarantor of quality *The Bookseller's* discussion of the survey's findings presented the targeting book clubs to achieve word of mouth recommendation as ideal; however a direct approach to the reader required caution. Covers were seen to be significant in the process of choosing a book, but the inclusion of professional endorsement was off-putting for readers. Terry Jackson marketing director for the Time Warner Group was quoted as saying "they often don't believe them. They don't want to know about previous books either – what they need is a quick précis of what they're buying" (Holman 2005b). Marketing strategies such as refreshing backlist covers for established authors in order to attract new interest demonstrated the industry's newly acquired understanding of the heterogeneous nature of potential book buyers. Such approaches were proposed in order to break down preconceptions, or indeed to eschew values held by the first wave of readers who had originally taken up the author when they were first published.

When books are understood as experience commodities, then it follows that they can only be evaluated, and their quality determined, after their sale through their consumption (Alvisi 2006, 64). Promotion can damage the sustainability of the market if a reader fails to finish the purchase and is left feeling disappointed and suspicious of subsequent advertising. Therefore particular strategies have to be put in place that establish the quality of the product yet also manage to negotiate fiction, which is categorized outside of genre or immediate mass market appeal. Marketers have to find a means of demonstrating the product to potential readers and motivating them to experiment with authors who are unknown to them. Often this will take the form of associating the book with other successful cultural products, practices and experiences and securing a reputable endorsement. For consumers who were alienated by such marketing strategies, and for whom books were consumed as experience commodities, the RJBC sticker became the cultural authority to license, support and validate the risk-taking necessary for sustaining reading as an ongoing leisure activity through the introduction of new authors.

Assumption of Cultural Authority

In her assessment of changes in the US book trade in relation to the growth of chain bookstores, based in the shopping mall, Laura Miller (2006) interviewed readers to find out how they thought and spoke about reading and book buying.

She found that amongst booksellers and readers competing cultural frameworks were used to define consumer motivation and responsibility in managing risk (2006, 12). The chain stores represented "the belief that readers' individualised preferences should override booksellers' tastes" (Miller 2006, 57) but this now left them adrift in the market place because new titles were literally unknown quantities where saleability was difficult to ascertain. Bookselling is not necessarily unique in the way that culture mediates economic transaction, but the audience may be looking for more than entertainment through popular reading. In interviews with booksellers and readers Miller found "for those who see books as different from other commodities reading effects a transformation of the mind that is thoroughly intangible, unpredictable and ethereal – and there lies its great value" (2006, 80). Thus perseverance, expectation and reward become aspects of the reading experience. Such aspects were continually acknowledged in reviews by RJBC readers.

Miller found that in her interviews readers tended to compare books favorably with television. Television was derided because it required little imaginative engagement on the part of the audience; thus it constituted the antithesis to how they perceived a satisfying or successful reading experience (2006, 136). However television, especially drama, is discussed more readily in listing magazines, national newspapers, breakfast television and amongst colleagues, leading to the popular understanding of television as both a commodity and part of culture. However as Miller acknowledges because books are not so prevalent in everyday culture they hide their commodity status particularly well. Thus bookshops have to work hard to overcome tensions between commercial imperatives and the cultural values associated with books (Wright 2005, 306; Miller 2006, 127).

Miller's interviewees reported that elitist attitudes regarding the moral and educational value of books still prevented some of them from enjoying the environment of a specialist retailer; instead they preferred the more casual location of the chain store. Thus in working with the middlebrow market of daytime television RJBC had to negotiate a vast array of attitudes towards the value of reading. As well as the opposition between high culture and the populist aesthetic, the book club needed to dispel an understanding of reading as either an exclusive activity associated with intellectual labor, or its opposite extreme, a self-indulgent, undifferentiated pastime. Reading for pleasure needed to be validated in the face of the collective anxiety expressed by the subjects of the many surveys that researched the nature of declining literacy and reluctant readers.

Therefore, despite the immense success of OBC, featured on the *Oprah Winfrey Show* from 1996, which influenced the Channel Four program, the RJBC developed and tested its inclusion of books very carefully. It did so in high profile stages, which involved the industry, the writer and the reader. In the first instance the show became the long sought after broadcast partner for the British Book Awards known as the Nibbies. As part of the special broadcast in 2004 Channel Four sponsored a new award "The Richard and Judy Best Read of the Year." The winner was determined by viewers from a shortlist chosen by the presenters and debated on a regular 10-minute Reading Club slot in the post Christmas season. This format then continued into the spring schedule with the selection of books for summer reads. The impact of this initiative was dramatic with "more than one in every 50 books bought in the UK" in 2004 being an RJBC selection (Elliot 2005). This trend was expected to be sustained in 2005 (Elliot 2005). Enjoyment featured as the major criteria in rating favorite titles for both the Nibbies award and the popular choice of the Summer Reads, which were the more prominent selection of the RJBC and its promotion by the industry.

While for RJBC enjoyment featured as an important indicator of pleasure associated with adult reading, when it came to literacy initiatives, promoting intergenerational reading pleasure became problematic for two interrelated reasons: loss of vitality and pressure of time. During The Big Read participants had commented on the loss of vitality found in the books they associated with their childhood. This memorable pleasure had not survived the transition to adult reading, which they saw governed by a literary paradigm that legitimated intellectual pleasure but dismissed the affective pleasures of childhood experience of books. This situation created an ambivalence towards childhood reading, the effect of which could be found being addressed in government literacy initiatives. In 1999 the Government's Reading and Literacy Campaign adopted a strategy of jettisoning books in order to motivate parental involvement and support for their child's reading practice. In addition research had shown that:

> The immediate association with children's reading was the book at bedtime, an occasion which in theory was joyous and intimate, but in practice was when everyone was tired, and was often cut short. For many the occasion turned into a chore. (Broadbent 2000, 41)

Another of the main issues for reading books with children was the pressure of time. Therefore in order to reach lower educational and income groups, and especially fathers, the public information campaign had to validate alternative reading moments that were open to parents. Therefore they promoted

> natural reading opportunities that occurred spontaneously in everyday life. They were far removed from the recommended 20-minute reading period or the daunting book at bedtime. Parents recognised these occasions, but seemed uncertain about them asking 'Is that proper reading?' (Broadbent 2000, 42)

Reading was to be associated with a fun and easy exchange between parent and child, but one that was not based on books. Thus the campaign represented functional literacy as the last resort to combat increasing illiteracy figures.

However for adult readers of the RJBC, enjoyment and emotional response to narrative remained the predominant criteria used by the presenters, the viewers and celebrities in the evaluation of new books. Its recommendations were differentiated from literary judgment in the way in which readers refused to become distanced from the text, although markers of literary value such as moral improvement, interpretation, style and complexity featured in the way that a book was discussed and then recommended. As Elizabeth Long's study of book clubs in Houston proposes, "collective and institutional processes shape reading practices by authoritatively defining what is worth reading and how to read it" (1992, 192) and the RJBC format displaced that authoritarian definition of worth and the cultural value of reading matter with that of popular opinion and debate.

Long's (2003) study of book clubs is concerned with the problems of researching and validating middle class culture, recognizing that such readers exist in between the appreciation of literature and the consumption of mass market popular fiction. Her ethnographic study confirmed that her readers believed that reading is transformative (2003, 24) and that their activity was motivated by the anticipation of such experience. Her study concluded that reading groups do more than just recommend and assist in the selection of books that might offer personal development; it combines the pleasures of reading with sociability (Long 2003, 74). Long found that as a collective, the reading group both challenges and conforms to cultural authority in different stages of its career, but that it is consistently engaged with the interrogation of knowledge, either social or personal, in a setting that permits the assumption of different subjectivities and perspectives (2003, 152). Likewise frequently the reviews posted by readers on the RJBC website acknowledge that the selections have introduced them to reading matter that they would have otherwise overlooked, rejected or not believed themselves capable of attempting. Through this contributors conceded that the book club's aim of broadening their reading experience had worked.

Throughout 2005 the impact that the RJBC selections had on book sales, library lending and reading habits became referred to as the "Richard and Judy Effect." In 2006 RJBC was the winner of The Harper Collins Award for Expanding the Retail Market. The award was given in this instance for the program's role in increasing sales but also because it made its selections in the first quarter of the year, which is traditionally a quiet period, when RJBC encouraged multiple book buying. The judges commented on how RJBC acted to dispel any feeling of intimidation about book buying or reading through discussion and sharing of ideas and opinions about books. Moreover the RJBC focus on new authors would contribute to long term development, supporting writers at the start of their careers and taking risks in promoting unknown authors.

At this point Amanda Ross, managing director of Cactus television, which produced the *Richard and Judy* show for Channel Four, was acknowledged as a powerful force in the book trade. She was credited with the "adventurous picks" made by the program (Elliott 2005). In 2008 when the industry was assessing the potential impact of RJBC's move to the cable channel Watch, *The Bookseller* noted that what had built the RJBC brand was "the astute picking of titles. In the past four-and-a-half years, R&J selections have built a rock-solid credibility with the public; customers know they will get a good read" (Anon 2008). When, in June 2009, the program was cancelled, it was the contribution to the industry made by the show's producer which was emphasized in a *Bookseller* editorial:

Ross's success is unarguable: the 100 books picked since 2004 (including this summer's club) have sold 30 million copies in total with a combined value of £180m. When you factor in the creation of author brands that otherwise might not have emerged, plus backlist sales for picked authors and second book sales for debutants, we can estimate the total sales values at perhaps £250m over the five years. (Denny 2009)

The value of the show was its ability to interpellate a wider demographic than other television or radio book programs. However in 2006 as, following a change in Ofcom regulations, RJBC began to sell discounted books online (Bone 2006) it also became recognized as a brand that had handed the authority to recommend to supermarkets; this had previously been the way that specialists were able to differentiate themselves. The supermarkets now had an arbiter for the books that they discounted (Henderson 2006). Furthermore up until RJBC's involvement in bookselling the online site had said that the books were available from libraries and "all good bookshops." Good bookshops were retailers who led by investing in new books prior to their recognition as bestsellers, and in new authors rather than proven ones or those supported by genre. Thus from 2006, by the omission of the general promotion of the traditional trade, RJBC became the focus for anxieties about the fate of independent booksellers, the bellwether of industry crisis.

The Richard & Judy Book Club Online Reviews[1]

The website was originally established as a forum for users to discuss the selections and post comments about the books. These recommendations will be analyzed as a way of understanding the discourse that emerged through which to recommend, rather than formally review, books in a way that encouraged broader readership in an imagined community of readers. The site was launched in 2005 to expand the presence of the book club beyond the television show and the material posted on the site complemented decisions about whether to participate in reading and debating each book. It also served to cement relationships with real readers' groups. The RJBC was quick to acknowledge groups who had taken on their selections and to make a feature of them. Structured around the individual book the site provided a synopsis, short reviews from Richard Madeley and Judy Finnigan themselves, a record of the celebrity review featured on the program and excerpts of reviews from the quality press. Readers were also provided with a biography of the author that concentrated on their character, inspiration and homeland. When online sales were added in 2006 the home page for each book changed making the cover of the books the central focus in order to feature the recommended price and the site's discounted price as well as details about ordering. More frictionless forms of electronic shopping followed.

---

[1]   I am grateful to my research assistant for this project, Ria Cheyne, who carried out the coding and analysis of the review sample.

Reading groups were directly addressed as having something to contribute to the debate about the books and their discussions were featured on the page given to each book. The survey of the site carried out for this discussion therefore checked for reviews to register acknowledgment of the diversity of opinion associated with a book. As Long notes, for book groups the ability of a book to generate different viewpoints is a key aspect in selection, which can then be successfully discussed by participants in the group (Long 2003, 118). However the research found that only one book per season was considered and evaluated in these terms by the RJBC readers who posted on the site. The RJBC reviews concentrated on private reading, which sometimes drew on the context of the prior history of the reviewer's reading experience, and the book's subsequent impact on their reading career.

In order to post a review, readers needed to register with the site. They were advised that their reviews would be subject to moderation, and possibly edited, before they appeared. Some of the reviews appeared anonymously but most appeared with the reader's name and these show that often the same people reviewed the majority of the 50 books considered in the survey. According to these names the reviewers were predominantly female, but male readers were not exceptional. Teenage readers tended to state their age and were allowed to use more colloquial speech in their reviews. The protocols of the site did not encourage direct comparison of books and so this happened in only a few instances, such as the reviews for *Labyrinth* (2006) and *A Quiet Belief in Angels* (2008), which received a significantly higher number of responses than the average of eight postings.

To examine the process of recommendations made by members of the RJBC this study examined 390 reviews posted online, commenting on 50 books, taken from selections promoted during 2004–2008. The average length of review was 55 words and ranged from six words to 480. Most of the reviews were overwhelmingly positive. In response to this, the coding scheme was designed to analyze and acknowledge positive (reasons to recommend) and negative (doubtful about the reading experience) responses to the books across a range of aspects suggested by the participants themselves: emotional reaction, characters, the difficulty posed by the book, the reading experience, perceived markers of quality and the presence or strength of recommendation to other readers. The coding schema was more sensitive to fictional narrative than non-fiction, but both types of books were considered in the sample. Many of the positive comments on the books expressed a desire to see the book made into a film, something that reflected commentary and evaluation by Richard and Judy themselves as reviewers and that has subsequently been realized for many of the novels. Positive comments also included statements about the willingness to re-read a book and anticipation of the author's next publication.

The reader reviews from the RJBC website are being considered as implicit recommendations and advice for other readers as well as personal testimony about the reading experience. Many of the reviews intimated that their writers were new to the process of reading, discussing or evaluating books and had been highly motivated by the RJBC. Thirty-three books were explicitly given either qualified, unqualified or non-recommendations to other readers. Education and personal development were often cited as evidence for recommendation, or used as justification for reading and not only in the case of the book currently being considered by the review. This was conveyed as a distinction between learning and transformation, with transformation occurring when the book was then viewed as a catalyst for change in the readers' ways of thinking. Recommendation therefore went beyond the expected affirmation of enjoyment, strong response or lack of disappointment elicited by the book.

The analysis was prompted in part by an interest in the extent to which recommendation and comment were based on reference to affective reading rather than literary worth. Littau (2006), researching how the acknowledgment of reading as a sensory experience fuelled various debates about the pathology of reading for pleasure across the eighteenth and nineteenth centuries, charts how part of the process of developing literary criticism was to curb the legitimacy of affective reading and subject it to repudiation. Therefore a hierarchy was established that valued "sense-making, thinking and reason over a whole array of sensory experience, such as pleasure, feeling and passion" (Littau 2006, 98). Moreover, readers who read in quantity and voraciously were seen as endangered and such reading became configured as a pathology (Littau 2006, 41) When Janice Radway, who has also considered the discursive power of reading understood as consumption, looked at the selections made by Book-of-the-Month Club editors, she located an interest in finding a book that was sufficiently absorbing to "transport" the subscriber, which outweighed literary considerations of the text (1997, 72). Affective reading in the RJBC reviews manifested itself in the repetition of two phrases: "compulsion," being unable to put the book down, and "immersion," being fully involved in the story. The antithesis of this praise was to use the terms dull or slow as a criticism of the book overall or of stages in its narrative development. Reviewers also demonstrated a willingness not only to refer to emotional responses but physical ones as well: tears, laughter and astonishment.

In terms of effort and investment in the texts readers commonly liked to state how many hours it had taken them to read a longer book. *Labyrinth* (2006) was a particular example and reviewers wanted to advise other readers not to be put off by the number of pages. Difficulty was another predominant theme, which occurred when a book was intellectual and hard to read because of its complexity, or when readers had issues with the writer's style or the book's narrative structure. "Difficulty" also referred to finding a book hard to read because it addressed troubling subject matter or contained disturbing content. "Difficulty" in these reviews was resolved either by advising others to persevere because the book was worth continuing with and they had found it enjoyable and interesting in the end or stating (rather than confessing) that they had given up. However, in these cases, it was often noted that they had done so in favor of another book. This concern with whether a book was worth reading took on two other forms. Readers identified concerns arising from the start of the book, which led them to doubt its appeal but reported that it did justify tenacity. Secondly, for a fifth of the titles, reviews that might praise a book also expressed dissatisfaction with the ending but these were commonly observations rather than warnings to future readers.

The protocols of the site discouraged extra-textual comments, but readers were keen to say if the book had been a gift. This was particularly the case if the giver was a spouse. Similarly readers wanted to acknowledge the source of their recommendation if it was outside RJBC and especially if it formed an intergenerational connection. Discussions of where and when books were read were included to add emphasis to recommendations about the book's ability to deliver absorption, especially in environments that might be hostile to the reader.

In comment that had a more literary tone, the dominant themes were originality; personal development; aesthetics in the sense that a text was artistically pleasing; and assertions of quality; often expressed as good writing achieving realism. The frequently used term for this was the truthfulness of a story. Long explains:

> First, readers may desire immersion rather than analysis to form the kinds of connections with a book that can allow it to have the weight of reality in their imagination. In a sense, the novel may have to have the ontological equivalence of the real world in order to become comparable to personal experience. (2003, 152)

They may also, as found in this survey, resist novels "that transport them to a world that they do not *want* to imagine" (Long 2003, 152) leading to qualified recommendations, expressions of difficult emotional engagements with texts and exhortations to persevere with the novel.

Truth was a referent for at least one novel in each seasonal selection and those readers who chose to comment in this manner referred to having to remind themselves that the characters were not real. Long's observation of reading group discussions leads her to state:

> The spark of recognition and insight that reading group members evoke when they discuss identification entails a momentary loss of barriers between self and fictional 'other' that can reintegrate aspects of the reader's self in almost therapeutic fashion. (Long 2003, 154)

The scale of the RJBC readership offers this experience and interaction between text and reader to an expanded audience, delivering the desired experience of commodified reading.

Reviews did not use literary terms but they were interested in characterization and language. This is an emphasis modeled by the television discussion of books. Indicating that literary approaches are considered too uptight to address modern popular fiction Ross observed "I would never have a book critic or someone who wants to be esoteric and wordy about literature on the show" (Langley 2007).

Radway observed a similar approach in the editor's written reports for the Book-of-the-Month Club, which exhibited a tendency to react negatively to literary excess as it was felt that this would "prove a hindrance to readers seeking specific reading pleasures" (1997, 67) because it failed to communicate with those readers.

Opportunities for education and learning were far more likely to be a distinguishing feature of a text in the reviews. Readers were interested in encounters with cultures and experience that were foreign to them, rather than a direct alignment with their own lives and social sphere. Long observed that reading groups offered the possibility of "inhabiting different subjectivities" (2003, 152) even though the aspects of these subject positions identified with were most likely to embrace conservatism (2003, 162). In the RJBC readers' reviews books were valued because they had contributed towards learning and personal development. The educational element, however, might be downplayed with reviewers stressing that it was not intrusive. Terms such as "revealing," "insight," "understanding" and "opening up" were used in response to concepts, the experience and beliefs of others and about representations of particular groups of people.

Twenty-first Century Book Trade in Crisis

As Britain experienced the banking crisis and moved into a declared state of recession in 2008, the book trade redoubled its efforts to understand and therefore be able to communicate with book buyers. The book trade's most visible casualty of the recession was the closure of Borders Oxford Street superstore in August 2009. The opening of this store had been indicative of a pattern of investment in the early part of the century that had created an exemplary environment for conducive book buying. However running parallel to these trade initiatives the use of electronic media forms to create the sociability of a reading community, which can then be used to market books as an experience commodity, would prove to be the most successful means of promoting reading and book buying.

The RJBC was not the only website available for readers to post and share their experience of reading or personal rating of books under discussion. From the 1990s reviews and personal comment were central to the way that Jeff Bezos created the Amazon.com site so that it emulated the experience of browsing in a bookshop. Not only could readers review, they could share their lists of favorite books, recommend new discoveries and offer appreciation of authors; cultural practices that existed on a whole host of websites that may or may not be connected to bookselling. The mall, according to Miller, had already "lessened the elite aura that had formerly encircled the bookshop [by making an] association with other consumer-friendly businesses of the shopping centre" (2006, 91). Long also found that the members of her reading groups appreciated "their wide range of titles and inclusive, non-judgemental atmosphere" (2003, 117). At the start of the present century, superstores and chain book retailers became committed to entertainment retail concentrating on social environment rather than exhibitions of distinction and taste. Late twentieth-century bookshops coupled discounts and promotions with the inclusion of cafes, ambient decoration, author talks, connections with other consumer goods and making the location sociable; Bezos wanted to recreate this online. He also wanted to utilize interactive information technology to rationalize book retailing, especially with regard to the circulation of credit and receipt of payment (Kotha 1998). However, books for Bezos were loss leaders so that he could create a reputable and recognizable portal, a brand name for much broader online consumption.

It is useful to understand why Bezos chose books as the commodity to experiment with and build up an understanding of online consumption. Despite the difficulties that we have observed with a lack of confidence in what an unread book has to offer its reader, unlike other goods sold online, Bezos saw a novel as a fixed concept. The book you saw on the screen was the same one that would be dispatched to you. The bookselling industry in the US during the 1990s, when Bezos carried out his market research, was fragmented and lacked a single prominent brand. However the market had steady growth and over half of American book sales took place through mail order. He identified that 17 titles each year sold over 1 million copies and these if discounted would encourage traffic on the site. Furthermore it was publishers who bore the costs and risks of advertising and promotion.

Most significant of all, Bezos's previous career lay in banking and the security of electronic financial transactions. Therefore he was in a position to deal securely with the monetary traffic that he aimed to attract to his site. Thus his knowledge of financial markets and information systems enabled him to resolve the problem of warehousing and display issues, which had led to the creation and investment of major book store chain retailers in the superstore. Bezos capitalized upon the fact that the internet offered an "exhaustive selection" of titles that could be both displayed and navigated. In Bekken's analysis of Amazon.com's impact on the market he concluded that the company's expansive investment in online operators and distribution infrastructure, including warehouse facilities to ensure reliability, had developed very effective barriers to competition (2002, 236).

The Amazon.com retailing model for books, like many who had used books as a loss leader before, offered a positive book buying experience by providing an interface that understood the consumers' interests and reading history in order to build individual profiles. These could smoothly connect the reader to other types of merchandise and position this as serendipity in the manner of browsing. The site was able to resolve the inefficiencies of offline trading that had to wait for buyers and economies of scale that did not allow for discounting. It also enabled the sale of backlists, small presses and second hand books all through one site, whereas for the store at the mall the same ability to display vast quantities of stock often intimidated readers. Bekken suggests that Borders' failure to compete with Amazon.com led it to concentrate on overseas operations, where it could reproduce the social environment for bookselling in countries still using the older model predicated on the aura of the book rather than its entertainment value (2002, 323). As an online retailer the distinction that Amazon.com had and sought to sustain was that all of this activity was underwritten by Bezos's understanding not of books but investment banking, security for internet shopping and by the facilitation of frictionless shopping. Reader reviews and the exchanging of reading lists became a central feature of this experience and of the site's strategy to seek and retain book buyers.

As already noted, in order to develop the Amazon.com site as an expanding market place in the manner of an electronic department store, Bezos chose to use books as a loss leader. He was not however the first to do so and earlier incursions by department stores into this market has often proved a damaging challenge to the book trade's monopoly in this sector (Miller 2006). Books have many advantages to entrepreneurs seeking to establish a central site for varied consumption in that they attract a middle/upper class clientele who will regularly visit the site and become familiar with the other retail opportunities it may offer. These consumers appreciate good service, positive response to consumer demand, convenience and competitive pricing. All of these aspects of a pleasurable shopping experience foster trust and brand loyalty. However, as Bekken (2002) argues, the book trade is an ecosystem that is reliant on the experience commodity, and different parts contribute to the supply of marketable product. New authors have to come forward and readers have to be induced to take risks in order for the book trade to sustain itself. By recreating the book club experience Amazon.com has been able to participate in that ecosystem while using it to expand its own retail market.

During the 1990s and the early twenty-first century, supermarkets, book superstores and internet book retailing all took their toll on the independent bookstore. In an assessment of the industry made at the beginning of 2009, *The Bookseller* commented on the loss of bookshops between 1995, the year that the Net Book Agreement ended, and 2009, the year that the RJBC closed. The British price maintenance mechanism had been in effect for nearly a century and the RJBC did little to halt the fall of closed book shop numbers from 1,900 to 1,400 in the 15 years after it collapsed. Bekken (2002) also argues that book superstores and internet book retailing seized market dominance because of investors' willingness to continue to provide finance without evidence of profit. As a result the diffuse retail market of the independent bookshop, which did the work of helping unpublicized and untried authors and books find a public, has been eroded if not destroyed. RJBC offered a consolidated period of cultural arbitration, exploited more by non-specialist retailers than booksellers, which, now it has been lost, will be difficult for the industry to reproduce in a sustainable and heterogeneously inclusive form.

Reference List

Alexander, Clare. 2009. Waiting for Oprah. *The Bookseller*. May 15.
Alvisi, Alberto. 2006. The Economics of Digital Games. In *Understanding Digital Games*, eds Jason Rutter and Jo Bryce, 58–74. London: Sage.
Anon. 2003. C4 to broadcast Nibbies. *The Bookseller*. November 7.
Anon. 2004. The Richard and Judy effect. *The Bookseller*. January 30.

Anon. 2004. Books bask in television spotlight. *The Bookseller*. April 30.

Anon. 2004. Richard and Judy effect spreads. *The Bookseller*. December 3.

Anon. 2005a. Bookclub back with a bang. *The Bookseller*. January 14.

Anon. 2005b. Millions say no to reading books. *The Bookseller*. March 11.

Anon. 2006. The Harper Collins Award for Expanding the Retail Market: The Richard and Judy Book Club. *The Bookseller*. September 22.

Anon. 2008. The Richard and Judy brand can grow. *The Bookseller*. August 15.

Anon. 2009. An ill-wind is blowing. *The Bookseller*. January 30.

Barnsley, Victoria. 2005. Get Connected. *The Bookseller*. February 11, Expanding the Market Supplement.

Bekken, Jon. 2002. Books and commerce in an age of virtual capital: The changing political economy of bookselling. In *Citizenship and Participation in the Information Age*, eds Manjunath Pendakur and Roma M. Harris, 231–49. Ottawa: Garamond Press.

Bone, Alison. 2006. Richard and Judy site under fire *The Bookseller*. April 21.

Broadbent, Tim. 2000. Reading and literacy – how advertising mobilised parents to help improve the reading ability of their children. *Advertising Works 11*. Henley-on-Thames: World Advertising Research Centre.

Bury, Liz. 2005. Playing the price game. *The Bookseller*. February 11, Expanding the Market Supplement.

The Richard and Judy Book Club [website]. 2008. http://www.channel4.com/entertainment/tv/microsites/R/richardandjudy/book_club_shadow_plus.html.

Dean, Jonathan. 2005. Readers like us. *The Bookseller*. February 11, Expanding the Market Supplement.

Denny, Neill. 2009. Editorial: The empty sofa. *The Bookseller*. May 15.

Elliot, Giles. 2005. Richard and Judy picks powers on. *The Bookseller*. February 18.

Hartley, Jenny. 2002. Maverick readers. *The Bookseller*. December 6.

Hartley, Jenny. 2003. The way we read now. *The Bookseller*. April 11.

Henderson, Paul. 2006. The sticker point. *The Bookseller*. April 14.

Holman, Tom. 2003. Building on the Big Read. *The Bookseller*. May 23.

Holman, Tom. 2005a. Reach for the universe. *The Bookseller*. February 11, Expanding the Market Supplement.

Holman, Tom. 2005b. Like that? Try this… *The Bookseller*. February 11, Expanding the Market Supplement.

Jones, Philip. 2005. Killing off non-readers. *The Bookseller*. February 11, Expanding the Market Supplement.

Kaufman, Rona. 2004. "That my dear is called reading": Oprah's book club and the construction of a readership. In *Reading Sites: Social Difference and Reader Response*, eds Patrocinio P. Schweickart and Elizabeth A. Flynn, 221–54 New York: Modern Language Association.

Kean, Danuta. 2003a. A book is forever. *The Bookseller*. January 1.

Kean, Danuta. 2003b. Big Read makes a big splash. *The Bookseller*. July 11.

Kean, Danuta. 2003c. Seven seasons to zero. *The Bookseller*. November 21.

Kotha, Suresh. 1998. Competing on the Internet: The case of Amazon.com. *European Management Journal* 16 (2): 212–22.

Langley, William. 2007. Profile of the bookmaker: Amanda Ross. *The Telegraph*. December 30.

Littau, Karin. 2006. *Theories of Reading: Books, Bodies and Bibliomania*. Cambridge: Polity.

Long, Elizabeth. 1992. Textual interpretation as collective action. In *The Ethnography of Reading*, ed. Jonathan Boyarin, 180–211. Berkeley and Los Angeles: The University of California Press.

Long, Elizabeth. 2003. *Book Clubs: Women and the Uses of Reading in Everyday Life*. London: The University of Chicago Press.

Miller, Laura J. 2006. *Reluctant Capitalists: Bookselling and the Culture of Consumption*. London: University of Chicago Press.

Radway, Janice A. 1986. Reading is not eating: mass-produced literature and the theoretical, methodological and political consequences of a metaphor. *Book Research Quarterly* 2, Fall: 7–29.

Radway, Janice A. 1991 [1984]. *Reading the Romance. Women, Patriarchy, and Popular Literature*. Chapel Hill: University of North Carolina Press.

Radway, Janice A. 1997. *A Feeling for Books: The Book-of-the-Month Club, Literary Taste, and Middle-Class Desire*. London: The University of North Carolina Press.

Rickett, Joel. 2003. If you build it, they will come. *The Bookseller*. February 28.

Ruppin, Jonathan. 2008. Richard and Judy and beyond. *The Bookseller*. June 7.

Spector, Robert. 2000. *Amazon.com Get Big Fast*. London: Random House.

Wright, David. 2005. Commodifying respectability; distinctions at work in the bookshop. *Journal of Consumer Culture* 5 (3): 295–314.

Chapter 3
Different Spaces, Same Old Stories?
On Being a Reader in
The Richard & Judy Book Club

Alex Kendall and Julian McDougall

The phenomena of the Richard & Judy Book Club would appear to offer a challenge to the classificatory relations that define what it is to read and be a reader in the modern context and to reclaim talking about reading as a popular leisure pursuit that has value independently from indexes of cultural distinction. In this chapter we draw on theoretical frameworks from cultural studies to explore some of the ways in which the book club might be understood to frame and classify the processes and practices of reading. Focusing on Reading Notes as a pedagogical (Bernstein 2000) mechanism of the club we consider whether new possibilities of reading together for pleasure are opened up that are distinct and different from more conventional, established paradigmatic traditions such as those that might be found in "schooled" contexts where reading relations have tended to be predicated on models of meaning making and taking (Peim 1993, Kendall 2008) that emphasize transmission and valorize acts of cultural distinction (Kendall 2008).

This chapter posits that categories of reading are challenged by both the emergence of "new literacies" in digital spaces (video uploading, blogs, gaming, virtual world play and online gaming) with their attendant obscuring of boundaries and by the "hosting" of a book club by Richard and Judy – two "star-texts" firmly rooted in the world of popular culture, their meanings being so grounded in daytime television. However, our analysis of the discourses of reading and of being a reader that the book club circulates leads us to argue that these kinds of framing maintain conservative arrangements of textual value and even extend them.

In addition, this chapter explores the versions of being a reader that are at work in and around the Richard & Judy Book Club and is informed by various theories of power, knowledge and culture. Our theorizing draws on work in education and literacy to illuminate the grammar of what counts in different contexts and modalities and how these ideas are employed to identify the ontology of being a reader as framed by the Richard & Judy Book Club. We argue that while the Richard & Judy Book Club format promises much potential to offer new affordances to readers, in the sense of a new paradigm for reading and being a reader, in practice the book club offers a particular configuration of literacy that reinforces a traditional ontology and serves to reproduce culture.

New spaces

In contemporary Media and Cultural Studies and in the study of literacy, debate proliferates around the significance of Media 2.0 for reframing literacy practices (see Marsh 2007, McDougall and Dixon 2009, Kendall and McDougall 2009). Media 2.0, then, refers to a range of "prosumer" online activity where amateurs produce original material and share it instantly with potentially large audiences or where audience members of orthodox mass media are able to remix and parody or homage cultural products according to a set of user-generated conventions. Media 2.0 is characterized by a rejection of what Gauntlett calls the "fetishisation of 'expert' readings of media texts" (Gauntlett 2006: 1) and the "patronising belief that students should be taught how to 'read'" (ibid.) in favor of "a focus on the everyday meanings produced by the diverse array of audience members" (ibid.) towards an inversion of conventional concerns with power and politics. This set of ideas resonates with the kinds of accounts of reading emerging from the new literacy studies where rather than a technical process of transmission and decoding reading is understood to be "practice" constituted in social and cultural relations (Barton and Hamilton 1998).

With this notion of a temporal shift to a new modality in mind, we can speculate that the combination of the popular culture origins of _Richard and Judy_ as texts with the use of online discussion around the chosen books allow us to include the book club – perhaps unexpectedly – within an extended definition of Media 2.0. However, the emancipatory discourse surrounding Media 2.0 rests on a notion of transgression and also liberation – citizens become journalists, film-makers, artists, musicians. In reality, much digital space is currently occupied by conservative practices in which culture is reproduced rather than remixed (Buckingham and Willett 2009).

Examples of the status of literature being preserved within digital spaces are many. As Chindu Sreedharan (2009) re-tells the Mahabharata using Twitter he seeks not to resist the dominant reading of the epic or use the idioms of 24 character storytelling (posts on twitter, known as "tweets" are restricted to this number of letters, numbers or symbols) to subvert the text, but instead to extend and preserve its status as heritage:

> This is not quite about capturing the philosophical richness of the original Mahabharata – but presenting a version that will, hopefully, suit the medium (Sreedharan 2009:1)

Likewise, Rylands' (2007) educational work with low-achieving boys in Bristol schools may appear to be transgressive. Rylands uses the videogame series _Myst_ to stimulate creative writing and can prove the success of this through a remarkable increase in achievement measured by SAT results. However, the videogame is, while undoubtedly successful in its difference to forms of stimulus material that may be more alienating to this audience (for example, Dickens's descriptive detail or epic poetry), merely a contextual departure – the category of creative writing as an exclusive form of cultural practice to which students should aspire (to produce) is maintained.

To map out the duality of old and new media set against the question of cultural reproduction, which will be a sustained arrangement for this chapter, the comparison of McLuhan and Williams offered by Lister et al. (2009) is very helpful:

> While McLuhan was wholly concerned with identifying the major cultural effects that he saw new technological forms bringing about, Williams sought to show that there is nothing in a particular technology which guarantees the cultural or social outcomes it will have. McLuhan's arguments are at the core of claims that 'new media change everything'. If, as McLuhan argued, media determine consciousness then clearly we are living through times of profound change. On the other hand, albeit in a somewhat reduced way, the 'business as usual' camp is deeply indebted to Williams for the way in which they argue that media can only take effect through already present social pressures and structures and will therefore reproduce existing patterns of use and basically sustain existing power relations. (Lister et al. 2009, 77–8)

Although we are not primarily concerned with technology itself in this chapter, we *are* interested in the dual presence of the book club on television and online and how the latter provides a "peer sharing" context for the social functions of the reading experience. Without the internet, the discussion of reading in networks would be much less tangible. So our interest here is in the potential for the Richard & Judy Book Club to challenge, partly through the popular culture context from which the stars generate their currency and partly through web 2.0 networking, "existing patterns of use" and "existing power relations" that are already in circulation.

In the specific domain of literature, the duality of old and new categories and, crucially, the hybrid nature of reading in this "space in between" is evident in the way that the Richard & Judy Book Club provides a multimodal space for reading as an act of performance. *Richard and Judy* can be read as a rich text from the perspective of fan ethnography: seeking to bear witness to the "produced meaninglessness" of *Richard and Judy*, formed as this is by the conventions of daytime television as social practice as lived in relation to ritualistic uses of media. As *Richard and Judy* become a more complex "star text," the distribution of meanings about their celebrity are clearly the subject of a great many resistant and/ or ironic readings and as such they become "hyperdiegetic," described by Hills as:

> The creation of a vast and detailed narrative space, only a fraction of which is ever directly seen or encountered within the text, but which nevertheless appears to operate according to principles of internal logic and extension. (2002, 137)

Thus the relationship between *Richard and Judy* as "star text" framed by the conventions of daytime television within the domain of mass culture and the "always-already" legitimized nature of literature must be read in tandem. The interplay of the potentially subversive or against-the-grain nature of daytime television acting as a facilitator of "book reading" is in a proximal relation with the socio-cultural framing of literature itself as an exclusive category to be "appreciated." While this insulation of literature from other forms of culture is more complex than a simple binary between high and low culture would suggest, the discourse of derision that circulates around Media Studies in comparison with English Literature, which has moved from derision to legitimation, illustrates the way such boundaries operate and exercise power. A further element in the distribution of such meanings is the invitation to join a social network and thus to distribute personal responses to books with others, a peer to peer context very much in keeping with the flavor of reading lists and recommendations that proliferate in the "long tail" of digital consumption (in which consumers are seen to acquire the power to share responses to cultural products, gaining new forms of audience influence). However, the potential for emancipatory or at least progressive discourses of resistance to be mobilized by this "new media" forum are mitigated against by the provision of reading strategies, in the form of "notes," that serve to frame the discussion as a horizontal discourse. That is to say the notes stand in for an "expert" reading to be handed down to a new audience who might, in turn, pass on this knowledge to their peers and offspring.

Elsewhere in this reader authors explore the methods employed by the Richard & Judy Book Club to disrupt conventional notions of reading and to promote reading for pleasure. Peim (1993), in his sustained theoretical critique of the cultural politics of "Subject English" as institutionally framed in schooling, asks why literacy education does not require its students to question the idea of literacy itself, the ideological component of literacy. Peim's critique is based on a concern with the "normative" and "correcting" function of English teaching and he draws on Stow's (cited in Peim 2000) configuration of the playground as an architectural apparatus for behavioral supervision to extend the argument to view "Subject English" as a panoptical technology for moral surveillance (after Foucault 1991). To what extent, then, does the Richard & Judy Book Club, with its multimodal reach, question the ideological component of the performance of reading in relation to the exchange of cultural capital?

The idea of literature as a special category worthy of attention in itself, with its own special qualities and specific effects, and its very own modes of engagement is really a very dubious affair. Teachers of English have believed, in a necessary ideological move, that literature really does exist – in itself, somehow – and that it really does have intrinsic qualities that make it worthy of study in itself. They have maintained, one way or another, that literature is generally very good for you, if you're lucky enough – or sensitive enough – to appreciate it. If you're not able to appreciate it this is likely to be due to innate insensitivity or poor social conditioning, or maybe the general decline of culture into technological mindlessness and media intoxication. (Peim 1993, 176)

To view the Richard and Judy intervention through the lens of Peim's critique of the "precepts" of literature is interesting. On the one hand, the multimodal distribution of the club and its origin in the "basement" of popular culture makes it a curious hybrid of the Leavisite enrichment and "we media" (the idea that the audience has become the producers) that web 2.0 has mobilized. The kind of democratization of media content and distribution that is most visible in the emergence of "citizen journalism" and "eye witness news." But on the other hand Buckingham and Willett (2009) provide substantial evidence to explore the (perhaps disappointing) argument that amateur video distribution on the internet tends to reproduce existing and conservative modes of classic realism. This suggests that the simplistic idea that access to uploading necessarily enables either alternative patterns of creative practice or adherence to conservative ways of "self-representing" is in need of challenge, as they conclude:

> This portrait of the field complicates several of the generalisations that recur throughout the popular debates with which we began. On the one hand, it challenges a simple binary opposition between amateur and professional; and it disputes the notion that technology in and of itself can act as a force of empowerment, for example by virtue of its simplicity and accessibility. On the other hand, it questions the monolithic construction of the home mode – at least in its contemporary form, as an essentially naïve practice, or indeed as inevitably conservative (either aesthetically or ideologically). (Buckingham and Willett 2009, 69)

We wish to draw a parallel with this discussion in our exploration of the ways in which the Richard & Judy Book Club exists in a space in between schooled and "non-schooled" reading practices. However our view is that, ideologically, conservatism and naivety are both reproduced in the version of being a reader that is constructed.

On "being a reader"

It can be persuasively argued that popular ideas about what constitutes reading are likely to be informed by the discursivities that dominate the places and spaces of formal education. Bourdieu (1990) reads educational institutions as exercising a "monopolising power" that is pervasive and influential.

Bourdieu argues that texts are cultural artefacts that operate within an economy of "symbolic exchange." That is to say that as cultural objects, texts have "value" defined in terms of both their context of production *and* the nature of the discursive social/cultural trajectories through which they are "reflexively mobilised" (Gauntlett 2008) by agents and institutions towards the management of self and the exercising of power. Texts in this sense are understood as signifiers, as material and visible sites around and upon which discursivities are structured/imposed and thus enact and perform power relations through a process of "orchestrated transformation." Texts as "cultural objects operate for Bourdieu within their own economy of symbolic value" (Colebrook 1997, 103) functioning as currency within markets of social, cultural and capital exchange. We would like to extend this argument to encompass not only texts but also the reading practices to which texts are central.

For Bourdieu markets are characterized as micro, that is to say locally, socially and historically situated and they "differ as to what they accord value to, there can be no general description of symbolic exchange without considering its particular divisions (class, tribal, ethnic, political) and values (honour, display, power, aesthetics)" (Colebrook 1997, 103). Colebrook goes on to argue that an exploration of the market of the kind that Bourdieu undertakes in *Distinction* makes it possible to explore "how specific literary texts create aesthetic boundaries and how these boundaries relate to other forms of social power" (Bourdieu and Passeron 1990, 91). We would argue that a similar operation is true for the observation and inculturation of textual practices – that is to say not only the texts that get chosen (or not) but also their purpose in textual practice.

Bourdieu identifies educational institutions as "sites" that occupy a "state of domination" within the discursive market. Through enactment of their specific practices and their rite/right to speak value – a right acquired through a long term strategic, political and historical positioning within relations of power – educational institutions claim a rite/right to name the legitimate both within the boundaries of the specialists fields and beyond. They have a key role in determining and setting the value of the signifier through "rite" of a particular and strategic historical positioning within relations of power. Thus within a particular field and beyond:

> The family and the school function as sites in which the competences deemed necessary at a given time are constituted by usage itself, and, simultaneously, as sites in which the *price* of those competences is determined, i.e. as markets which, by their positive or negative sanctions, evaluate performance, reinforcing what is acceptable, discouraging what is not, condemning valueless dispositions to extinction. In other words, the acquisition of cultural competence is inseparable from insensible acquisition of 'sense' for sound cultural investment. (Bourdieu 2002, 85)

Through a "game" of "continuous creation" educational institutions compete for the "monopolistic power" within the "field of specialised production" to impose *recognition* of the "legitimised mode of expression" (Bourdieu 1992, 85). Thus Bourdieu sees the school, or in this case college, as constantly producing and reproducing the game, not just within the institutional stakeholders but the wider cultural nexus within which it participates/is situated:

> The struggle tends constantly to produce and reproduce the game and its stakes by reproducing, primarily in those who are directly involved, but not in them alone, the practical commitment to the value of the game and its stake which defines the recognition of legitimacy. (Bourdieu 1992, 58)

So what do schooled reading practices look like? Kendall's (2008) work with young adult readers offers insights into the often unspoken "common sense" of how reading works. Participants in the study found it difficult to articulate a response to the question "what is reading?" and most often offered a "pictures in the head" explanation of the reading process. The "pictures in the head" notion identifies a reader ("you"), an author ("they") and an experience, "the text" that is shared between the two generally with the "author" or creator of text *acting on* and *directing* "the reader" to achieve particular responses. This constructs the reader (passive) as one who must come to know what it is that the writer (active) knows already. Reading in these terms is an acquisitive experience through which the reader might come to know more, from darkness to enlightenment. One is minded of Foucault's notion of the author functioning as an ideological product:

> the functional principle by which in our culture one limits, excludes, and chooses; in short, by which one impedes the free circulation, the free manipulation, the free composition, decomposition, and recomposition of fiction. If fact, we are accustomed to presenting the author as a genius, as a perpetual sign of invention. (1991, 119)

Utterances relating to – sometimes expressed as concern about – "understanding" and/or "misunderstanding" the "message" permeated the responses, suggesting perhaps an acquiescence to this discursive construction of "an author." Gee's (2003) notion of how reading is learned in schools perhaps offers a way of interrogating and interpreting this. Gee argues that the teaching of reading fixates on "reading as silently saying the sounds of letters and words and being able to answer general, factual and dictionary like questions about written texts" (Gee 2003, 16). This, he contends, engenders readers who can de-code but not *really* read:

> You do have to silently say the sounds of letters and words when you read (or, at least, this greatly speeds up reading). You do have to be able to answer general, factual, and dictionary like questions about what you read: This means you know the 'literal' meaning of the text. But what so many people – unfortunately so many educators and policymakers – fail to see is that if this is all you can do, then you can't really read. You will fail to be able to read well and appropriately in contexts associated with specific types of texts and specific types of social practice. (Gee 2003, 16)

While readers may then feel comfortable with literal meanings they may be less sure about the other ways in which texts mediate the meaning of social situations – that is to say the practices of reading as manifest in the language or literacy classroom, whereby the notion of the literary text carrying meaning beyond the literal is at once made obligatory yet restricted. The young adult readers tended to comply with a hegemonic model of reading when comparing "reading" books with "watching" films or TV:

> If it's on TV there's only one way you can take it because there's only one way to portray it unless it's like a documentary or something. If it's like... a soap then they're telling you a story so it can be told [only] one way.

> You can picture in your head what's happening [when you read a book] but that's only if you get into it though, if you don't get into it the words start to slip out of your mind, they just go in one side and out the other

> Because when you're reading you can picture it how you wanna picture it but if you're watching a film the pictures are already there for you. (Kendall 2008, 19)

With both kinds of text "meaning" is seen to inhabit a space "outside" the reader. But unlike making sense of TV or film the meaning of books is seen as less easy to pin down in the sense that the author's meaning is sometimes difficult to grasp. The possibility of multiple meanings was often explained as a straightforward "getting it wrong":

> [A film] actually shows you what happens instead of describing it to you, because some people might misinterpret the writing and get the wrong picture, they might not get the picture the writer was trying to put forward. (Kendall 2008, 20)

While Kendall's participants did express an awareness of different reading practices, they did not attach a politics to these different choices or demands, neither did they see them as social practices organizing power relations between different subject identities within disciplinary groups, rather they saw and accepted them as simple common sense. Furthermore different reading practices were not understood to impact on possibilities for meaning taking and making. These accounts illustrate the complexities of attempting to make sense of the meaning making and taking of reading and raise some interesting and important questions about the ways readers construct, represent, manage and value their own reading identities and practices. Readers generally have little experience of the range of theoretical ideas and frameworks they might draw upon, the kinds of theories of author, genre and narrative that are learned in school for example, to think through their experience of text or, perhaps more significantly, little awareness that this is a contested field.

While readers may then feel comfortable with literal meanings they may be less sure about the other ways in which texts mediate the meanings of social situations – that is to say the practices of reading as manifest in the literature classroom and in the Richard & Judy Book Club. Putting together Peim and Gee, the provision of the "reading notes" seem to amplify both the discourse of sensitivity and the shared practice of "de-coding" but not "really reading." Whether or not the provided notes are ever used by readers, the impulse to produce these is the discursive intervention at stake and in the lens of our analysis as we bear witness to the way in which this gesture situates the book club in a proximal relation to Subject English's powerfully conservative and exclusive model of what it is to be a reader. That is to say as reproducing the certainties of "techniques" and "strategies" such as narrative, genre and author as keys to textual meaning.

In the reading notes for Stephen L. Carter's *Palace Council*, one of the Summer Reads that would be more likely to be framed as "fiction" as opposed to "literature" by Subject English, participants are encouraged to discuss the relationship between the narrative of the book and Obama's election as American president and to evaluate the success with which the author blends fact and fiction. These prompts are articulated in an "everyday" discourse, firmly within the textual "language game" of *Richard and Judy* but at the same time they reinforce the assumption that the book is the product of authorial intention and that authenticity of representation can be measured straightforwardly against political events in the real world.

The reading notes are differently constructed in mode of address, seemingly according to the status of each book as more or less elusive to amateur discussion. In comparison with the more conversational prompts for Carter's thriller, the notes for Khaled Hosseini's *A Thousand Splendid Suns* ask the participants to consider the intertextual reference in the title (from a poem, a marker of cultural value) and to discuss the "thematic significance" of this. It would appear, then, that decisions are made in the construction of each set of reading notes based on the "imagined reader" for each genre, with genre itself represented as a meaning making category. These assumptions, of course, preserve intact the socio-cultural framing of literature, set against mere fiction. For this to be the intervention made by the Richard & Judy Book Club, set against the conditions of possibility for new perceptions of literacy, as discussed by Marsh (2007) and Bazalgette (2008) is a highly conservative act of cultural reproduction. It would seem to be apparent that the "members" of the club are positioned between community and hierarchy (Hills 2002) but that hierarchy is granted an apparently neutral privilege in the framing of the discourse. As Hills describes: "The same regime of value can break down into a fine web of distinctions while retaining effects at the level of larger conceptual structures" (2002, 62). Hills's thesis on fandom as cultural expression asserts that a theory of fandom robust enough to bear witness to the complexity of how people attribute meanings to texts (including celebrities) cannot be reduced to merely analyzing interpretation, but must instead extend to analysis of how they invest emotionally in the objects of their "fan culture." Clearly, in some cases, Richard and Judy fandom (in the more complex understanding of this practice, from Hills, in which we see Richard and Judy as in between a different arrangement of the distribution of reading) will play a role in people making the choice to read books. Given that the meanings attributed to Richard and Judy are very different to those traditionally circulating around literature, here is a "new space" for being a reader.

Research into the way people construct representations of themselves as readers raises some interesting and important questions about the ways readers construct, represent, manage and value their own reading identities and practices. A schooled normative construction of reading serves to deny a space for the development of theoretical ideas and frameworks that readers might draw upon to think through their experience of text or, perhaps more significantly, raise awareness that this is a contested field. As a result readers may be over-reliant on the "common sense" of methodologies that would seem to draw heavily upon structuralist orientations (from which ideas about authors, narrative and genre are generated), which may serve to situate them as deficient readers: inexperienced, naive detectives seeking out, but too often "failing" to locate, the neutral "truth" of the texts they encounter. As Web 2.0 technologies open up the possibilities to *be* as readers it is clear that an intervention such as the Richard & Judy Book Club may be an agent in bridging the gap between "in school" and "out of school" literacies.

It seems, then, that the Richard & Judy Book Club potentially offers a different framing to traditional classificatory relations of reading because of its relatively weak indexing to schooled regimes of "distinction" and the subsequent lack of insulation. Here potentially is a much freer paradigm within which ways of being as a reader and thinking/talking about reading might be re-thought. The book club offers the potential to be about "undoing," yet the readers' notes, as a pedagogical technology (in Bernstein's (2000) terms) seem to undermine the potential for reflexive ways of thinking about reading and the practice of reading together for pleasure because they steer (back) towards a more conventional paradigm of reading/being a reader.

Steering the Group

The discussion prompts provided both on the website and in the Richard & Judy Book Club branded editions of recommended reads signpost ways in to reading and understanding literature and as such are worthy of a more forensic analysis in order to further explore these concerns with critical literacy set against Gee's (2003) "unreading" – the critically bankrupt form of the act of reading that is framed by a discourse of "appreciation," through which the conditions of possibility for the literature to be read are never questioned or explored as discourse.

Here we explore the prompts for *A Thousand Splendid Suns* which are re-ordered below in groups of discursive practices that exercise various forms of power. What follows is a deconstruction of the structuralist arrangements at work in these framing devices, with a view to asking questions about the ways in which they might serve to reinforce regimes of value and to re-locate readers as deficient "seekers" of external enlightenment, like Kafka's man from the country before the gates of the Law.

Reading Notes: Questions about Themes (that "exist" outside of the reader)

The Reading Notes document begins with a prompt that asserts a group of facts about a phrase that appears in the novel:

> The phrase "a thousand splendid suns," from the poem by Saib-e-Tabrizi, is quoted twice in the novel – once as Laila's family prepares to leave Kabul, and again when she decides to return there from Pakistan. It is also echoed in one of the final lines: "Miriam is in Laila's own heart, where she shines with the bursting radiance of a thousand suns." Discuss the thematic significance of this phrase.

Yet, the idea of a phrase being echoed by another sentence and the subsequent notion of thematic significance are metaphorical and discursive. Readers are interpellated into the act of discussing something that is assumed to exist – thematic significance. This is presented as objective, such a theme can only be significant if it exists and can be looked at and known as such, outside of the thinking of the reader. There is no space for the reader to think that the phrase is not thematically significant, or that themes are questionable or that the idea of lines from a novel echoing other lines is subjective. A further example again makes an assumption about themes:

> Mariam's mother tells her: "Women like us. We endure. It's all we have." Discuss how this sentiment informs Mariam's life and how it relates to the larger themes of the novel.

Again, larger themes from the novel are treated as neutral, real, substantial. A statement is transformed into a sentiment. Mariam, a fictional construct, is attributed meaning beyond the words on the page; she takes life outside of the novel but how she takes this extratextual existence is already decided and not negotiated by the readers in this discursive arrangement.

The notion of "larger themes" in the one prompt, along with the "thematic significance" in the other, serve to illustrate the duality at work in the "schooled" construction of being a reader. On the one hand, readers are invited to be critical – the personal response is foregrounded: what do the readers think about the obligation for women to "endure" and how might this be related to personal experience? And what do we think of when we read about bursting radiance? And yet the delimiting of these discussions serves manifestly to mirror institutional pedagogy – the "answer" may be partly polysemic but ultimately we are led to identify a set of themes that are "of the novel" and to focus on the choice of title (by the author) and how this anchors the nomenclature of what follows in the book. These prompts might have been worded differently in order for book club members to reflect critically on the idea of the book itself. An alternative question might be: "what do you think the title of a book is for?" The "thematic significance" question is derived entirely from the language game of Subject English; "thematic significance" is something to be understood on the path to literary enlightenment – it is there, in the book, to be located and comprehended.

Fairclough's method of critical discourse analysis (1995) views discourse as triangular. It combines the spoken or written language text (in this case the combined texts of the novel and the prompts), interaction between people to interpret the text (the channeling effect here of attesting certain areas for discussion – themes that are "significant," with no discussion of who chose these things to call "themes" in the first place and for what purpose) and social practice (the combined effect, we argue, of offering access to literature through the book club and reinforcing the symbolic power structures work in textual pedagogy at the same time).

Reading Notes: Questions about Characters' actions (that can be explained)

Readers are asked by the Reading Notes prompts:

> By the time Laila is rescued from the rubble of her home by Rasheed and Mariam, Mariam's marriage has become a miserable existence of neglect and abuse. Yet when she realises that Rasheed intends to marry Laila, she reacts with

outrage. Given that Laila's presence actually tempers Rasheed's abuse, why is Mariam so hostile toward her?

This idea of character motivation is a classic premise of Subject English at both primary and secondary school levels. We might argue instead that an author has provided a narrative but there are no absolute motivations or reasons and there is no "world of the text." Novels are commercial and cultural products to which Subject English ascribes a range of ideological precepts, and the Reading Notes take their cue from this model. A further question involves the characters' relationship:

> Laila's friendship with Mariam begins when she defends Mariam from a beating by Rasheed. Why does Laila take this action, despite the contempt Mariam has consistently shown her?

Again the readers are called upon to find an answer to a question, an answer that is presented as existing in some extratextual reality where the author's constructions of characters serve as a partly revealed puzzle. This is extended when the Reading Notes assume that the characters have psychologies that can be analyzed in real-world ways:

> Laila's father tells her, "You're a very, very bright girl. Truly you are. You can be anything that you want." Discuss Laila's relationship with her father. What aspects of his character does she inherit? In what ways is she different?

The phrasing of these prompts is consistently powerful in reproducing a particular discursive framing of literature and such phrasing is familiar from the institutional artefacts of Subject English – exam questions, textbook discussion activities, revision guides. The question begins with actions from the novel presented as facts; these things happen and are followed by the call to discuss something that is seemingly open to interpretation but is clearly skewed towards the idea of author intention – the reader equipped with sufficient cultural capital will be able to go beyond what happens (part of each prompt) to discuss these in-between ideas that exist/don't exist, are partly formed, in need of (delimited) realization by the reader. Similarly, the emancipated reader will be able to know the answer to the next question:

> Mariam refuses to see visitors while she is imprisoned, and she calls no witnesses at her trial. Why does she make these decisions?

And yet there is no space for a discussion of the idea of fictional characters having reasons beyond their actions described on the page – of the category of literature and the idea of reader interpretation. The novel is "unread" in this practice.

Again we must bear witness to the duality of discursive practice here. Readers are encouraged to interpret the motivations of characters. This is open-ended and there is room for discussion (the whole point of the exercise) and for a high level of personal engagement – agreement is not guaranteed. However, the questions are framed in such a way as to suggest the existence of a "right answer" or at least an answer that will be arrived at by someone who "understands" the novel. We are minded of Peim's observation that the idea of literature existing at all is dubious and open to skeptical interrogation. So too is the idea that there are existing "reasons" for Mariam's decisions and that the pages of the novel can be decoded to the level that we can discuss a relationship between father and daughter as "real." The prompts might have been worded so that Richard & Judy Book Club members might critically explore the way that a novel such as this might either challenge or reinforce dominant discourses about various things – family, for instance – and why a novel such as this, with the way it sets up family in fiction, is so critically acclaimed. What are the "constitutive effects" of the novel *as* discourse?

Reading Notes: Questions about the Author employing devices (that "work" in the real world)

Irony is a technique deployed by the author, and as such the author is marked out as someone whose practices are to be understood, in the question:

> One of the Taliban judges at Mariam's trial tells her, "God has made us different, you women and us men. Our brains are different. You are not able to think like we can. Western doctors and their science have proven this." What is the irony in this statement? How is irony employed throughout the novel?

We might ask why the following stylistic issue is of interest to readers:

> While the first three parts of the novel are written in the past tense, the final part is written in present tense. What do you think was the author's intent in making this shift? How does it change the effect of this final section?

Does formulating a response to this question in any way change the final section? Where is the space for the reader to discuss the relationship between this cultural product and their experience of the world in relation to socio-cultural categories? Why is the notion of the author's intent privileged? Discourse is realized in social practice, and power is exercised, not held in reserve, as Foucault (1991) argues. The way that these prompts appear neutral, obvious, helpful – and the way that our interrogation of them might seem pedantic, negative, excessive – merely reinforce the power exercised by the orthodox framing of discussions of literature: author as architect of meaning, reader in the mode of appreciation and understanding, uncritical, constrained, deficient.

These prompts are most clearly configured in relation to the institutionalized framing of discourse around literature: we are asked to contemplate (and ultimately to understand) the author's various "techniques" that are, of course, used by other authors for other novels and thus form part of the horizontal discourse of literature. The *use* of tense, the *use* of irony, the *use* of effect – the "employment" of these, are very much the "meat and drink" of the literature classroom. These are largely closed questions in the sense that we would expect there to be an answer – if we can't find it in ourselves it is probably available to us in the words of the author (in interviews, perhaps) or in the existing words of reviewers or academics. These three sets of discursive operations reinforce orthodox classificatory relations of reading through their delimiting of any space for a more reflexive discussion of how the book comes to be. Critical discourse analysis leads us to the view that in so doing these "microstructures" of language reinforce "macrostructures" of society (Mayr 2008, 9).

These prompts appear on the "branded" edition of the novel itself. In this form they are, of course, part of a commercial product. On the website, the prompts appear after a celebratory collection of statements about the book that are entirely in keeping with promotional discourse. The relationship of critical discussion to pedagogic legitimation is rarely, if ever discussed within the idioms of Subject English and yet this is highly conspicuous by its absence. The book club does not encourage its members to view the promotional statements as "texts" to discuss.

What alternative prompts might have been provided that would avoid the constraining effects of those we have deconstructed above? How might similar ideas circulating in the novel have been set up for a more critical and theoretical, a more reflexive discussion? A question such as "what do you think is the purpose of a novel featuring fictional characters as Taliban members?" would do more than, in Bourdieu's (1990) terms, merely recirculate and reaffirm the legitimate mode of expression at hand – to be recognized and not challenged. We can very easily suggest further prompts:

> Why do you think this book has been selected for this book club?

> What ideas about the world are reinforced in the novel?

> How does the way the book is described on its back cover identify it as 'suitable' for certain kinds of readers but not others?

> Why do you think the book cover was designed this way?

or even,

> Who is the publisher and what other kinds of books did they publish in the same format?

These questions, about institutional discourse, are central to the self-appointed status of literature in the "real world" and yet only one set of relations to that "reality" are bookmarked for the book club's attention – the idea of the novel relating to an externally "known" world, not a commercial one.

On Being a Reader with Richard and Judy

We have in this chapter explored the duality of the experience of reading as framed by the Richard & Judy Book Club. We have found that there are spaces set up for new ways of being a reader and that these can be included in an extended definition of Media 2.0 and that these are partly the result of new media technologies (the multimodel dissemination of the invitation to read and to discuss reading and potentially to reflect on being a reader). However, we conclude with the realization that a discourse analysis of the prompts for discussion provided in both old and new media contexts serve to reinforce and reproduce existing discursive framings of being a reader. Further research might productively do ethnographic work with readers to "count the ways" in which they make sense of and, crucially, read against the grain of the discussion prompts we have deconstructed in this account. Such an extended exploration of the social practices set up by the Richard & Judy Book Club in the context of the commercial publishers' adherence to the insulations (between reader and author, text and reader, understanding and not understanding) of schooled literature education will go further to measure the balance between new spaces and the same old stories.

Reference List

Barton, D. and M. Hamilton (1998) *Local Literacies*. London: Routledge.

Bazalgette, Cary (2008) "Literacy in Time and Space." *Points of View* 01.

Bernstein, Basil (2000) *Pedagogy, Symbolic Control and Identity: Theory, Research, Critique*. London: Taylor and Francis.

Bourdieu, P. (1991) *Language and Symbolic Power*. (Raymond, G. and Adamson, M. trans.). Oxford: Polity Press.

Bourdieu, P. (1992) *Language and Symbolic Power*. (Raymond, G. and Adamson, M. trans.). Oxford: Polity Press.

Bourdieu, P. and J-C Passeron (1990) *Reproduction in Education, Society and Culture*. London: Routledge.

Bourdieu, P. reprinted (2002) *Distinction, A Social Critique of the Judgement of Taste*. London: Routledge.

Buckingham, David and Rebekah Willett, eds (2009) *Video Cultures: Media Technology and Everyday Creativity*. London: Polity.

Colebrook, Claire (1997) *New Literary Histories: New Historicism and Contemporary Criticism*. Manchester: Manchester University Press.

Fairclough, Norman (1995) *Critical Discourse Analysis: The Critical Study of Language*. London: Longman.

Foucault, Michel (1991) What is an author? In *The Foucault Reader*, ed. Rabinow, Paul, 101–20. London: Penguin.

Gauntlett, David (2008) Participation, Creativity and Social Change. http://www.youtube.com/watch?v=MNqgXbI1_o8&feature=channel_page (accessed 28 July 2009).

Gauntlett, David (2009) Media and Everyday Life. http://www.theory.org.uk (accessed 9 July 2009).

Gauntlett, David (2006) Media Studies 2.0. http://www.theory.org.uk/mediastudies2.htm (accessed 2 August 2010).

Gee, James Paul (2003) *What Video Games Have to Teach about Language and Literacy*. New York: Palgrave Macmillan.

Hills, Matt (2002) *Fan Cultures*. London: Routledge.

Kendall, Alex (2008) Giving up reading: re-imagining reading with young adult readers. *Journal of Research and Practice in Adult Literacy* 65: 14–22.

Kendall, Alex and Julian McDougall (2009) Just gaming: on being differently literate. *Eludamos: Journal for Computer Game Culture* 3 (2): 245–60.

Lister, John et al. (2009) *New Media: A Critical Introduction*. 2nd edn. London: Routledge.

Marsh, Jackie (2007) New Literacies and Old Pedagogies; Recontextualising Rules and Practices. *International Journal of Inclusive Education* 11(3): 267–81.

Mayr, A. (2008) *Language and Power: An Introduction to Institutional Discourse*. London: Continuum.

McDougall, Julian and Steve Dixon (2009) Doing Media 2.0. *Networks* 08.

McLuhan, Marshal (1967) *Understanding Media – The Extensions of Man*. London: Sphere.

Merrin, W. (2008) Media Studies 2.0. http://twopointzeroforum.blogspot.com/ (accessed 3 July 2009).

Peim, Nick (1993) *Critical Theory and the English Teacher*. London: Routledge.

Peim, Nick (2000) The Cultural Politics of English Teaching. *Issues in English Teaching*. London: Routledge.

Richard & Judy Book Club Reading Notes (2009) http://www. richardandjudybookclub.co.uk/siteimages/RandJ/pdfdownload/4TSS.pdf

Rylands, T. (2007) Myst in Action. http://www.youtube.com/ watch?v=X5xFMmK5Ujs.

Sreedharan, C. (2009) Reuters e-mail interview. http://in.reuters.com/article/ technologyNews/idINIndia-41551220090805

Chapter 4
Richard and Judy Behind Bars

Jenny Hartley

Inside the prisons of the United Kingdom, Richard, Judy and their Book Club have done good work: as messengers, as authorizers of affect, and as cultural brokers. This brief chapter analyses their role and impact, through the Richard & Judy Book Club books chosen by prison reading groups, and one book in particular. Audrey Niffenegger's *The Time Traveler's Wife* in jail was an example of perfect convergence. Book and group came together in an unlikely and successful encounter.

The library is often the most congenial room in a prison. Since the mid 1980s prison libraries in the United Kingdom have been staffed, though not exclusively, by professional librarians (prison libraries are part of the public lending library service). The high quality publicity material promoting the Richard & Judy Book Club (RJBC) – the fliers and advertisements – has been a boon to librarians on the hunt to attract new readers, and to flag up new and diverse material. By these means word has got through about books that readers might not have met before, and about reading practices too, although prison libraries have had a long-standing interest in such matters. Back in 1987 an article in the *Prison Libraries Group Newsletter* introduced its readers to bibliotherapy, explaining: "the basic idea is to choose the right book for the right inmate at a time when he can absorb the material and then to discuss the work and his interpretations of it" (*Newsletter* 1987). This was the pre-reading-group era but with similar aims and goals. In 1989 the Council of Europe's report, *Education in Prison*, advocated "establishing the library as a lively place, where events such as readings, debates, exhibitions and lectures take place" (*Newsletter* 1990). However, 20 years later there is still, according to one prison librarian, "no wholehearted agreement that reading for pleasure is a valuable activity in its own right." In this respect the RJBC has had a legitimizing role. A book club, it reassures unconvinced prison officers and inmates, is worthwhile, something regular, ordinary people do.

Reading groups in prisons often run much like any other reading group, deciding on a book that the members will all read in order to discuss at the next meeting. For the past 10 years Sarah Turvey and I have been running reading groups in UK prisons. These are not bibliotherapy groups with prescribed texts, nor are they classes, nor courses following pedagogic paradigms, such as the successful Changing Lives Through Literature program in the United States (their philosophy and practice are outlined by Trounstine and Waxler 2005). For any reading group anywhere, choosing the books can take a long time. As one 17-year-old group commented in the survey of UK groups that Sarah Turvey and I conducted in

2001, "our biggest problem is always 'what do we read next'" (Hartley 2001, 45). How much more difficult this perennial challenge is for a reading group inside a prison. The stimulus of the bookshop, the chat in the coffee shop, or the cue from what is being read on the London Underground: many of the ways in which a reading group finds its way to its next book are denied to the prisoner. At the same time, prison is a place that puts a high premium on choice. A prisoner is not able to make many choices, and the choice of what to read next in a prison reading group is freighted with importance. The process may involve negotiating, persuading, voting: all skills a prisoner often needs to develop.

One of the principles guiding choice is that prisoners want to feel that they are part of the reading world, reading on the same page as everyone else. In this respect, the RJBC has been an enabler: not so much for its television presence as for the virtual reading group it invites the prisoner to participate in. Richard and Judy are already familiar figures, friends on the outside, and a link to that ongoing outside life. As hosts they beckon and usher the would-be and perhaps uncertain reader into a reassuring, non-threatening space. Nor only have they been ambassadors and escorts in the choice process; just as importantly, they have helped expand reading horizons. This is the bonus of the reading group often identified by members generally in comments such as "We're reading books we would never have tackled independently," or "I read books I never would have chosen for myself" (Hartley 2001, 126).

Nearly 20 of the RJBC's recommendations have been chosen and read since 2004 by prison reading groups; these are the books I will be referring to in the rest of this chapter. They include Joseph O'Connor's *Star of the Sea* (2003), Asne Seierstad's *The Bookseller of Kabul* (2003), and Tim Butcher's *Blood River* (2007): books that can be challenging and that groups might not have found their way to otherwise. The women's group have chosen more – and more fiction – than the men's groups. But the men are surprisingly well-represented in the fiction choices, especially given their often expressed wariness of the genre in general.

Virtual friends though they may be, Richard and Judy's seal of approval is not an uncontestable imprimatur. Their books have not been invariably accepted, and if chosen, not always admired. Like other reading groups, prison reading groups pride themselves on their independence of judgment. RJBC books that disappointed included Julian Fellowes's *Snobs* ("trivial and rather unpleasant"), and Mark Mills's *The Savage Garden* ("main character too thin, plot too obvious"). Jim Lynch's *The Highest Tide* divided opinion in time-honored reading group tradition: half the group thought it was rubbish, the other half thought it "visionary." And while the ethical issues raised by Jodi Picoult's *My Sister's Keeper* engrossed the women's group, this same group rejected the dilemmas of Kim Edwards's *The Memory Keeper's Daughter* as too obviously contrived.

Liking or disliking, however, may not be the point, as a discussion at a women's prison of Kate Morton's *The House at Riverton* suggests. The session started with a reported response from a member who could not be present, but sent a message to say it was the best book she had read in the group. Respecting such an opinion, the group tactfully agreed that it was "a good read." One member had noted a couple of phrases she particularly liked: for example, during an argument between two sisters, everything in the room took sides. While we could all recognize that, opinion shifted over the next quarter of an hour. Yes, this was easy to read, but as a historical novel it just did not convince. Would women wear tights in the years before the First World War? Just how much could a housemaid earn? The structure was picked apart: why did quite so many characters have to die? Why did the author give away her plot climaxes? But even if the group found fault with the book, there was as always the dividend of the unexpected insight. Discussion turned, on that cold and wet February evening, to the narrator's choice to stay in service at the big house rather than marry the man she loved. "It's a bit like prison, isn't it" commented a member of the group. "It's a comforting world, all your decisions taken for you. It's warm, a world she knows."

To the RJBC then, our groups owe many good discussions, many unforeseen moments of perception. Other benefits have accrued from their choices. For the unaccustomed reader, who claimed that she had only read six books in her life before being brought to the group by a woman on her corridor, Mitch Albom's *The Five People You Meet in Heaven* brought such solace that she copied out passages to stick up on her cell wall. The group reading *The Star of the Sea* appreciated how much it told them about the plight of the Irish in the nineteenth century. Sometimes the insights are about how books work. A group member who had enjoyed William Boyd's *Restless* complained about what she called the "let-down" of the ending: why was it left so open, why couldn't the woman settle? I pointed to the title of the book; others, including the complainer, then picked up ideas about restlessness throughout the book, before she asked, "do you think William thought about all that?" Sometimes the insights are about how book discussions work. After a heated argument about the motives of the teacher in *Mr Pip*, a member new to the group commented, "Ah I see, it's not like school, it's OK to disagree." And sometimes a group member may find himself in an unaccustomed readerly position, such as the stance revealed in a comment by a male prisoner on Kate Summerscale's *The Suspicions of Mr Whicher*: "I never thought to say it but I'm feeling sorry for the detective here; they've got him involved far too late."

In 2007 a survey of reading groups currently running in prisons throughout the UK put Audrey Niffenegger's *The Time Traveler's Wife* (2004) at the top of the list of books that had gone well (Hartley and Turvey 2008). It had been featured by Richard and Judy's Book Club in 2005. A facilitator for a group where members do not always read the same books as each other was surprised by its popularity, "despite me telling the guys it was a love story!" She described the book's progress:

> The first man who read it was so enthusiastic about it that a second reader wanted to read it and it eventually made its way around the whole group, even being read by one man who was convinced it wasn't for him. It also opened up the group to the idea of reading genres previously discounted as 'girlie' and we followed up by reading James Frey's *Million Little Pieces* which is very emotive and powerfully written.

A member of this group wrote that he "enjoyed these books very much and although they are fiction they gave me a lot of insight on various things including the many ways of different authors have in telling their stories." Another prisoner answered the survey question, "Has talking about a book in the group ever made you change your mind about it?" by saying "I did not want to read *The Time Traveler's Wife* until I heard about it because I thought it was a woman's story about love." Members of other men's groups were also enthusiastic: "a fantastic book, wonderful, very emotional."

These endorsements by men, who are usually wary of both fiction, and female authors, are striking. Here it is precisely what one would expect to put them off (love, emotion) that they respond to. But there is a precedent for the success of *The Time Traveler's Wife*. In 1910 the then Home Secretary, Winston Churchill, commissioned a report on the supply of books in prisons, which included an Appendix of "Favourite Prison Authors" (*Report* 1911). Leading the field by a long way, was Mrs Henry Wood. Her best-seller, *East Lynne*, had been published 50 years previously in 1861, and again, this must have included many male endorsements, as men's prisons have always much outnumbered women's prisons. Like *The Time Traveler's Wife*, *East Lynne* seems an unlikely favorite for this male constituency; do the two novels share any common features or themes?

East Lynne is a reverse *Jane Eyre*, with a trajectory for its heroine from duchess to governess. And in a parallel slide, a man also becomes déclassé: wrongly suspected of murder, a magistrate's son is on the run for most of the book. Working in stables, because horses are all he knows about, he now addresses the gentlemen from his old life as "sir." Waiting is the great motif of the book. "'Ay, to wait on'" murmurs Barbara, in unrequited love over many years and pages; "'to wait on in dreary pain; to wait on, perhaps for years, perhaps for ever! And poor Richard – wearing out his days in poverty and exile!'" (Wood 1861, 145). Being pursued and victimized are also important: "Poor hunted Richard!" (266). The book's highest virtue is fidelity, even after the beloved has betrayed.

Fidelity is also the crucial value in *The Time Traveler's Wife*, which has waiting at its heart. "I won't ever leave you," declares Clare, the wife of the title, "even though you're always leaving me" (105). Her husband Henry is a reluctant time traveler, the victim of a genetic mutation that whisks him away suddenly, and involuntarily. Like *East Lynne*'s Richard Hare, Henry finds himself wrongly persecuted as his time travelling deposits him naked, sick and vulnerable, forced to steal clothes and food in the interests of survival. If this is a flattering perspective of the prisoner, his wife's point of view is well represented too. "Our life together in this too-small apartment," observes Clare, "is punctuated by Henry's small absences. Sometimes he disappears unobtrusively; I might be walking from the kitchen into the hall and find a pile of clothing on the floor. I might get out of bed in the morning and find the shower running and no one in it. Sometimes it's frightening" (274–5). Henry's life rhythms would be all too recognizable to many of the prison population, and "Love After Love," the Derek Walcott poem used as one of the book's epigraphs, seems to speak straight to the prisoner in its first stanza:

> The time will come
> when, with elation,
> you will greet yourself arriving
> at your own door, in your own mirror,
> and each will smile at the other's welcome.

This "elation" of the return home is the sustaining narrative in the prisoner's head, even though he or she may know that the reality will be rather different.

"A modern fairy tale," as the *New Statesman* calls it in the blurb on its book-jacket, *The Time Traveler's Wife* confers a knowingly ridiculous but transfiguring gloss on to both sides of the prison experience: on to the one who reluctantly departs and the one who faithfully waits. Further, Niffenegger's methodology offers a good fit to the prisoner, as she splits Henry into two, one a good citizen librarian, while the time traveler is a "disappearing artist," "inverted, changed into a desperate version of myself . . . a thief, a vagrant, an animal who runs and hides" (3). And the book also has it both ways in that time travelling is not always disastrous; it has its consolations, its wish-fulfilling aspects. Henry's travels take him back to his childhood and grant him the wish of seeing his dead and much missed mother again. They also grant evasion: "We escape," says Henry (348): surely another prisoner fantasy. Intermittently absent through reasons beyond his control, Henry is the husband or father the male prisoner might wish to be: devoted and attentive when present, and, crucially, emotionally articulate. From its first page onwards the book is a flowing tour-de-force of expressed emotion. Clare begins the book avowing what is so dear to the prisoner's belief system: unshakeable fidelity, "love intensified by absence" (1); 500 pages later Henry ends the book acknowledging his responsibility – "I have given you a life of suspended animation" (503) he tells Clare.

If this is a "modern fairy tale" about time travel, it is also a very old story indeed, harking back as it does explicitly on more than one occasion to the figures of Odysseus and Penelope. The novel finally concludes with a quotation from Robert Fitzgerald's celebrated translation of *The Odyssey*, the moment, inevitably, of the wanderer's return to his wife Penelope, "her white arms round him pressed as though for ever." Homer's poem has itself found responsive readers in prison. A group in California's San Quentin jail, who particularly enjoy "stories about women who wait for their men," picked *The Odyssey* as a significant book for them: the son who has to grow up without the father, the father who has to leave his son and, at the heart of it: Penelope waiting.

The persecuted man, the waiting woman, the emotionally expressive form: the similarities between *The Odyssey*, *East Lynne*, and *The Time Traveler's Wife* suggest the appeal of certain themes and motifs to men in prison. These elements found – or created – an audience that became temporarily and unusually open to affect: a response all the more apparent because of its absence in a reading group in a women's prison. This group enjoys the pleasures of sentimental and sensational fiction, to being swept along and identifying with characters and so on; but in their responses to this novel they voiced their suspicions about what they saw as Henry's manipulation of Clare. For them, this novel was not such an unusual reading experience.

For the men, however, this was a unique reading experience. Here was a book they would not otherwise have glanced at; and this reminds us of the importance of the reading situation. Interestingly, a similar phenomenon was observed a century ago, in the evidence collected by Florence Bell for her survey of reading habits among working people in the Yorkshire iron-town of Middlesbrough. As in the prison reading survey of 1911, Mrs Henry Wood is the most popular named author by far. And it is not only the women who read her. Men often like her too; but more than that: she features explicitly in scenes of shared reading. Reading aloud is often mentioned; in one family "Sister very fond of reading, and reads Mrs Henry Wood and Shakespeare to the rest of the family"; in another family the husband "Reads aloud to his wife, chiefly Mrs Henry Wood's books." Yet another "reads aloud to his wife in the evening Mrs Henry Wood's books and Dickens's" (Bell 1907, 147–62). These convivial shared settings that host *East Lynne* can be compared to the welcome proffered by Richard and Judy and their extended group. In both cases, male hostility to the genre of sensational/sentimental fiction and male wariness of the literature of affect – literature that has designs on their emotional lives – has been lulled by the presence of the reading companion, whether real or virtual.

Context, we may conclude, is all. Reader response is a plant of unpredictable growth. Discoveries and connection have to be made by the reader for him or herself; they are indeed part of the act of reading, what gives reading its value. Some members of prison reading groups are adventurous readers but the majority are – like most of the population outside prison – wary of experimenting, of reading genres they perceive as not for them. Prisoners also suspect literature that they feel is presented to them with specific designs upon them: prescribed texts, for example or the Enhanced Thinking Skills material, which forms part of the HM Prison Service's Offending Behaviour Programme. They are also wary of laying themselves open to exposure, and emotional vulnerability. For the feats achieved by their Book Club in introducing and accompanying these readers on new journeys, Richard and Judy and their team should be warmly applauded.

Reference List

Bell, Lady Florence. 1985 [1907]. *At the Works: A Study of a Manufacturing Town*. London: Virago Press.

Hartley, Jenny. 2001. *Reading Groups*. Oxford: Oxford University Press.

Hartley, Jenny, and Sarah Turvey. 2008. What Can a Book Do Behind Bars? *The Reader* 32 (Winter): 60–68.

Niffenegger, Audrey. 2004. *The Time Traveler's Wife*. London: Jonathan Cape.

Prison Libraries Group Newsletter. 1987. Prison Libraries Group of the Library Association.

Prison Libraries Group Newsletter. 1990. Prison Libraries Group of the Library Association.

Report of the Departmental Committee on the Supply of Books to Prisoners in HM Prisons and to the Inmates of HM Borstal Institutions. 1911. London: HMSO.

Trounstine, Jean, and Robert P. Waxler. 2005. *Finding a Voice: The Practice of Changing Lives Though Literature*. Michigan: Michigan University Press.

Wood, Mrs Henry. 1901 [1861]. *East Lynne*. London: Macmillan.

PART 2
Reading The Richard & Judy Book Club Selections

Chapter 5
You Can't Judge a Book by Its Coverage: The Body that Writes and the Television Book Club

Kerry Myler

Writing is that neutral, composite, oblique space where our subject slips away, the negative where all identity is lost, starting with the very identity of the body writing.

—Roland Barthes, "The Death of the Author"

Words leak from my brain. Seep out of my ear. Burble from my crooked mouth. Splash on my shirt. Trickle into my keyboard. Pool on my warped parquet floor. At least they're not gushing from my heart. Or, God forbid, my ass. I catch the words as they fall. My hands smell. And the place is a wreck. From all the spilled words.

—Lori Lansens, *The Girls*

The author's body *is* important – and not only the hand that writes but also the mouth that speaks, the face that photographs, the hand that shakes and signs and, for the purposes of the television book club, the body that sits upon the comfy sofa and/or wanders thoughtfully around the location in which their current novel happens to be set. And yet when Roland Barthes infamously announced the death of the author in 1968, the body was the first thing to go: the "subject slips away," he writes, starting with the "very identity of the body writing" (1995, 125). The body that Barthes seemingly erases with such ease (the rest of his essay focuses on the more "metaphysical" traces of authorial presence) is, in the world of modern publishing, a body that is not simply necessary in order to produce the text, but also to function as a visible and active promotional tool in the marketing of that text *as product*. Rather than "the author enter[ing] into his own death" when the "writing begins" (Barthes 1995, 125), the author enters into a diverse and competitive arena of marketing and promotion that requires them to be very much alive when the writing ends. And, in being so very much alive, the problems that Barthes attempts to escape – those metaphysical assumptions regarding authorial intentions as well as those always troublesome, material bodies – reappear in new, potentially problematic, but also revelatory, ways.

In the year following the publication of "The Death of the Author," Michel Foucault rephrases Barthes's central question through Samuel Beckett's *Texts for Nothing*: he asks "what does it matter who is speaking" (1986, 101)? Foucault reconsiders notions of authorship as functions of discourse. As a discursive construct the concept of the author is utilized in order to instate and perpetuate certain "truths" about the nature of not only literature and how we read, but the industry, legalities and institutions involved in the distribution, regulation and promotion of literature and knowledge. However, while Foucault's "author function" (1986, 108) can be used in order to construct the notion of, for instance, a "body of work," it is in no sense resuscitating the "body of the author." The author as function only reclaims the author as a *concept*; for the most part the author here is little more than a name that can be used in order to categorize works, or allow one to lay legal claim to works or, indeed, assign blame for works. Foucault, then, does not attempt to revive the body of Barthes's dead author – rather he erects the headstone by which one can mark and inscribe, and so utilize, a name, a date, a brief "generic" epitaph. That said, if Foucault can reply yes, it does matter "who is speaking," perhaps we might be permitted to ask if it might also matter what body is writing. And, by extension, what of the "matter" of the body that writes?

These are questions an emerging second wave of feminist literary theory was required to confront. The significance of the author was being challenged just as feminist critics were attempting to instate and theorize a new/recovered gendered category of literature, a category based on the sex of the author, the *body* of the author. Nancy K. Miller, in her 1985 essay "Changing the Subject: Authorship, Writing and the Reader," argues that the debates surrounding the nature of authorship from 1968 onwards displace notions of "authority" from the author to the text, to language itself, to the extent that such theoretical practices actively *suppress* the author in order to create a "disembodied and ownerless *écriture*" (1995, 194). Second-wave feminist critics were faced with the difficulty of having to forge, collate and theorize a body of work under the heading of, for instance, "women's writing" or "black women's writing," while simultaneously the body of the author was being considered no longer desirable or applicable to the study of literature. Problematic though genre categories such as "women's writing" or "black women's writing" can be, they, at the very least, serve to identify and make visible texts *and authors* that have historically been disregarded, undervalued, unread, unable to write. How can Spivak's subaltern ever be heard if as soon as she opens her mouth any trace of the body that speaks is expunged from her text?

In *Figuring the Woman Author in Contemporary Fiction*, Mary Eagleton discusses the difficulties faced by feminist literary critics in the wake of Barthes's and Foucault's essays:

> If we accept the loss of 'the very identity of the body writing' then certain conclusions follow: the name and gender of the author become irrelevant; the fact that all the authors mentioned by Barthes are male and that only three of the more than forty authors mentioned by Foucault are female is inconsequential; and the preoccupation of literary feminists to find lost women authors and to focus on women's literary production has been misplaced. (2005, 17)

Eagleton's head count reveals the implicit assumption in "The Death of the Author" and "What is an Author?" that the body that writes is a *male* body. It matters what body is writing then because a body made invisible is presumed to be the already disavowed and disowned body of the archetypal possessor of knowledge, language and power. Foucault writes that the author function is "the result of a complex operation which constructs a *certain rational being* that we call 'author' … this *intelligible* being" (1986, 110, *emphasis added*). The author function is generated by way of a particular construct of the author as that which is rational and intelligible – that is, the transcendent, white, heterosexual, male voice that second-wave feminist theory argues has historically (if metaphorically) transcended the materiality of the (feminine) body. The authorial body, in this case, is always already "immaterial" to the concept of authorship; it is the bodies that do not conform to this model, those "irrational" or "unintelligible" bodies, that are conveniently made invisible in order to protect the sanctity of the "disembodied and ownerless" text.

There is then, one might argue (as, indeed, Miller does), a "political need" (Eagleton 2005, 19) for the visibility of the female author's body and, as Eagleton writes, a continuing "need for women to claim cultural legitimacy through authorising themselves" (2005, 2). Foucault's author functions are historically and culturally determined categories, which, as such, are susceptible to change. The work of second-wave feminist critics has changed the landscape of literary history and production by reinstating a neglected body of women's writing and forging the way for a new genre of feminist literature, as well as paving the way for other previously disregarded or marginalized texts and their authors. The concept of the author has had to adapt to encompass this more inclusive cultural moment as well as the re-emergence of the authorial body that has suddenly, in a Western media-driven, visually orientated, capitalist-consumerist society, become highly visible and highly sought.

This visible authorial presence is a key component of the television book club format. In 1968 Barthes wrote that "the *author* still reigns in histories of literature, biographies of writers, interviews, magazines" (1995, 126), and so, in the twenty-first century the author still reigns in the television book club format – a popular and powerful phenomenon that has been associated with, in particular, promoting women's writing. The author whose text is selected for the television book club must emerge from their early grave, construct their media image and confront the talk show host, the panel of readers and the audience of millions watching at home. To what extent, then, does this uncovering of the authorial body trouble the disembodied sanctity of the text? What happens when the body that writes fails to match up to the archetypal author image, or, indeed, is unable to construct a media image that meets the standards of current Western perceptions of bodily intelligibility? How, for instance, might the prominence of the authorial body within the television book club format serve to complicate the author function in terms of issues surrounding gender, sexuality, race, age, attractiveness, illness or, as I will discuss later in this chapter, disability? What kinds of questions concerning the body that writes, and perhaps the concept of a "right" body to write, are generated when the author's body is transported from the shady confines of the home-office to the small screen of the day-time television book club?

Oprah's Authors

The Oprah Winfrey Show established the book club television chat show format in 1996. That format has become the template, or, at the very least, a reference point, for all subsequent television book clubs, including its British equivalent, the Richard & Judy Book Club. Oprah's Book Club began as a small segment within the show but quickly became a substantial cog in the Oprah corporate machine as well as a major presence in the US publishing industry and beyond. The appeal of Oprah's Book Club is in its ability to make an onscreen reading group discussion visually stimulating, inclusive and entertaining. The presence of the author has proven integral to this process. Oprah's Book Club is not troubled by Barthes's warning against attempting to seek "the *explanation* of a work … in the man or woman who produced it" (1995, 126). Oprah's Book Club, in fact, revolves around and relies upon precisely this notion. Studying the role of the authorial body in Oprah's Book Club, and how that role has evolved over the course of the club's 15 years, reveals the various ways in which the author can functions in terms of the television book club and helps to establish how and why the Richard & Judy Book Club chose to alter the format established by Oprah.

Oprah's Book Club begins with an introduction to the text and its author, who is captured in a VT usually filmed "on location." The segment might then involve some superficial discussion with the chat show audience before introducing the lucky few who have been invited to meet the author to discuss the book. After various clips of the viewers in their homes reading the letters that awarded them this opportunity, the segment moves on to the main section of the format: the dinner party. Here Oprah wines and dines her selected author in the presence of the suitably reverent and deferential viewers she has selected. The author is venerated, displacing even Oprah from the head of the table, and, allowing for the usually highly personal and subjective responses to the text offered by the guests, the author offers the final and definitive word on *their* work. Oprah and her dinner guests look to the author for clarification, amplification, "*explanation*."

In an interview with Marilyn Johnson, Oprah declared that "writers are in a class by themselves. I have the ultimate respect for them" (1997, 6). In Oprah's Book Club the author is the authority on the text. There is no need to analyze or interpret the text when the author is present to tell the reader what it means. And, once the issue of what the text is *about* is settled the show is free to discuss the issues and topics raised by the text as opposed to the text itself. Cecilia Konchar Farr, in *Reading Oprah: How Oprah's Book Club Changed the Way America Reads*, explains that "later Book Club shows were often advertised as issue orientated shows, a proven format, where the issue (domestic abuse for *Black and Blue* or illiteracy for *The Reader*, for example) took centre stage over the book" (2005, 10). The reading group discussion revolves around a theme generated by the selected text but is addressed in terms of how the (carefully selected) guests respond to that theme, or how the book reflects their own personal experiences or how the novel has impacted upon their lives; it is no sense an *analysis* of the text. This is not a requirement of the format. The author, for Oprah's Book Club, functions in order to negate such a requirement. The author functions in order to fix meaning, to "furnish" the text "with a final signified, to close the writing" (Barthes 1995, 128–9).

And yet the author, as a visible presence on the screen, can also function in other more liberating ways. Oprah's authors have been a diverse and multi-cultural group. In the first seven seasons of the book club, 1996–2002, of the 39 authors featured six were African America, one Armenian American, one Haitian American, one Canadian, one Chilean, one Indian, one Irish, two German, one Moroccan, and 29 of the 39 were women. In the foreword to Farr's *Reading Oprah*, Elizabeth Long observes the "'oprahfying' effect" that has "elevat[ed] unexpected books and authors due to her personal taste or critical charisma" by "selecting unknown authors and authors of color" (Long 2005, xi). Oprah's Book Club was actively involved in raising the profile of the non-white, non-male body that writes and, in the process, generating a huge upsurge in the sales of novels that had been or might otherwise have been overlooked. Oprah's book club selections and the sales generated by them have, according to Farr, "made a significant inroad" in what is "a largely white audience in an industry dominated by white writers ... one that demonstrates, again, that Oprah had a meaningful agenda for the Book Club" (2005, 22). This agenda, to promote and champion writers who have been previously under represented in the literary market, earned Oprah's Book Club a reputation for selecting, in particular, African American and women's writing – a reputation for making visible the marginalized bodies that produced the same kinds of neglected works that second-wave feminist literary critics had fought so hard to reclaim and canonize.

While improving the visibility and sales of previously overlooked writers, the book club's author-orientated format proved to have inherent dangers. By bestowing such importance on the author and making the "present" author a central feature of the segment, the book club was dependent on that author's cooperation and their willingness to submit to the necessary onscreen (and later online) commitments that such a format demands. But the body that writes can also be a body that bites, and in Oprah's case it was not the unruly female body that proved troublesome but the white, male American, Jonathan Franzen. *The Corrections*, Franzen's third and critically acclaimed novel, was announced as an Oprah's Book Club "pick" on September 24, 2001. *The Corrections* signaled a marked turn to the "literary" for the book club. Oprah's penchant for women's writing had led to some critics deriding the book club for promoting "women's books" at the expense of other more notable texts and (male) authors. By selecting *The Corrections*, Oprah appeared to be accepting (or submitting to) the challenge set by her critics: to get America reading (what they considered) more "serious" works of literature. However, it was precisely this perception of Oprah's past gender bias that contributed to Franzen's disastrous dealings with the book club.

Franzen gives an account of his foreshortened Oprah's Book Club experience in an essay entitled "Meet me in St. Louis" (2001). In the essay he describes the process of filming for the VT segment of the show which is set "on location" in his home town. Not only does Oprah's Book Club happily, even greedily, seek out authorial intentions, it also actively pursues that other route of critical enquiry discounted by Barthes – it conflates text and author to the extent that one simply mirrors the other (Barthes 1995, 126). So Franzen is filmed in his old neighborhood, outside of his old home, looking at a tree planted after his father's death "contemplatively" (Franzen 2005, 297). These shots, Franzen explains, will "produce a short visual biography of me and an impressionistic summary of *The Corrections*" (2005, 289). In the VT footage the authorial body functions in two ways: it is the origin of the text and, by extension, the embodiment of the textual content. Foucault writes that "it would be wrong to equate the author with the real writer as to equate him with the fictitious speaker; the author function is carried out and operates in the scission itself, in this division and this distance" (1986, 112). Wrong though the merging of author, writer and character might be according to Foucault, the television book club thrives on such associations. While Franzen speaks as the authorial "third self … to tell the work's meaning, the obstacles encountered, the results obtained, and the remaining problems" (Foucault 1986, 122), his body functions as a visual image of the other two selves – writer and character/narrator – which, in the process, become conflated.

When asked to return to his home town to film the VT, Franzen complied because "when I accepted Winfrey's endorsement of my book … I understood that television is propelled by images, the simpler and more vivid the better. If the producers wanted me to be Midwestern, I would try to be Midwestern" (Franzen 2004, 290). However, the producers, and Franzen too I suspect,[1] wanted the image to be less one of geographical origins as one of literary origins, of "literariness." Franzen's function on the screen is to project that which the novel signifies for Oprah's Book Club – the turn to the literary, to the heavyweight novel, to a "serious" text. Franzen not only had to walk around the Midwest and act Midwestern, he also had to emulate a "great" writer, to *embody* the literary. Conveniently, this author of "high art" (Franzen 2004, 300) equates with that archetypal image of the possessor of knowledge and power: he is white, western, heterosexual and male. And yet Franzen remembers feeling distinctly uncomfortable in this body during filming and fails to give the director what he wants: "rendering emotion is what I do as a writer, and this tree is my material, and now I'm helping to ruin it" because "I'm failing to emote" (Franzen 2004, 297). The tree is a signifier of origins: the origin of life; the origin of knowledge; the origin of Franzen (it symbolizes the father here); and, quite literally, the origin of the paper on which he writes. Beside it Franzen is supposed to signify as an origin too – his body is the "origin" of the words on the paper. But, just as you can't turn the pages of a tree, so Franzen's body fails to "emote" as the origin of his own "high art." This is partly because the *body* is not part of the concept of the "Author–God" (Barthes 1995, 218) – the

---

[1]   Franzen is also eager to film in his current location – New York, that metropolis of art, culture and intellectual endeavor (Franzen 2005, 289).

Author–God is the transcendent, the immaterial, the "mind." The white, male body is a body already assumed and then disavowed. And it is also partly because the seriousness and weightiness of the "literary" that Franzen is supposed to embody is directly contradicted by the sentimental, "schmaltz[y]" "emoting" (Franzen 2004, 297) required by the popular television format that seeks to simplistically conflate author/writer and character/narrator upon the authorial body. Indeed, throughout the essay Franzen symbolizes his discomfort at becoming an "Oprah author" (Franzen 2004, 297) in terms of a body that has turned against him: "I try not to claw myself where I itch," he writes (2004, 295).

Bodies continued to be problematic for Franzen as he sets about getting himself disinvited from the book club. In the weeks leading up to the book club dinner Franzen voiced various concerns about his role as an "Oprah author," including a disinclination to have the Oprah's Book Club corporate logo on the jacket of the book and the issue of popular fiction versus "high art" (Franzen 2004, 300). More interestingly, these were concerns that were also caught up with the gender of Oprah's previous authors and the gender of her target audience. Franzen, in an interview with Terry Gross on NPR's *Fresh Air*, explains that

> Now I'm actually at the point with this book where I worry – I'm sorry that it's – I had some hope of actually reaching a male audience. … And I've heard more than one reader in signing lines now in bookstores say, 'You know if I hadn't heard of you, I would've been put off by the fact that it is an Oprah pick. I figure those books are for women, and I never touch it.' (quoted in Rooney 2005, 43)

Though Franzen's concerns are seemingly about the gender of his potential readership, they also reflect anxieties about how Oprah's Book Club might threaten his own masculinity. By accepting Oprah's invitation, by becoming an "Oprah author," Franzen finds himself in an arena that is not only predominately occupied by supposedly "popular" texts but also by women writers. In an effort to establish himself within this arena he resorts to denigrating the readership that appearing on the club will bestow upon him and his novel. He appeals, instead, to that supposedly elusive "male audience" that he now believes Oprah's Book Club is serving to further alienate. His inclusion on a long list of female and/or "popular" authors causes Franzen, it seems, to feel himself categorized as less "literary," and indeed, less masculine.

Ironically, Franzen's concerns, which eventually resulted in his dinner party being cancelled,[2] would serve to found a new direction for the book club over the following years – a direction that was to become a lot more "literary" and a lot more masculine. While in the year after the Franzen incident the book club took a short break – Oprah cited difficulties in finding books worth recommending (Rooney 2005, 163) – from 2003 onwards the book club took a curious new turn. The club had gained a reputation for promoting first time and early career

---

[2]   Despite the "misunderstanding" (Rooney 2005, 66), *The Corrections* does remain an official selection of the club.

novelists, as well as women writers, African American writers and writers from other ethnic minorities; but, for the three series following the break, the majority of texts reviewed by the club were written by authors now dead – really dead – and *male*. Toni Morrison's 2002 appearance for *Sula* (1973) was the final time a woman would appear live on the book club. In the past eight years the book club has selected 17 authors, all of whom have been men with the exception of Pearl S. Buck and Carson McCullers. Before 2003 all of Oprah's Book Club picks were written by authors currently living and who (with the exception of Franzen) had made appearances on the show. But between 2003 and 2005 the book club featured novels by Alan Paton, John Steinbeck, Leo Tolstoy and William Faulkner, as well as Buck and McCullers. According to Farr, a spokesperson for *The Oprah Winfrey Show* explained that the book club was to "focus on 'great books that have stood the test of time' – not necessarily classics … not necessarily old books and not necessarily dead authors, but 'great books'" (2005, 122). However, one might speculate that, after the Franzen incident, Winfrey chose these "great books" by mostly dead authors because the dead author is not (usually) a troublesome author.

The lack of female authors chosen for the book club over the last eight years is less easily explained. In one sense, a turn to canonical, nineteenth- and early twentieth-century texts is necessarily a turn to the white, male author; but even after the "classics" phase ended in 2005 the female author failed to reappear. Despite the reliability of her female authors and the unreliability of the author of "high art," the club's new direction was decidedly "literary" and male. Franzen's main criticisms concerning Oprah's Book Club, that it favors female authors, panders to a predominantly female audience and that, hence, a male readership is discouraged when a book is selected by the club (Rooney 2005, 42–3), seem to have been "righted" by the club's more recent incarnation. At the expense of the under represented writers Oprah's Book Club once helped to promote, the book club has submitted to those detractors who criticized Oprah for not choosing more "literary" works by more "literary" authors, as well as the rather narrow view of what constitutes the literary: male, white and, ideally, dead. For the contemporary women writers Oprah so purposefully promoted in the early years of the book club this not only means the loss of the visibility they were once afforded but also, by comparison to the new "literary" direction of the club, "women's writing" is once more equated with the *non*-literary, the "popular."

Although Oprah's Book Club continued to be powerful (in terms of enhanced sales) during the "classics" phase, the format as a whole suffered. The three William Faulkner novels, selected for the Summer of 2005, did not even feature on the television show but were instead confined to the Oprah.com website (Wyatt 2005, 1). Even Oprah had to admit that "some recent selections did not draw the enthusiasm of some of her early ones" (Wyatt 2005, 1). Part of the reason that the "classics" phase of the book club did not quite emulate the success of the pre-Franzen days might be attributed to the lack of author and the difficulties of translating a book onto the screen without a visible, tangible presence to embody that text. Indeed, when Oprah explained that she "wanted to open the door and broaden the field" by choosing contemporary novels again, she added that this allows her to "do what I like to do most, which is sit and talk to authors about their work. It's kind of hard to do that when they're dead" (Wyatt 2005, 1). Without the author as a focus for the book discussion, particularly when that book is a literary "classic," the segment risks becoming more "educational" than entertaining. The author is vital to bringing "to life" the words on the page – to translating what is, after all, the extremely camera-unfriendly medium of writing, into an entertaining and visually stimulating representation of the text. The absence of the author also reinstated the need to *interpret* the text. Without the present author to carry out this function the host and her guests were left with the task of seeking the author "beneath the work" to "explain" the text: "victory to the critic" says Barthes (1995, 129). But not, alas, victory to Oprah. However more critically and analytically aware such a book club discussion might be, an author-less format fails to capture the same sense of immediacy, surety and intimacy generated by the presence of the (a)live author.

Consequently, in 2005, the (a)live author returned with James Frey and, unfortunately, another controversy, this time over the extent to which his "memoir," *A Million Little Pieces* (2003), pushed at the fact/fiction boundary of that genre. But this time Oprah brought back her troublesome author to confront on air. Maureen Dowd, in *The New York Times*, writes that "watching Oprah flay Frey was riveting" (2006, 17) and, in the process, she "rescu[ed] her reputation" (2006, 17). And, with the author back in line, Oprah's reputation intact and her no-nonsense attitude made plain to all potential book club authors, the next couple of years saw Oprah's Book Club return to its original format of live author chats and dinner parties, albeit without quite the same range and diversity of the original book club. But in 2008 the club changed direction again, this time with Eckhart Tolle's *The New Earth*. This book, a non-fiction spiritual guide, prompted Oprah to dedicate not just one meal and a handful of guests to the author but a whole 10 weeks of "webinars" (online seminars) that viewers/readers could log onto in order to "attend" class and afterwards submit questions to the author via Skype (Walker 2008, 26). With *The New Earth* the pedagogical leanings of the "classics" phase became a full blown course in new age spirituality, personal development and self-improvement. The return of the living author, it seems, signaled the return of the Romantic notion of poet as prophet. *The New Earth*, for Oprah, *is* "a line of words releasing a single 'theological' meaning (the 'message' of the Author–God)" (Barthes 1995, 128). The author is, once more, the *A*uthor, a spiritual guide and teacher – white, male and even European.

The Oprah Winfrey Show will end (at least on the *ABC* network) in September 2011. The book club has evolved significantly over its 15 years on air, not least in its turn to more heavyweight texts and authors; however, despite some deviations, it has retained a basic format over those 15 years, a format that relies upon the participation of a living author. The final series of *The Oprah Winfrey Show* continues with this basic format as well as the favoring of a "heavyweight" author. In fact, the first text announced for the final series is the highly publicized and long-awaited novel *Freedom* by Jonathan Franzen. In an on-air announcement, a benevolent Oprah extends the hand of reconciliatory friendship to Franzen who, she says, approached *her* with his new book. In choosing *Freedom* for the final series, Oprah effectively erases that dark moment in the book club's history. Franzen, once more granted the incredibly powerful endorsement of Oprah's Book Club, appears, this time, to have eagerly participated in all televised and online commitments. As a book club selection, *Freedom* (which happens to feature a male author who achieves commercial success in 2001 – the year *The Corrections* was published) embodies all the required elements of the perfect book club segment, including that most crucial of components – a willing author.

Richard & Judy's Authors

The success of Oprah's Book Club has not only spawned numerous other television book clubs around the world but also provided a tried and tested format for capturing a text and a book group discussion on air. In Britain that template was most famously employed by Amanda Ross for the television chat show *Richard & Judy*. The Richard & Judy Book Club began in 2004 and appeared to model itself upon the early incarnation of Oprah's Book Club. The British club featured contemporary texts (fiction and non-fiction) from authors who ranged in sex, race, age and nationality. On the first series, six of the 10 authors were women and the list included writers as diverse as Monica Ali and Martina Cole. The book club did not shy away from "popular" fiction, as Oprah's Book Club was then currently in the process of doing, but selected a variety of texts that crossed both genre and perceived high/low cultural boundaries. The Richard & Judy Book Club, as well as embracing the "popular," also prided itself on supporting new authors, even "creating" new authors: 2005 saw the launch of Richard & Judy's How to Get Published competition. Like Oprah's Book Club, this club also appeared to have an agenda – an agenda that sought to promote contemporary novels and support new novelists, as well as challenge the boundaries of the television book club format and, by extension, the literary and cultural boundaries it helped to constitute and perpetuate.

The Richard & Judy Book Club segment begins, like Oprah's Book Club, with a VT in which the author introduces the text. The Richard & Judy Book Club author wanders contemplatively around the location in which the novel is set, much like Franzen describes in "Meet Me in St Louis." In this setting, the author, for the most part, simply describes the plot and themes of the text. However, the format then deviates from the Oprah's Book Club template. Instead of following the VT with an Oprah style book club dinner party or author interview, Richard, Judy and two or three celebrity panelists discuss – and, indeed, debate – various aspects of the text live in the studio. The author is not a participant in this section of the segment and therefore the hosts and panelists are free to interpret, critique and even *dislike* the text. In an interview with *The Sunday Times*, Ross says, "We knew it wouldn't work in the same way as Oprah's – we needed more criticism. Oprah is too sugary. She has the author in the studio and is never critical about the books" (Appleyard 2008, 8). When Oprah selects a text the assumption is that the book is good. There is no discussion about the quality or value of the text during her dinner parties; Oprah has already settled this question by selecting the book. But, in the Richard & Judy Book Club, quality and value is very much up for debate and, famously, Richard and Judy do not always agree. The final section of the segment switches to another VT, this time featuring a local reading group who are usually filmed in a library and also offer their opinions, good or bad, on the text. The Richard & Judy Book Club quickly established itself as an engaging, popular and, like Oprah's Book Club, very powerful segment – the club generated phenomenal sales and earned itself privileged shelf space and promotional campaigns in libraries and leading UK bookshops.

While an "alive" author, it seems, remains necessary as an image to be projected onto the screen as part of an introductory VT, a "live" author, an "interactive" author, is not desired for this particular television book club. This differs significantly from Oprah's Book Club's reliance (save for the "classics" phase) on the author as an active participant in, and the focus of, the book group discussion. In Oprah's Book Club the author is multi-functioning – as in the Franzen example, the author functions to signify the origin of the text, the meaning of the text and the significance of that text for the book club. The author might also already function as a "celebrity," either as a literary name or as a popular media figure.[3] If not, their exposure as an Oprah author will grant them a certain degree of celebrity (or, for Franzen and Frey, infamy) and, at the very least, an author persona will be created during the dinner party. In The Richard & Judy Book Club the author's function, it seems, is much less varied. There is no preoccupation with authorial intention or author as origin of meaning or author as celebrity.[4] Although the VT encapsulates and safeguards the author's comments on "their" book, they actually offer very little interpretation of the text and instead simply provide a synopsis of the story and introduce the main characters. Moreover, these new or relatively unknown authors are not afforded the opportunity to construct an author persona – restricted to the VT, their function is limited to a visual image that simply acts as an embodiment of, and spokesperson for, textual content.

The emphasis of this book club is not on the author, it seems, but the reader. As Barthes argues, to relinquish notions of the author as the location of textual origin and meaning is to allow for "the birth of the reader" (1995, 130). Rather than associating meaning and celebrity status with the author, the Richard & Judy Book Club prefers to associate these with the reader, as represented by the panel of

---

[3]   Examples include Isabel Allende, Maya Angelou, Jeffrey Eugenides, Gabriel Garcia Márquez, Toni Morrison, Joyce Carol Oates as well as the "classics" phase authors. Popular celebrity authors include Bill Cosby and Sidney Poitier.

[4]   Exceptions include Julian Barnes, Justin Cartwright and celebrity author Griff Rhys Jones.

celebrity guests and the local reading groups who offer their interpretations of, and opinions on, the selected text. The Richard & Judy Book Club seemingly adheres to Barthes's main argument – that meaning is located (and proliferates) in the interaction between text and reader, not author and text. The effect is to encourage the audience at home to identify with the celebrities and book group members and the position of authority they assume as readers. It is the role of the reader, not the author, which is privileged in this format. The reader gets to sit on the comfy sofa and give their interpretation of the text, while the author is left "on location," on film, confined to the VT.

However, the television book club viewer is not necessarily (as yet) a *reader*. While some viewers may "read along" as the book club selections are aired on television, a large majority of the audience will not have read the text. As "viewer," as opposed to "reader," the audience may find themselves adrift between a text they have not read and a panel of readers with perhaps significantly differing interpretations of, and opinions on, that text. Oprah's Book Club circumvented this issue by locating and fixing meaning in the figure of the author and by refusing to debate a text's quality or value. But the Richard & Judy Book Club's Barthesian dismissal of the author as origin and provider of meaning in favor of a more reader-led format, meant that they risked alienating their audience both as viewers of the show and as potential readers. By retaining the VT segment the audience is provided with a "taster" of the text before it is discussed by the hosts and guests. This "taster," presented by the author, offers an impression of the textual content in order to help acquaint the viewer with the text's story and main concerns in preparation for the discussion that follows.

The VT "taster" is not, however, simply an innocent orientating device for the viewer who is not yet a reader; the VT is also a promotional tool, an *advertisement*, targeting a viewer who is also a potential *consumer*. The book club's emphasis on the reader as opposed to the author is, in fact, *not* about valuing a reader response method of criticism in the way that Barthes's endorses, but rather about generating audience figures and sales. Although Ross, like Oprah, is "keeping herself pure" (Appleyard 2008, 8) by not receiving any direct profits from the sales generated by the club, book sales and television book club audience figures directly impact one another. The text selected by the book club is a product and the book club audience is the potential consumer of that product, who, based on the quality of the selection, will return to "view" the book club for further recommendations. A television book club is not successful if the viewers do not buy and read the books. Appleyard writes that "the mystery of how to sell decent books consistently has eluded publishers and booksellers. The R&J Book Club has cracked it" (2008, 8). The Richard & Judy Book Club segment is not simply a televised reading group discussion, but also an advertisement designed to market the selected text to as wide an audience/consumer base as possible. And, because this book club has a critical edge and the guest panelists might not always agree on whether a book is a "good read," the "objective" VT portion of the segment becomes crucial to this marketing process.

The VT "promo" is, then, a powerful tool in the marketing of the text, as is the figure of the author who features in it. Claire Squires, in *Marketing Literature: The Making of Contemporary Writing in Britain*, writes that "marketing is conceived *as a form of representation and interpretation*, situated in spaces between the author and the reader – but which authors and readers also take part in – and surrounding the production, dissemination and reception of texts" (2007, 3). As such the authorial body on the screen, framed within the VT "taster," comes to figure not simply as representative of the textual content but also as a *mediator* between that text and the viewer as potential consumer. The Richard & Judy Book Club authorial body is *only* an image, there is no "persona" attached to this body, and, for this very reason, that image becomes malleable, adaptable, exploitable. As a visual image that is situated between the text and the potential consumer of that text within the VT, the author functions as a marketing device in much the same way as the book's dust jacket.

Indeed, book covers are another key feature within the television book club format. In both Oprah's Book Club and the Richard & Judy Book Club the cover of the book will appear numerous times during the segment, slowly spinning around the screen and fading in and out as the VT cuts between frames. The function of the book cover as a marketing device is to appeal aesthetically to the potential consumer while simultaneously providing an insight into the book's content and its particular genre category. One of Richard & Judy's Summer Read selections, Sam Bourne's *The Righteous Man* (2006), does this by way of association with an already established (and phenomenally successful) text and its author. The book cover design for *The Righteous Man*, as well as the author's name (Sam Bourne is a pseudonym), function by visual association with the cover of *The Da Vinci Code* (2003) and the name of its author, Dan Brown. This marketing device, exploitative though it may seem, faithfully renders visible the textual content of the book – Sam Bourne's novel *does* belong to the same genre category as *The Da Vinci Code* – but not all covers function so straightforwardly. Squires writes that "the book [cover] is used as a vehicle to express certain interpretations of and aspirations for the book, which may in fact be contradicted by textual readings" (2007, 89). This is particularly pertinent for television book club selections that, instead of targeting a specific market, must attempt to appeal to as wide a consumer base as possible. *Richard & Judy*'s Amanda Ross certainly recognizes the potential of the book cover as a marketing vehicle. Sarah Lyall, in *The New York Times*, reports that "HarperCollins … agreed to change the cover of Cecelia Ahern's *PS, I Love You*, the tale of a young widow recovering from her husband's death, to blue from pink after Ms. Ross said that pink would turn off male readers" (2006, 7). By changing the color of the book cover, Ross was attempting to conceal the book's "chick lit" genre category and thereby target a male readership as well as a female one. In this case the book cover design works not by attempting to associate the book with a specific genre category or established text/author, but rather to conceal the genre and textual content in order to appeal to a wider audience and potential consumer base.

As significant as the book cover image is in terms of marketing by way of representing (or misrepresenting) textual content, its potential is limited for the purposes of the television book club. A two-dimensional image of the book cover floating across the screen can only function so far. However, these vital functions of representation and marketability need not be restricted to the image on the cover. By valuing the role of the reader, by restricting the author to the VT, by dismissing notions of the author as the origin of textual meaning and by withholding the privilege of authorial celebrity or even persona, the Richard & Judy Book Club has effectively reduced their authors to three-dimensional, talking, walking equivalents of a book cover. Within the Richard & Judy Book Club VT, the author articulates what amounts to little more than an extended back cover "blurb," while their image functions in order to convey an impression of textual content *and* as the packaging designed to appeal to and target the potential consumer. This is not to diminish the relevance or significance of the author function within this television book club format. The authorial body, as mediator between the book club selection and its potential consumer, must, like the book cover, also serve to conceal or resolve any inconsistencies that might exist between the textual content and the text's potential market and media appeal.

Lori Lansens and *The Girls*

The Girls (2005), by the Canadian author Lori Lansens, is a book club selection that demonstrates particularly well the complexities of this author function within the television book club format. *The Girls* was the 34th Richard & Judy Book Club selection and the book club segment was aired February 7. 2007. The novel is the fictional autobiography of Rose and Ruby Darlen, craniopagus twins who live in a small Canadian town with their adoptive parents. This is a text, then, that is highly concerned with the body and with notions of bodily normalcy and ideals. The two protagonists, through their first person accounts, are offering an insight into the experience of living in – and attached to – a disabled body. Disability Studies is a relatively new critical field and it, like Feminism and Queer Theory studies before it, has sought to examine and challenge normative representations and conceptions of "the body," including who does and should speak for that particular body.[5] *The Girls* engages with this debate in the sense that it is written in the first person as the autobiography of the two disabled girls – here the disabled speak for themselves. Rose is a writer and she is composing her autobiography before the aneurism in her brain kills both her and her sister. Ruby, who is not a writer but asserts the right to tell her side (quite literally) of their story, also contributes to the narrative with shorter, chatty chapters. The conjoined bodies of Rose and Ruby are deformed, disabled and dying and therefore represent what Susan Wendell terms the "rejected" or "neglected" body. These terms "refer to aspects of bodily

---

[5]   For a recent detailed account of the history and critical scope of Disability Studies see *Disability Theory* by Tobin Siebers (2008).

life (such as illness, disability, weakness, and dying), bodily appearance (such as deviations from the cultural ideals of the body), and bodily experience (including most forms of bodily suffering) that are feared, ignored, despised, and/or rejected in a society and its culture" (Wendell 1996, 85). Indeed, the book begins with a roll call of names the girls have been called, including "freaks, horrors, monsters, devils, witches, retards" (Lansens 2007, 3). The conjoined twins represent the "Other-ed" body – a body that fails to conform to current standards of Western cultural intelligibility and so is "rejected" and "neglected" as something "Other," something monstrous, something potentially threatening – but it is represented from the perspective of the twins, from "within" that "Other-ed" body.

But this is, of course, a *fictional* autobiography. The "real" writer here is Lori Lansens and she is not disabled. In fact, Lori Lansens's media image is the embodiment of current Western perceptions of (female) bodily normalcy. The "real" author writing about the experience of disability is doing so from "within" a non-disabled body, a "normal" body, and this body becomes crucial to the marketability of the text within the television book club format. Lansens is not the archetypal disembodied, transcendent Author – she is a "woman writer" and therefore an "embodied author." And as a marketing device – as a *visible* authorial body – the "woman writer" is subject to those same pervasive gender-specific norms that govern all women who enter into the popular media. She is expected to be attractive, photogenic, glamorous, sexy even. The 2007 Virago paperback edition of *The Girls* features an author photograph on the inside of the back cover.[6] In this promotional image Lansens bends ever so slightly forwards, her long blonde hair falling over one eye, her hands clasped in front of her; with a wide-eyed gaze she half smiles for the camera. Her subtle jewelry, fair complexion and the expanse of pale skin above her décolletage are contrasted against the dark shade of her soft knit clothing; she appears luminous, youthful, pretty. The photograph presents a relaxed, inviting, slightly coy and overtly feminine image of the author that conforms to culturally prescribed norms of female attractiveness.

Stephanie Harzewski writes that "in today's highly competitive publishing environment, the contemporary woman author cannot do without the media but instead must negotiate her status as a producer of writing and an object of visual consumption. She writes and is written upon – by agents, marketing departments, critics, fans, book reviewers, and journalists" (2007, 24) – *and* the television book club. As a Richard & Judy Book Club author, Lansens is all but dead in the Barthesian sense: she does not function in terms of authorial origins, to uncover textual meaning or even as an authorial persona. But her body is not buried. In the television book club format Lansens is present – visible – and she functions purely in terms of *image*. This image, however, is not functioning as an embodiment of the text, as Franzen was in the Oprah's Book Club VT. Instead, Lansens's body image

---

[6]   This was the edition marketed for The Richard & Judy Book Club. The inclusion of an author photograph on the inside of the back cover is uncommon, although Virago often reproduces a small image as part of the author biography on the first page of the book.

functions as the "normal" body that is used to "normalise" those "rejected" textual bodies that, though they might "speak" in the text, are denied visual representation on the television screen or, for that matter, the book's cover. Lansens's author function in the VT is not to then to "uncover" the text but rather to provide a cover *for* the text. The author image "packages" this novel about deformity, disability and dying – about bodies that are "feared, ignored, despised, and/or rejected" – not by attempting to faithfully "embody" them but by way of functioning as an acceptable, and thereby "normalising," "object of visual consumption." Thus Lansens's author image acts as the "normal" body that *mis*represents and thereby conceals the "rejected" bodies contained within her text. Like a book cover or an advertisement, the authorial body in the VT intercedes and mediates between textual content and potential consumer for the purposes of marketability. In fact, the book cover for the 2007 Virago edition of *The Girls*, which also features in the VT, does just that.

The book cover image consists of two pairs of legs dangling over the edge of riverbank. They skim the surface of the clear blue water that is dotted with white flowers. The legs appear Caucasian, adolescent, smooth and shapely. All four legs are the same length. And yet Rose, at the very beginning of *The Girls*, narrates: "presently, my right leg is a full three inches shorted than my left, my spine compressed, my right hip cocked … Ruby's thin thighs astride my hip, my arm supporting her posterior, her arm forever around my neck" (Lansens 2007, 4). The legs on the book cover do not belong to the bodies described beneath that cover. The cover image, while suggesting the text's generic category (the female legs, the flowers and the pastel colors all imply that this is a "woman's novel"), and some sense of the text's content (that this is a story about two young women, about bodies, about bodily sensations, about issues of "nature" and the "natural" perhaps), nevertheless misrepresents the "unnatural" bodies hidden beneath that cover. The cover packages the textual bodies within by using an image that normalizes and idealizes those bodies. Judging this book by its cover would not garner an accurate impression of its content. Michael Legat writes that "good jacket/cover artists understand that they should reflect the content of the book with a fair degree of accuracy, but many feel that they have a licence to adapt in order to make what they consider a better picture" (1998, 82). Although the cover image is representative of certain (non-threatening) aspects of this text it is also purposely misleading – it "rejects" the problematic textual bodies in order to present a "better picture."

Legs are, in fact, featured on the covers of all three of Lansens novels and in each case fail to faithfully represent the bodies contained within. The 2008 Virago edition of *Rush Road Home* (2002) features a pair of girl's legs in long white socks; this is a novel primarily about a body marked both by race and old age. The 2010 Virago edition of *The Wife's Tale* (2009) has a pair of slim, muscled female legs hopping from a rock on the cover; this is a novel primarily about obesity. Squires calls a reoccurring book cover image for a particular author's texts the "consistent image" (2007, 86), but, in terms of the bodies they claim to represent, these cover images prove decidedly inconsistent. While (very) broadly representative of the content and genre of each text, these three covers conceal the problematic textual bodies that are unmarketable in a media culture saturated with images of the "right" kinds of bodies. In *The Girls*, Ruby reveals that Rose had "already thought of a book design" for their autobiography: "she says the design is very important" (Lansens 2007, 69). Indeed, covers are important, especially when they function to conceal potentially troublesome textual content by way of a sanitized and "normalized" (mis)representation of the bodies contained within.

Just as the cover serves to intercede between these "Other-ed" textual bodies and the potential consumer, so too does Lori Lansens in her function as author image in the Richard & Judy Book Club VT. Like the book cover, Lansens's authorial body must act as the "normal" and "normalizing" body that mediates between Rose and Ruby's "rejected" bodies and the book club audience in order to successfully market the text. The VT begins with a close up of this cover. The book is held up to the camera by Lansens, as if she is reading the text. The book cover image and the author image are immediately conflated. The authorial body is not being associated with the bodies that appear *in* the text, but rather with the inaccurate bodies that appear on the cover. Not long into the segment, Lansens is filmed dangling her feet over the edge of a riverbank. This shot directly mirrors the book cover image – minus the second body. Significantly, the two bodies represented in the text and on the cover are reduced back to a single ("normal") body in this shot.

This process is reversed when Lansens's body is doubled on the screen. Using a split screen edit the image of Lansens is reflected on each side of the screen in order to appear as representative of the textual content of the book – that is, as representative of the textual bodies, the identical twins. But, as Rose explains, though the twins are identical they are not "identical looking": "Ruby's face is arranged quite nicely (in fact, Ruby is very beautiful), whereas my features are misshapen and frankly grotesque" (Lansens 2007, 4). In no sense is the viewer confronted with Rose's "grotesque" features by way of this attempt to create a visual impression of the twins. Moreover, the two images of Lansens, which reappear throughout the VT, remain divided by the landscape in the background of the shot – they are not conjoined. When the screen does merge into the central divide the doubled image of Lansens is replaced by a doubled image of a tree that fuses in the center of the screen to become one tree. Just as Franzen's tree functioned symbolically (in terms of origins), so this tree functions symbolically, this time in terms of the "natural." The fusing of the doubled image of the tree serves to "naturalize" and render non-threatening the "unnatural" conjoined bodies in the text. Lansens's image, though doubled, remains divided – to merge her doubled image would be to represent too explicit, too accurate, an impression of the textual bodies. Similarly, towards the beginning of the VT, Lansens describes the girls' point of conjunction by gently cupping the side of her head with her hand. This gesture also appears in the text when Rose asks her reader to "press the base of your palm to the lobe of your right ear" (Lansens 2007, 4) to locate the point where their skulls fuse. But this performative gesture does not serve to render the site of conjunction visible or even conceivable – it is only a vague impression that fails to convey the visual impact of the girls' physical condition.

A potential challenge to Lansens's "normalizing" function is posed by a series of photographs that appear in the VT of real-life conjoined twins Chang and Eng Bunker and Ladan and Laleh Bijani (all of whom are also mentioned in the novel). However, like the legs on the book cover, these images are either already normalized by way of the picture's composition (the site of conjunction is not obvious), its context (the medical or carnivalesque, for instance) or simply in the brevity of the image's appearance on the screen. As Rose explains, "if you glance at us, you might think we're two women embracing, leaning against each other tête-à-tête, the way sisters do" (Lansens 2007, 4). These pictures, the book cover and the VT "taster" as a whole, constitute only a "glance" that misreads/misrepresents the bodies it purports to represent. These impressionistic images sentimentalize, sanitize and normalize the potentially disturbing visual particularities and peculiarities of the "abnormal" textual bodies. Lansens's author image, as the primary bodily image within the VT, functions to make "normal," and thereby marketable, the "rejected" bodies contained within the text.

However, once the viewer, having watched the Richard & Judy Book Club segment, purchases the text and becomes a *reader*, those "rejected" textual bodies are no longer mediated through the image of the author. If the author function is limited to the author image as marketing device, then when sold the text once more becomes the "disembodied and ownerless *écriture*," which, in the interaction between text and reader, can generate a proliferation of interpretations, meanings and readings. That said, one of those possible readings might serve to again raise questions about the figure of the author and their function. Rose and Ruby Darlen are, after all, not only textual bodies but also *authorial* bodies. This text is, in the context of the novel, *theirs* – it constitutes their autobiography. The disjuncture between the "rejected" bodies encountered in the text and the "normal" authorial body used to sell the text, then comes into play in a potentially new and revelatory way. Wendell writes that "people who do not appear or act physically 'normal' draw attention to the disciplines of normality" (1996, 89). Thus, Rose and Ruby's "abnormal" textual body/ies might draw attention back to Lansens' "normal" authorial body and challenge the very basis upon which that body makes a claim to "normalcy" and, therefore, to cultural perceptions of the "right" kind of body to write.

This is made clear when Rose fantasizes about what her life might have been like had she been born "singular":

> Still, I have an elaborate fantasy life in which I am a singular woman. My right arm belongs to me. My right leg is the exact length of my left, and I tote nothing on my hip but a funky leather bag. My features have been surgically corrected and I have my sister's pretty face. … I am a well-known author and I have a poet boyfriend … for whom I dress provocatively. (Oh yes, in this fantasy I also have large, shapely breasts.) (Lansens 2007, 50)

Rose has, at the beginning of this chapter, said that she types "quickly with my wrong hand. I sense that I'm naturally a right-handed person, but my right arm belongs to Ruby" (Lansens 2007, 47). Rose's right arm is the arm that holds Ruby in place on her hip. When Rose fantasizes about a "right arm" that "belongs to me" she is wishing for the hand that writes. By reconstructing her body into a "normal," single body, Rose also constructs the fantasy of the "right" body to write. This author image is "pretty," fashionable, heterosexual and sexy – she is, like Lansens, the "normal" authorial body. Her fantasy reveals her fear that in order to be a "well-known author" her body must conform to certain standards of cultural intelligibility. But "this other me, the one that only I can see, a girl called She, who is not We, [is] a girl who I will never be" (Lansens 2007, 181). And yet Rose *is* writing. These fears about not having the "right" body to write are undermined by the very fact they are being articulated *in writing*. Rose might have to write with the "wrong hand" and in the "wrong" kind of body, but she is still a writer.

Eagleton argues that women writers have often been drawn to the fictional "figure of the woman author [because her] subaltern status alongside her potential for critical expression makes her a figure of rich narrative interest" as well as a "key figure for exploring problems of authorial power" (2005, 5). In featuring two women authors, *The Girls* does explore problems regarding "authorial power" in terms of gender, but it also extends that issue to consider the disabled author too. In fact, the two are intimately bound together. Rose and Ruby are women writers but also disabled writers; they are doubly "subaltern" (in terms of gender and disability) but also doubly "expressive" (in terms of the text's double perspective). By way of the girls, as writers and as conjoined twins, this text contains the potential to explore "problems of authorial power" not only by dispelling the fantasy that there is a "right" body to write, but also by challenging the very boundaries that constitute that authorial body and the writing it produces.

According to Eagleton, the first problem Rose should encounter as narrator of her own life story is her claim to the authorial "I." And yet her autobiography begins with what appears to be a confident display of the author's claim to the personal pronoun – it appears 12 times in the first, short paragraph. However, the prevalence of the authorial "I" and the affected style of Rose's opening paragraph (it is full of rhymes and repetition and ends with three rhyming lines of iambic tetrameter) might suggest an effort to conceal and overcompensate for her "anxieties of authorship." Sandra M. Gilbert and Susan Gubar famously argue that women writers have historically been plagued by "an anxiety built from complex and often barely conscious fears of that authority which seems to the female artist to be by definition inappropriate to her sex" (2000, 51). The anxieties of authorship, which are "based on the woman's socially determined sense of her own biology" (Gilbert and Gubar 2000, 51), are, in the case of this particular female writer, much more complex and difficult to negotiate.

Rose writes not only as a woman and not only as the "rejected" body, but also as one half of a conjoined twin. Her "sense of her own biology" is complicated by the fact that she shares that biology with another body. Rose is never only an "I": "I understand that I am *me*, but that I am also *we*" (Lansens 2007, 8). Despite Rose's attempts to construct and determine herself as a single authorial voice, her textual body resists such definite borders – Rose is Rose but she is also Ruby and, together, they are also "The Girls" (Lansens 2007, 3). The conjoined bodies of the twins disrupt the division between "I" and "we." This body – which is also two bodies (*three* bodies when Rose is pregnant) – is a body that merges, that proliferates and that exceeds and transgresses bodily boundaries. Their body/ies thus trouble notions of an identity that is singular, fixed, self-contained, autonomous. How then can Rose make claim to an authorial "I" that depends on a perception of "one's" self as singular, as an individual subject? How can she fulfill Aunt Lovey's advice to write "not just as a conjoined twin but as a human being and a woman" (Lansens 2007, 12).

Rose begins by constructing a set of personal qualities and physical borders that differentiate and divide the "I" from the "we." This requires Rose to locate and negotiate the bodily and psychical boundaries that determine her individual selfhood – what exactly separates "her" from Ruby? Rose asserts that despite the fact that their "cerebral tissue is fully enmeshed, our vascular system snarled like briar bushes … our brains themselves are separate and functioning. Our thoughts are distinctly our own. Our selves have struggled fiercely to be unique" (Lansens 2007, 5). Interestingly, this "struggle" for "uniqueness" manifests itself in terms of both the literary and the gendered: "I like sports, but I'm also bookish, while Ruby is girlie and prefers television" (5). Rose is the masculine authorial body and Ruby is the feminine body against which Rose can assert herself as "writer." Yet Rose's autobiography, however many personal pronouns litter its first pages, is also necessarily Ruby's autobiography: "my sister claims that it can't technically ('technically' is Ruby's current favourite word) be considered an *auto*biography and is opposed to my telling what she considers *our* story" (6). Ruby insists that Rose's story is also her story and that she should therefore tell her side of that story. Of course, the fact that there is another side reveals that this is *not* one story, but two separate narratives from two perspectives that happen to share a bodily boundary. But Ruby's decision to contribute to the narrative of the autobiography further complicates the distinction between Rose as "author," who makes claim to the authorial "I," and Ruby as contributor, who makes no claim to literary prowess. Just as the single "rejected" body is made up of both the "grotesque" Rose and the "beautiful" Ruby, so the unified autobiography is made up from the literary narrative of masculine and "bookish" Rose and the chatty chapters by "girlie" Ruby who "prefers television." The singular "rejected" body and the unified text turn out to be "hybrid" – to be a fusion of various entities and oppositions. As such, these bodies and this text trouble and challenge the boundaries that separate and determine self and other, normal and "Other," the beautiful and the grotesque, the masculine and the feminine, the literary and the popular.

The Girls is a "popular," sentimental novel featured on a tea-time television show and yet it poses a challenge to the disciplinary structures and boundaries that determine selfhood, that constitute a culturally intelligible bodily identity and that construct the "right" kind of body to write. It is ironic, then, that, in a text obsessed with the "identity of the body writing" (Barthes 1995, 125), these textual bodies that are also authorial bodies are, in fact, dead. Rose and Ruby's fictional autobiography is published, we must assume, posthumously. Rose writes that "the aneurysm isn't going away. But I hope it can contain itself for a while. Until our effects are sorted out. Until this book is done" (Lansens 2007, 178). Once more we are confronted with the death of the author/s. But this is *not* a dead author in the Barthesian sense – "the very identity of the body writing" here is not an authorial body that can be severed from the text. These bodies that write reside *within* the text, and as such are bodies preserved *as text*, as part of that "disembodied and ownerless *écriture*." Because these authorial bodies are also textual bodies they cannot be erased or reduced to an author image and, for this reason, they remain to oppose the idea that there is a "right" body to write – and to market – literature. The textual authorial bodies function to challenge the very methods by which the text within which they are contained has been marketed and sold. The process by which the potentially disruptive textual bodies have been "normalized" by the image of Lansens is, in the *reading* of the text, now reversed and the textual bodies emerge as a challenge to the idea that there might be a "normal" or "right" body to write as well as the boundaries and discourses that constitute those culturally determined categories.

Clare Hanson, in "Marketing the 'Woman Writer'," summarizes Hilary Radner's argument that "women's novels" find themselves caught between the canonical and the popular and "thus always remain 'out-of-category'" (1998, 69). Radner sees being located "out-of-category" negatively but Hanson argues that the "hybridity" of women's writing is "integral to the challenge which it offers to the divisions between high and low culture, masculine and feminine, the transcendent and the bodily" (70). Similarly, in *The Girls*, the "hybrid" body/ies of Rose and Ruby Darlen function to question the validity and boundaries of such cultural, identity and literary categories. By extension, the Richard & Judy Book Club has also contributed to this "integral" challenge. Despite reducing the author function to a mere image, the Richard & Judy Book Club choose texts that challenged cultural, gendered and bodily boundaries. Their choices included works by both female and male authors, authors from a range of ethnicities, the popular and the literary, fiction and non-fiction, texts that refused to conform to gendered genres or were marketed to appeal to those who might not otherwise read them (the blue cover of *PS, I Love You*, for instance) and, notably, novels that included those problematic textual bodies that, once read, troubled the very methods by which the television book club's manipulation of the author image might have served to market them.

If the body that writes is not, in fact, subject to Barthes's death sentence, but continues to function in the promotion, marketing and commodification of literature in a Western, visually orientated, image-saturated, media culture, then that body is central to the construction and perpetuation of ideas about who can write, what they can write and what kind of writing is the "right" kind to read. The television book club, as currently at the forefront of literary mass culture, therefore has a responsibility to continue to extend the boundaries of these categories. And if the authorial body is to remain within the television book club format then it too must play its part in widening cultural perceptions of the kinds of bodies that write, whether as "real" or textual, be it in terms of gender, sexuality, race, age, attractiveness, illness and/or disability, and thus make visible that body's legitimate claim to the authorial "I."

Reference List

Appleyard, Bryan. 2008. How daytime telly killed the literary snob. *The Sunday Times*, June 15. Culture section.

Barthes, Roland. 1995 [1977]. The Death of the Author. In *Authorship: From Plato to the Postmodern. A Reader*, ed. Seán Burke, 125–30. Edinburgh: Edinburgh University Press.

Dowd, Maureen. 2006. Oprah's Bunk Club. *The New York Times*, January 28.

Eagleton, Mary. 2005. *Figuring the Woman Author in Contemporary Fiction*. Basingstoke: Palgrave Macmillan.

Farr, Cecilia Konchar. 2005. *Reading Oprah: How Oprah's Book Club Changed the Way America Reads*. Albany, NY: State University of New York Press.

Foucault, Michel. 1986 [1980]. What is an Author? In *The Foucault Reader*, ed. Paul Rabinow, 101–20. Harmondsworth: Penguin.

Franzen, Jonathan. 2005. Meet Me in St Louis. In *How to be Alone*, ed. Jonathan Franzen, 286–302. London: Harper Perennial.

Gilbert, Sandra M., and Susan Gubar. 2000 [1979]. *The Madwoman in the Attic: The Woman Writer and the Nineteenth-Century Imagination*, 2nd edn. New Haven and London: Yale University Press.

Hanson, Clare. 1998. Marketing the 'women writer.' In *Writing: A Woman's Business, Women, Writing and the Marketplace*, ed. Judy Simons and Kate Fullbrook, 66–80. Manchester and New York: Manchester University Press.

Harzewski, Stephanie. 2007. New Voice, Old Body: the Case of Penelope Fitzgerald. *Contemporary Women's Writing* 1 (1/2): 24–33.

Johnson, Marilyn. 1997. Oprah Winfrey: A Life in Books. *Time*, Sept. Quoted in Kathleen Rooney, *Reading with Oprah: The Book Club that Changed America* (Fayetteville, AR: The University of Arkansas Press, 2005), 62.

Lansens, Lori. 2007 [2005]. *The Girls*. London: Virago.

Legat, Michael. 1998. *An Author's Guide to Publishing*. London: Robert Hale. Quoted in Claire Squires, *Marketing Literature: The Making of Contemporary Writing in Britain* (Basingstoke: Palgrave Macmillan, 2007), 74–5.

Long, Elizabeth. 2005. Foreword to *Reading Oprah: How Oprah's Book Club Changed the Way America Reads*, by Cecilia Konchar Farr, ix–xii. Albany, NY: State University of New York Press.

Lyall, Sarah. 2006. The British Version of Oprah's Book Club. *The New York Times*, July 29, Arts/Cultural Desk.

Miller, Nancy K. 1995. Changing the Subject: Authorship, Writing and the Reader. In *Authorship: From Plato to the Postmodern. A Reader*, ed. Seán Burke, 193–211. Edinburgh: Edinburgh University Press. Originally published in Nancy K. Miller, *Subject to Change: Reading Feminist Writing* (Ithaca, NY: Cornell University Press, 1988).

Richard & Judy. 2007. Channel 4, February 7. http://www.lorilansens.com/books.php

Rooney, Kathleen. 2005. *Reading with Oprah: The Book Club that Changed America*. Fayetteville, AR: The University of Arkansas Press.

Siebers, Tobin. 2008. *Disability Theory*. Ann Arbor: University of Michigan Press.

Squires, Claire. 2007. *Marketing Literature: The Making of Contemporary Writing in Britain*. Basingstoke: Palgrave Macmillan.

Walker, Esther. 2008. This Man Could Change Your Life. *Independent Magazine*, June 21.

Wendell, Susan. 1996. *The Rejected Body: Feminist Philosophical Reflections on Disability*. New York and London: Routledge.

Wyatt, Edward. 2005. Oprah's Book Club Reopening to Writers Who'll Sit and Chat. *The New York Times*, September 23, Business/Financial Desk.

Chapter 6
"Not the normal kind of chicklit"?
Richard & Judy and the
Feminized Middlebrow

Beth Driscoll

The gendered status of certain kinds of reading is spotlighted in a series of comments made by co-presenter of the Richard & Judy Book Club, Richard Madeley. Opening the episode discussing Dorothy Koomson's *My Best Friend's Girl* (2006), Madeley declares, "It's an unashamedly chicklit paperback this, but I must admit I still enjoyed it immensely. I did dab away a little tear as early as page 2! What a wuss" (Richard & Judy: My Best Friend's Girl). This contradiction between enjoyment and embarrassment is one Madeley returns to several times over the course of the episode: "I can't not say it, and I've said it a couple of times, I … I … it made me cry. I mean, I don't do chicklit." It even causes something of a crisis of gender identity, when he says to the rest of the discussion panel, "So what you're saying is for the last week I've been an honorary girl." Madeley defends his masculinity on the grounds that Winston Churchill admitted to being a "blubber" so "I don't feel too ashamed of it." Ultimately, though, it is the book club itself that provides the rationale for Madeley's enjoyment of the book. When his wife and co-presenter Judy Finnigan prompts him by saying, "It is definitely chicklit, I mean, which is why I'm surprised you liked it so much, Richard," Madeley responds:

> Well that's the strength of our book club … it makes you if you're going to play
> a part in it read books you wouldn't normally choose. I would *never* normally
> buy chicklit but I read this one, I had a ball with it (he throws his hands up).

Finnigan's somewhat exonerating response is, "It's not the normal kind of chicklit" (Richard & Judy: My Best Friend's Girl).

This phrase, "not the normal kind of chicklit," indicates the Richard & Judy Book Club's simultaneous embrace and disavowal of women's novels and women's reading. It is not only Madeley and Finnigan who express this: there are qualifications attending the other panelists' enthusiasm for *My Best Friend's Girl*. Actress Sian Reeves, for example, offers a potted history of this women's genre, from popularity to embarrassment:

> I remember, like 5 years ago, when we would say chicklit, you know, it was really
> at its peak and it was fantastic and I was really voraciously reading all of it but

this … you know, you shouldn't just say 'this is just chick literature you shouldn't buy it.' This is better than that and I think told very well and touches me.

Although Reeves distances herself from contemporary chicklit, her summary of reading *My Best Friend's Girl* invokes precisely the logics of this women's genre: "I felt like I'd had a brilliant evening … talking with my best girl friend about death, marriage, sex, men, children and felt everything was satisfied." As Finnigan notes, "Well, that's chicklit isn't it … That's the best of chicklit." Such a hedged endorsement, the "best of" caveat, signals some unease with heavily feminized reading, an attitude that extends beyond the Richard & Judy Book Club.

Dismissing women's reading as superficial is a common cultural trope. For example, the satirical television drama *Desperate Housewives* includes a scene where the characters meet for a book club:

> Woman: So, what did everybody think?
> Lynette: I thought the character of Madame Bovary was … very inspirational.
> Woman: Inspirational? She poisons herself with arsenic.
> Lynette: Really?
> Woman: You didn't read until the end?
> Lynette: I stopped after page 50.
> Woman: Am I the only one who read the book?
> Susan: I saw the movie. It was really good.
> Woman: Ladies! I'm sorry, but wh-wh-what is the point of having a book club if we don't read the book?
> Bree: More wine?

This barbed script trivializes the reading – or non-reading – practices of the suburban, all-female book club. The characters Lynette, Bree and Susan are modern versions of Emma Bovary, engaging only frivolously with literary works. They prioritize companionship and gossip over detailed examination of the texts.

As Andreas Huyssen (1986) observes, the novel *Madame Bovary* (1857) itself criticizes particular literary practices through the lens of gender, as Flaubert uses his protagonist to create a dichotomy between woman as the emotional, passive reader of inferior literature and man as the objective, ironic and active writer of authentic literature (1986, 47). Such negative associations between women and reading have a long history (see Lovell 1987, Tuchman 1989, Pykett 1992, Pearson 1999). Terry Lovell's influential study of literary women at the turn of the nineteenth century, *Consuming Fictions* (1987) suggests that the early novel was seen as a mass-market commodity, possessing popular appeal but not literary value (1987, 7). This disapproval built an association between commerce and gender: critics "linked the general shoddiness, as they judged it, of the novel not only to the female reader/writer, but also to the novel's commercial status: a commodity catering to 'infantile' female taste" (Lovell 1987, 54).

More recently, contempt for women's reading overlaps with contempt for middlebrow reading. Middlebrow is a term requiring careful definition. Most basically, it denotes a space between mass, popular culture and elite, or avant-garde culture. As a pejorative term, the middlebrow is cast as incomplete appropriation of high culture. In the first recorded use of the term in 1925, a *Punch* cartoon suggests "the BBC claim to have discovered a new type, the 'middlebrow'. It consists of people who are hoping that someday they will get used to the stuff they ought to like" (*Oxford English Dictionary* 2009). Dwight Macdonald also positions the middlebrow as negatively defined territory: his "midcult" (a synonym for middlebrow) is neither elite culture nor folk art and traditions (1960a, 1960b). Virginia Woolf, whose career trajectory challenges the link between women and degraded forms of literature, extends this idea by suggesting that the middlebrow mediates between the two forms of culture. She dismisses middlebrows as "go-betweens ... the busybodies who run from one to the other with their tittle tattle and make all the mischief" (1942, 115). This unsettling, mediating position creates an entanglement of economic, social and cultural factors:

> The middlebrow is the man, or woman, of middlebred intelligence who ambles and saunters now on this side of the hedge, now on that, in pursuit of no single object, neither art itself nor life itself, but both mixed indistinguishably and rather nastily, with money, fame, power, or prestige (1942, 155).

These assaults on the middlebrow thus focus on its role in the adulteration and dissemination of elite culture. As part of the attacks, middlebrow literary culture is routinely feminized both historically and in the contemporary literary sphere. Bridget Fowler (1991, 1997), Janice Radway (1997) and Nicola Humble (2001) all draw specific attention to the feminizing of the middlebrow in the twentieth century. Radway sees a "gender anxiety" in the realm of book publishing and distribution during the 1920s: "a form of deep distaste for the purported feminisation of culture and the emasculation of otherwise assertive artists and aggressively discriminating readers" (1997, 189). Book clubs that were distributive mechanisms reaching the middle class home were "greeted by their critics as a profound threat to independent American writers and readers, individuals gendered always as male" (1997, 190).

Two significant attempts to reclaim middlebrow literary culture were published in the late twentieth century. The first of these, Joan Shelley Rubin's *The Making of Middlebrow Culture* (1992), aims to "to redress both the disregard and the oversimplification of middlebrow culture in the 1920s, 1930s and 1940s" (1992, xv–xvi). She characterizes as middlebrow those institutions that include both entrepreneurs and an identifiable critical presence, and that engage in "activities aimed at making literature and other forms of 'high' culture available to a wide reading public" (1992, xi). These include the Book-of-the-Month Club, book reviews, book programs on commercial radios and the "Great Books" publishing initiative. An even stronger defense of middlebrow literary culture is provided by Radway's study, *A Feeling for Books: the Book-of-the-Month Club, Literary Taste, and Middle-class Desire* (1997). Her avowed task is "to present the middlebrow positively as a culture with its own particular substance and intellectual coherence" (1997, 5). She accomplishes this through her detailed analysis of the middlebrow practices of the Book-of-the-Month Club, including the founder's biography, the editorial board's decision-making processes and the club's commercial distribution system. These attributes distinguish the club from academia and comprise an alternative model of reading.

In an extension of Rubin's and Radway's historical investigations, the term middlebrow can also be applied non-pejoratively to aspects of contemporary literary culture. Certainly, there is still a large area of the contemporary literary field that is not strongly identified with either the avant-garde or mass production. David Carter suggests it is possible to describe this space as middlebrow: although the term may "ultimately be abandoned except as a historical trace," using the term might be "a mistake worth making for what it reveals about the new book cultures" (2007). Carter identifies the middlebrow's "contemporary resurgence" (2004, 195) in elements of literary culture such as bookstores with coffee shops, writers festivals, literary prizes, lists and book groups (2004, 195–7). It is productive to avoid a narrow view of this contemporary literary middlebrow. Rather than comprising particular texts, the middlebrow can usefully be considered as a set of meanings, attitudes and practices enacted by agents. This is the approach taken by Timothy Aubry, who sees the middlebrow "as a tactical, if sometimes automatic, mode of reading rather than as a fixed identity. Many people encounter texts at times as middlebrow readers and at other times through the lens of more scholarly postures" (2006, 353).

The reading practices of contemporary reading groups are particularly susceptible to characterization as middlebrow. Book clubs are middle-class institutions, part of the middle-class package of values that includes education and self-improvement. As Elizabeth Long notes, they offer a middle-class mechanism for building participants' cultural capital; for book club members, "literature becomes a cultural marker for distinction" (2003, 61). These members are overwhelmingly women. In separate surveys, all-female groups accounted for 69 percent of book groups in the United Kingdom (Hartley 2001) and 95 percent of groups in Victoria, Australia (Poole 2003, 264). In the United States, one estimate suggests that up to 85 percent of American book groups are comprised solely of women (Blewster 1998, 28).

The predominance of women has prompted the disparagement of book clubs in the media. Poole observes that book groups are "often undervalued as 'chat and chew' sessions or the 'equivalent of stitch and bitch sewing bees'" (2003, 1) and asks, "Is there some kind of cultural downgrading because this is a form of cultural consumption by women and is thus classified as a feminine activity?" (2003, 1). An example of the pejorative attitude towards women in book clubs is provided by American novelist and journalist Sarah Bird: "Above all else, it is essential to go with the all-female group. Introduce one straight man and Book Club will turn into, well, a book club" (2005, 1). This gendered ridicule of book clubs is not new. Long gives an example of nineteenth-century American opposition to reading groups; husbands of members of the Rhode Island Woman's club "nicknamed it the society for the prevention of home industry" (2003, 39). Such low regard for women's informal reading groups is evident not only in the media but in the neglect of book clubs by academia, and is a product of the historical marginalization of women's reading.

The Richard & Judy Book Club models a way of reading that places it in this tradition of feminized, middlebrow literary culture. There are a range of middlebrow literary behaviors, from commercial entrepreneurship to moral seriousness, but four, heavily gendered reading practices are of particular interest for this chapter. These are emphases on domesticity, emotion, personal connection to characters and social issues. Analysis of two episodes reveals how these reading practices work: the discussion of *My Best Friend's Girl* by Finnigan, Madeley and guests, and Lori Lansens's presentation of her novel *The Girls* (2006).

Despite being a mass-mediated and therefore public phenomenon, the Richard & Judy Book Club creates an atmosphere of domesticity, a private realm often associated with women and distinguished from academia. Humble observes that "the stylistic and thematic blue-prints of the sort of literature that came to be seen as middlebrow" include "a particular concentration on feminine aspects of life, a fascination with domestic space," although as she points out, these were also concerns of the mainstream novel (2001, 11). Domesticity is not only a feature of texts deemed middlebrow, but also of modes of reading. In the Richard & Judy Book Club, the focus on domesticity is partly achieved because reading is presented through the relationship between Madeley and Finnigan, a married couple whose banter communicates familiarity. Their knowledge of each other is evident in the *My Best Friend's Girl* discussion transcribed above, when Finnigan expresses surprise that Madeley enjoyed the book. The setting of the show enhances this sense of intimacy by recreating a domestic environment: discussion of books takes place on a set that recalls a suburban living room, complete with soft couches, vases of flowers and mugs on the coffee table. The use of domestic sets is also evident in the episode introducing Lori Lansens's *The Girls*. The author is interviewed in a comfortably furnished living room, with lit lamps and soft armchairs visible behind her. The coziness of this environment is emphasized by interspersed, contrasting shots of exterior landscapes: flocks of birds, fields, leafless trees and grey skies.

Discourses of home also feature in the presentation of the novels. Lansens's description of *The Girls*, for example, concentrates on the domestic situation of her novel's protagonists. Standing outside a farmhouse in Ontario, she says to camera, "This old farmhouse and this setting really reminds me of the sort of home the girls had." She then links this domesticity with her characters, using the home as a metaphor. It is "perfect in its imperfections ... I think it sort of represents the girls as well. They don't think they need to be fixed either" (The Girls Book Club). This metaphor is played out in detail in the novel itself. The narrator, Rose Darlen, identifies strongly with the farmhouse where she was raised. Towards the end of the narrative, with the knowledge that she is terminally ill, Rose describes a heavily idealized home: "I had this quick flash of heaven. And heaven was the den in the old farmhouse, with the orange shag and the big TV" (2006, 301). At other points, the house is described in a way that directly reflects events and emotions in the narrator's life. On a visit back to the farm following the twins' move to town, Rose declares, "The house, the old orange farmhouse, I had not underestimated. It looked shabbier than I remembered. Decrepit. I don't believe in ghosts, but I could have been convinced the place was haunted when we pulled up the graveled drive" (2006, 310). This gloomy depiction of the house foreshadows plot development: on leaving the farm, their adoptive mother dies in a car accident. In *The Girls*, the domestic environment is the filter through which the plot, characters and themes of the novel are presented, an authorial approach that invites a reading practice concentrated on domesticity.

At first glance, the Richard & Judy Summer Reads segments diverge from this focus on the domestic environment. For example, while discussion of *My Best Friend's Girl* takes place on the cozy lounges of the set, it also features a segment shot on the Italian island of Ischia. Here, against backgrounds of beaches, actress Donna Air outlines the plot of the book and explains why it constitutes ideal holiday reading. The show's emphasis on sun-drenched Italian landscapes defines Ischia against the domestic space of British readers, as an escape from home. However, similar reading practices are associated with both places. The island, like the home, is constructed as a non-work space. It is a place to read recreationally rather than professionally or academically. The show repeatedly combines references to leisure with the experience of reading Koomson's novel. Air says the book is "definitely recommended, especially in this sunshine," while back in the studio, Madeley follows the segment by saying "A lovely girl, a lovely island, and I have to say, I think it's a lovely book" ("Richard & Judy: My Best Friend's Girl"). Madeley's comment links gender with recreation, and this is also apparent in the concluding segment of the show, where a "party of ladies ... on a yoga holiday," as Finnigan describes them, is interviewed about the book. One of these readers says, "I would recommend this to a single girl on holiday," gendering the experience of leisure reading ("Richard & Judy: My Best Friend's Girl").

A second feature of middlebrow literary culture is its emphasis on emotional responses to books. As Radway writes, for the Book-of-the-Month Club, "reading was as much an event defined by affective response and reaction as it was an act structured by desires for guidance, education, and moral counsel" (1997, 262): reading provided a "sentimental education" (1997, 263). The Richard & Judy Book Club, too, privileges emotional reactions to texts over more intellectual analysis. This chapter has already described Madeley's emphatically emotional response to *My Best Friend's Girl*; he mentions three times that the book made him cry. Air, in her celebrity review of the text, also suggests the book inspires emotional reactions. She says, "I certainly cried, I definitely laughed," and extends the point: "Bit of a tearjerker though, especially if you were one of the ones who cried in *Beaches* or the last episode of *Cold Feet*." Here, Air links the book with well-known cinematic and television "weepies." The readers interviewed at the close of the segment also emphasize the feelings generated by the text. One pair relates,

Reader 1: It made me cry in places ...

Reader 2: Quite sad isn't it.

Reader 1: It brought out a lot of emotions that I thought, 'Ooh, I don't usually get this when I read a book.'

Another interviewed reader said, "I was on the verge of tears ... that was very powerful stuff." The novel strongly invites these reader responses. The opening pages, in which the character Adele describes her experience of cancer, include lines such as "I cried and sobbed and wailed. Yes, wailed. I made a hideous noise as I broke into a million, trillion pieces" and "Through all my sobs, all I could say was 'I've got to tell my little girl I'm going to die'" (Koomson 2006, 2). On the following page, there is a single word of text in large print: "'mummy?'" (Koomson 2006, 3).

A strong emotional pull is also evident in Lansens's televised introduction to her novel. She describes it as a "unique and special love story," signaling the importance of emotion in *The Girls*. She references an early passage in the novel where the narrator, Rose Darlen says she would "live a thousand lives as a conjoined twin with this sister Ruby because of the exponential love she feels" (The Girls Book Club). The word *exponential* is used here, as in the novel (Lansens 2006, 3), to suggest extreme emotion. The novel is strongly sentimental. Its last page includes the romantic, nostalgic lines, "I have never looked into my sister's eyes, but I've seen inside her soul. I have never worn a hat, but I *have* been kissed like *that*. I have never raised both arms at once, but the moon beguiled me still" (Lansens 2006, 343). Such writing encourages emotional reactions from readers.

The reading practice that enables this kind of emotional response involves readers making a personal connection with one or more characters. This mode of literacy is presented very strongly in the episode on *My Best Friend's Girl*. Air's review includes this line: "As the mother of a young girl myself, it certainly struck a few chords," while one of the interviewed holiday readers said, "It made me think of my children." Back in the studio, Reeves also draws attention to the connection she felt with the main character, saying "even the cover made me slightly nervous, cause I've got a little girl and I was like, oh God, what's it going to be about." Finnigan and Madeley validate this approach, encouraging identification between mothers and the text:

Finnigan: All parents – especially mothers I think – worry themselves sick when their children are little.

Reeves: Oh yeah, and that's why this book's really sort of poignant to me in the end because I've made a facility in my will where three of my best friends will take a part in her upbringing.

Madeley: Don't die on us! So you identified with her.

The other guest panelist, actress Lowri Turner, also promotes this way of reading but disputes the text's capacity to fulfill it, saying, "I did think the child in this book was incredibly well-behaved. I mean, my children wouldn't be that nice." In response, Madeley defends the psychological realism of the book, an important quality when a book is read for identification.

Finally, a feminized middlebrow reading practice evident in the Richard & Judy Book Club is a desire to connect recreational reading with social issues. Panel members praise the general seriousness of *My Best Friend's Girl*. After declaring the text "not the normal kind of chicklit," Finnigan continues: "It deals with much, much bigger issues." Reeves affirms, "It's much deeper than that" and Turner elaborates: "it's grown up ... I mean, if it was just a girl with cats, you know, it would be really dull ... It's grown up ... It's trying to bridge into a slightly different genre." As a specific example, panel members briefly discuss the book's treatment of racism. Turner approves of the book's subtle incorporation of race issues: "The heroine is black and I didn't pick that up until quite a long way into the book and that was clever." Madeley then suggests that race becomes important at a climactic moment in the plot: "It emerges when she's the target of a racist outburst in a supermarket ... 'that can't be your mummy because she's black.'"

The segment also draws attention to other serious themes. In her celebrity review, Air highlights the book's exploration of cancer and the real-world value of understanding the impacts of this disease: "Even though this book is fictional, people like Adele lose their battle with leukemia every day." She also values the book's theme of self-improvement: "I thoroughly enjoyed watching Kamryn learn to believe in herself." These are all claims for the social importance of the text, a distinctly middlebrow way of reading. The selected books enable this reading practice. Lansens's novel, for example, invites reflections on real-life disability and prejudice: in her presentation for the Richard & Judy Book Club, she discusses two historical sets of conjoined twins. She also claims that the book is about the quest for identity: "a lot of twins will tell you there is a personal struggle to see oneself as an individual" (The Girls Book Club). This theme resonates with middlebrow values of self-empowerment and self-improvement.

The feminized, middlebrow reading practices of the Richard & Judy Book Club have drawn some criticism. Literary author Andrew O'Hagan describes the phenomenon as contributing to "a coarsening" of literary culture, saying the hosts "oversell a reduced, unimaginative notion of what people's literary enjoyment might be" – presumably in contrast with more academic literary analysis (Boztas, 2008). Despite such barbs, however, the Richard & Judy Book Club has to some extent reclaimed the cultural status of women's middlebrow reading. Like Oprah's Book Club, the Richard & Judy Book Club's deployment of mass media and connection with celebrity has given the club and its model of literacy commercial and cultural clout.

As the excerpt from *Desperate Housewives* demonstrates, reading groups today operate in a multimedia environment. The Richard & Judy Book Club is part of what Long refers to as a "host of innovations in the technology and social organisation of communication" that affect the practice of reading (2003, 189).

Television is a mass medium, and a televised book club operates quite differently in the literary field to a solitary reader or neighborhood reading circle.

One way to conceive of this difference is through Nick Couldry's concept of media meta-capital (2003). That is, as a mass-mediated phenomenon that draws on celebrity, the Richard & Judy Book Club possesses a form of capital that is readily convertible to other forms of capital, including symbolic capital in the literary field. Due to its media meta-capital, the Richard & Judy Book Club holds a position of influence in the literary field. DeNel Rehberg Sedo (2008) perceptively captures the role of the media in producing literary value: "Broadcast book programming reflects a shift in the review and recommendation function of mass media and literary cultural authority. But in no way is it a smooth shift" (2008, 203). Such mediation of literary texts is a middlebrow function, as discussed above, but it also helps destabilize and refashion the cultural status of the middlebrow itself.

The Richard & Judy Book Club's deployment of media to shape reading practices suggests it might operate as what Deborah Brandt has called a *literacy sponsor* (1998). For Brandt, literacy sponsors are influential figures who affect "the course of an ordinary person's literacy learning – its occasions, materials, applications, potentials" (1998, 17). At the same time as they influence individuals' reading habits, however, literacy sponsors have a wider impact. They contribute to transformations within society as different forms of literacy are recognized or dismissed (1998, 177). In contemporary culture, their role may often be to unsettle existing hierarchies of value: Brandt argues that "sponsoring arrangements" are highly fluid in contemporary society and that "this phenomenon is what makes today's literacy ... so destabilized" (1998, 178). Brandt's model has been deployed in the context of Oprah's Book Club by R. Mark Hall, who examines "the club as a literacy system" (2003, 648) and argues that Winfrey's literacy practices hinge upon the use of television as a medium and an appeal to the personal and the emotional (2003, 664).

Like Winfrey's project, the Richard & Judy Book Club promotes a feminized middlebrow model of literacy that prizes the emotional, rather than cerebral, qualities of a text. The quotes that began this chapter suggest that the show engages ambiguously with the status of women's reading, both affirming and sometimes distancing itself from a gendered position, but the hosts deliberately distinguish their approach from more academic ways of reading. In a promotional interview for the club's 2006 Christmas Books Special, Finnigan states, "You've got to realise that most literary programmes, which are on late at night and concerned with 'Literature,' intimidate lots of people ... once people can see that a book, any book, is just a story about people, they can start to enjoy it" (Paxton 2006). The club presents books as "stories about people" through their emphasis on domestic, emotional, personal and social reading modes, four practices that are evident in the show's selected novels, visual imagery and the statements made by the hosts, celebrity guests and interviewed readers.

This model of literacy is influential. The authority wielded by the Richard & Judy Book Club as a contemporary literary sponsor is attested to by a 2006 article in *The Guardian* anointing Amanda Ross, producer and book selector for the

Richard & Judy Book Club, the most powerful person in UK publishing (McCrum 2006). The Richard & Judy Book Club also has an extremely significant economic impact, generating bestseller status for many of its selections. Its high visibility has unsettled the degraded status of some of the reading practices it promotes. Indeed, the overlap between selections for the club and other literary institutions suggests that the textual qualities the club values have a wider cachet. Club picks are also often major literary award winners: Geraldine Brooks's *March* (2006) won the Pulitzer Prize for Fiction, Chimamanda Ngozi Adichie's *Half of a Yellow Sun* (2006) won the Orange Prize for Fiction and several books including Julian Barnes's *Arthur and George* (2006), Lloyd Jones's *Mister Pip* (2007) and Joseph O'Neill's *Netherland* (2008) were shortlisted for the Man Booker Prize. Different values continue to conflict in the contemporary literary economy but the success of the Richard & Judy Book Club suggests the ascendant power of feminized, middlebrow reading.

Reference List

Aubry, Timothy. 2006. Beware the furrow of the middlebrow: Searching for *Paradise* on *The Oprah Winfrey Show*. *Modern Fiction Studies* 52 (2): 350–73.

Bird, Sarah. 2005. Read 'em and weep. *Texas Monthly*. October.

Boztas, Senay. 2008. Richard and Judy 'treat their audiences as stupid.' *The Guardian*, August 17. http://www.guardian.co.uk/books/2008/aug/17/edinburghbookfestival.fiction

Blewster, Kelley. 1998. A book club of one's own. *Bibli*, Aster (January): 28–9.

Brandt, Deborah. 1998. Sponsors of literacy. *College Composition and Communication* 49:165–85.

Brooks, Geraldine. 2006. *March*. Pymble, NSW: Harper Perennial.

Carter, David. 2004. The mystery of the missing middlebrow or the c(o)urse of good taste. In *Imagining Australia: Literature and Culture in the New New World*, ed. Judith Ryan and Chris Wallace-Crabbe, 173–201. Cambridge, MA: Harvard University Press.

Carter, David. 2007. *Learning to love the middlebrow: Middlebrow book culture in Australia*. MP3. The University of Queensland Public Lectures, 29 March. http://www.cccs.uq.edu.au/index.html?page=56003&pid=16377

Couldry, Nick. 2003. Media meta-capital: Extending the range of Bourdieu's field theory. *Theory and Society*. 32 (5/6): 653–77.

Desperate Housewives. 2004. Anything you can do. ABC. 21 November.

Fowler, Bridget. 1991. *The alienated reader: Women and Romantic literature in the twentieth century*. Hertfordshire: Harvester Wheatsheaf.

Fowler, Bridget. 1997. *Pierre Bourdieu and cultural theory: Critical investigations*. London: Sage.

The Girls Book Club. [nd]. *www.Youtube.com*. http://www.youtube.com/watch?v=uecehcjAna8 (accessed 9 February 2010).

Hall, R. Mark. 2003. The 'Oprahfication' of literacy: reading 'Oprah's Book Club.' *College English* 65 (6): 646–67.

Hartley, Jenny. 2001. *Reading groups*. Oxford: Oxford University Press.

Humble, Nicola. 2001. *The feminine middlebrow novel, 1920s to 1950s: class, domesticity, and bohemianism*. Oxford: Oxford University Press.

Huyssen, Andreas. 1986. *After the Great Divide*: *modernism, mass culture, postmodernism*. Bloomington: Indiana University Press.

Koomson, Dorothy. 2006. *My Best Friend's Girl*. London: Sphere.

Lansens, Lori. 2006. *The Girls*. London: Virago Press.

Long, Elizabeth. 2003. *Book Clubs: Women and the uses of reading in everyday life*. Chicago: The University of Chicago Press.

Lovell, Terry. 1987. *Consuming Fictions*. London and New York: Verso.

Macdonald, Dwight. 1960a. Masscult and Midcult I. *Partisan Review* (Spring): 203–33.

Macdonald, Dwight. 1960b. Masscult and Midcult II. *Partisan Review* (Fall): 589–631.

McCrum, Robert. 2006. Our top 50 players in the world of books. *The Guardian*, 5 March. http://www.guardian.co.uk/books/2006/mar/05/features.review

The Oxford English dictionary. Online edition, updated June 2009, s.v. 'Middlebrow.'

Paxton, Zoe. 2006. The Richard and Judy effect. *Times Online*, 9 December. http://entertainment.timesonline.co.uk/tol/arts_and_entertainment/books/article664016.ece

Pearson, Jacqueline. 1999. *Women's reading in Britain 1750–1835: A dangerous recreation*. Cambridge: Cambridge University Press.

Poole, Marilyn. 2003. The women's chapter: Women's reading groups in Victoria. *Feminist Media Studies* 3 (3): 263–81.

Pykett, Lyn. 1992. *The 'improper' feminine: The women's sensation novel and the new woman writing*. London; New York: Routledge.

Radway, Janice A. 1997. *A feeling for books: the Book-of-the-Month Club, literary taste, and middle-class desire*. Chapel Hill: University of North Carolina Press.

Richard & Judy: My Best Friend's Girl. Video clip [nd]. *www.Youtube.com*. http://www.youtube.com/watch?v=iYZfARvUHyo (accessed 9 February 2010).

Rubin, Joan Shelley. 1992. *The making of middlebrow culture*. Chapel Hill: University of North Carolina Press.

Sedo, DeNel Rehberg. 2008. Richard & Judy's Book Club and 'Canada Reads': Readers, books and cultural programming in a digital era. *Information, Communication & Society* 11 (2): 188–206.

Tuchman, Gaye. 1989. *Edging women out: Victorian novelists, publishers, and social change*. New Haven: Yale.

Woolf, Virginia. 1942. Middlebrow. *The death of the moth and other essays*. London: The Hogarth Press. 113–9.

Chapter 7
The Roles of the Storytellers: Richard and Judy Read
The Jane Austen Book Club

Jenni Ramone

'Storytelling happens in many situations, from kitchen-table conversation to religious ritual, from telling in the course of other work to performances for thousands of paying listeners. Some storytelling situations demand informality; others are highly formal. Some demand certain themes, attitudes, and artistic approaches. … the expectations about listener interaction and the nature of the story itself vary widely' (National Storytelling Network, 2009).

Richard and Judy, Oprah, the TV Book Club hosts and book club members who discuss the books in online forums or in the studio perform a storytelling role, and the texts discussed represent the stories that they tell. Positioning Richard and Judy and their readers as storytellers permits an examination of the way that commentators respond to the storyteller's authority and voice. As well as academic responses to storytellers, this essay considers the contemporary storyteller figure in the storytelling café, and the storyteller as presented by the Richard & Judy Book Club in its digital manifestation. In particular, I will examine the surprising responses of the Richard & Judy Book Club readers to the one book club choice that might be expected to be a sure hit, Karen Joy Fowler's *The Jane Austen Book Club*.

Kathleen Rooney objects towards Oprah's Book Club, observing that Oprah and Oprah's readers retell the stories they have read, reframing them from within their own experiences so that they become emotionally involved protagonists in the narrative instead of objective analysts, imposing their own voices – and metaphors – on to the texts and thus distorting them (Rooney, 2005: 22). To tell stories is to own, and in order to own it is necessary to be able to retell a story in the language of metaphor. Perhaps since the Death of the Author, ownership of the text in any form – by an author or by a reader – is automatically suspect in academic discourse. As a result, the kind of storytelling embarked upon by Oprah and her readers has come to be resented by academic commentators.

Like the traditional face to face reading group, broadcast book clubs like Oprah's Book Club (OBC) and the Richard & Judy Book Club form a context where people can retell a story in a number of ways. For Kathleen Rooney, Winfrey's manner of retelling stories falls short of the practices of reading group discussion, never mind objective academic analysis. This, she suggests, demonstrates a failing on Winfrey's part to enable her viewers to engage with the texts at a higher, more analytical level:

> Winfrey sadly underestimated her audience's ability and willingness to comprehend and to engage in discourse about the significance of their participation in such a revolutionary club, resorting more often than not to what amounted to little more than Reading is Fundamental – And Fun!–style sloganeering. This in turn was tied to Winfrey's tendency to underestimate her audience's ability to appreciate intelligent discussion of OBC-selected books themselves, and to resort instead to the imposition of various competing narratives – including those of her show, herself, and her readers – upon the novels. (Rooney, 2005: 22)

Oprah's Book Club operated primarily under a small group discussion format, often involving the author and other celebrity guests, and including hand-picked audience members, chosen on the basis of their letters, in which they set out reasons for their inclusion. This was a competition; successful readers were given the opportunity to have a meal with the writer and with Oprah, and among the winners were those with "the most relevant life experiences" (Farr, 2005: 10). This factor coincides with the common reading group assumption that the experience that a member can bring to the story makes their part in the discussion valuable: the reader with relevant experience becomes a storyteller by shaping the story to their context and becoming the expert reader, or storyteller. It is this act that Rooney disputes and considers an "imposition." However, Rooney's approach is somewhat contradictory. She makes academic complaints of a non-academic forum, and her complaints are echoed only by those who are also couched in academic reading practices: Cecelia Konchar Farr's students complain that with the OBC, Oprah is "'oprahfying' books" (Farr, 2005: 53). While Rooney celebrates the way that Winfrey's book club successfully set itself up in opposition to the academy and the literary establishment, growing to the extent that "five hundred thousand viewers had read at least part of the novel" under discussion, "and almost as many bought the book in ensuing weeks," at the same time she claims that:

> Winfrey … refused to allow her readers to discuss that material in any but the most superficial fashion … Winfrey instructed her audience to experience the books in terms of how they personally related to the main characters, focusing less on the novels themselves and more on how their own life stories could be understood and improved in the process. (Rooney, 2005: 24)

The kind of reading that Rooney wanted Oprah to engage in would have been reading that turns away from what reading groups do, in favor of academic discourse that is part of the literary establishment, the very thing that Oprah has been praised for avoiding, when she encourages "real" readers to engage with books.

Perhaps ultimately, Rooney has a problem with the purpose of Oprah's Book Club: "By encouraging her readers to sympathetically impose their own life stories over the ones they encountered in books, Winfrey caused OBC to have less to do with the books and more to do with the self-help narrative of her show itself" (Rooney, 2005: 28). In reading the novels in this way, for Rooney, "Winfrey seemed inclined to turn Oprah into the main character of each and every novel" (Rooney, 2005: 159). However, what Winfrey was doing seems very similar to the kind of reading produced by conventional reading groups. The difference, perhaps, came in the way that Oprah hosted every Book Club show as the dominant reader, and led the discussion. Reading groups generally share the hosting role in a more democratic format with each member taking turns to lead discussion. Being placed within the context of her well-established show, it was perhaps inevitable that both the narrative of her own life and of her show and its self-help format would come to determine the direction of the discussion. This is an interesting development in itself: surely the way that Oprah retells stories is just as valid an object for scholarly discussion as, for example, the way that the Sunjata epic has been retold in its particular and multiple contexts. The text isn't replaced by Oprah's summary and interpretation of it, just as one version of the Sunjata doesn't erase an alternative version but simply provides an additional frame of reference for later readers. The Sunjata epic is a very different kind of storytelling, yet some of the features of traditional oral storytelling – still practiced in organizations like the Storytelling Café – have resonance with the storytelling figure that emerges in the Richard & Judy Book Club.

The Storyteller's Intrusive Voice

Sunjata, the tale that celebrates the founder of the thirteenth-century Mali empire, is considered the most famous African epic. Traditionally recited as part of an oral storytelling tradition, text versions have also been published. This is a good example of an oral story that has been subject to the will of its teller: as Charles Bird claims, there are "many versions of the Sunjata story" (Bird, 1999: 275). Repeated retellings over hundreds of years have resulted in multiple versions of the tale, but the multiple tellings of this story have also had an impact on storytelling practices; Bird states: "I believe that the extraordinary diversity ... is not of recent invention, and I also believe that choices made in the distant past have left their traces in today's practices" (Bird, 1999: 275). This can be observed, frequently, in postcolonial literature that explicitly replicates the narrative form of traditional storytelling, while operating within print culture. Rushdie's *Midnight's Children*, for example, is an explicit attempt to replicate the structure and style of traditional Indian storytelling, for a new context and audience.

There are common characteristic structural and stylistic elements to oral storytelling. The storyteller punctuates the tale with repetitions and allusions, restructuring it to suit the audience. In traditional Western literary thinking, linear textual narrative has been seen as a privileged form of literature and oral, cyclical narrative as something primitive and less skillfully crafted: for example, as Ashcroft, Griffiths and Tiffin suggest, "features of African orature in novels ..., viewed with European assumptions about novel structure, may look like simple, even imitative reproductions of existing styles" (Ashcroft, Griffiths and Tiffin, 2002: 185). Linear and cyclical narratives offer contrasting concepts of time; cyclical narratives do not rely on the same desire for an ending that drives the linear narrative. Ashcroft, Griffiths and Tiffin suggest that the traditional techniques of the Indian oral narrative involves "circling back from the present to the past, of building tale within tale, and persistently delaying climaxes," suggesting that these "are all features of traditional narration and orature" (Ashcroft, Griffiths and Tiffin, 2002: 180–82). The traditional storyteller draws and holds an audience within a community setting by constructing a story told through cycles, repetitions and delays. These practical storytelling techniques remain in the tales performed in contemporary storytelling cafes, although the sense of community connection is somewhat lost: in storytelling cafes in the UK today, storytellers are international, travelling figures who tour with their stories. Storytellers often opt to tell stories from other places instead of their own local tales, as if the audience's experience of listening to stories is enhanced by the element of the mythical, unfamiliar or exotic. Recent storytelling events listed on the Storytelling Café's diary do include some local tales, but these outnumbered by those from "around the world" and even "fantastic worlds" (Storytelling Café, 2009). This shift in emphasis away from the local perhaps explains why the storyteller figure has become more peripheral in recent times, as the local community connection is severed.

Community storytelling was superseded by the publication of novels, and these novels were soon recognized as belonging to their author. Once the author was seen as an authority over their text, the practice of retelling and updating the story that characterizes oral narrative becomes more difficult: the text is instead understood as something permanent and fixed. In his work on the Victorian novel, Ivan Kreilkamp suggests that the storyteller figure is not lost, but rather, can be located within the realist novel. He disputes the notion that the storyteller has faded from prominence following the dominance of print culture. However, the storyteller figure he describes is very different from the traditional one who had a fluid and multiple community voice. Kreilkamp suggests that "the much-lamented storyteller came into being as a fiction within the very medium that is accused of having killed him off" (Kreilkamp, 2005: 2). The Victorian novel, for Kreilkamp, is "a fabricated struggle between multiple and complex forms of speech and writing" (2005: 3). Authorial narration and other voices within the novel represent the storyteller figure in Victorian literature, if this is the case. However, for Kreilkamp, ultimately the storyteller is interchangeable with the author, in the guise of the dominating Author-God figure: "from Dickens onward ... the figure of the storyteller emerges within British fiction as the sign of endangered intellectual authority, charisma, and personal presence" (2005: 3). Thus, while a more general form of capitalism was creating new hierarchies and divisions, the storyteller figure too became an authority and a privileged, canonized figure. While Kreilkamp identifies the novel as the storyteller's new location, this comes at a price: when the author took possession of the story by its print and publication the storyteller was replaced by the Author-God figure. This is bound to put in place restrictions regarding who may be considered a legitimate storyteller.

Today, within print culture, storytellers don't just exist within the text – they also thrive outside and alongside it. The book club and other public manifestations of literature can – even if unintentionally – challenge authorial status by retelling the stories in the manner of the storyteller in oral narrative. Though the author figure is often central to broadcast book clubs like Oprah's and Richard and Judy's, where the author is regularly invited to discuss their novels, the authority of this figure is challenged both by their presence in a non-academic context, and by the competing narratives that overlay their texts once other invited speakers start to read the novel from the perspective of their own personal stories.

In addition, literary festivals, poetry readings and book shops are locations where storytelling can still take place; here, people come together to discuss books and in doing so, they present those narratives according to their own reading practices and preferences. At the Hay Festival in 2008, for example, the Guardian recorded a reading of Gillian Clarke's poem "The Habit of Light" by multiple festival-goers, a recording that allows the readers to overlay the poem with their voice instead of deferring to the poet's voice. And although the numerous speakers are obviously reading from a text, no textual copy of the poem is published on the website where the video is held, so the poem retains nuances of oral literature (Hay festival, 2008). The Guardian also hosts a monthly online poetry workshop, and as a Hay Festival special edition, Gillian Clarke's workshop demonstrates the way that an object can have its story told in multiple ways, while providing another public place for the dissemination of literature. Clarke writes: "Just as I'd hoped, taking a familiar object for subject sent people rummaging for more than material remembered things. With the guitar, the vase, the T-shirt, the prayer shawl and all the other things, came all that surrounded it, and inner and outer landscapes are revealed" (Clarke, 2008).

But the storyteller is most clearly celebrated by the storytelling cafes that have emerged in recent decades and continue to operate in touring circuits and in regular venues in towns and cities. These events are often held together under the name of national organizations like the Society for Storytelling (UK), Storytellers of Canada (SC-CC) and the National Storytelling Network (USA). These organizations exist to promote and maintain storytelling as a community practice and as a skill, offering storytelling workshops as a way to recruit new storytellers. The host of the Storytelling Café event held at the Kitchen Garden Café in Birmingham on October 15, 2008, a motivational storyteller in schools and colleges with a firm belief (like Oprah's) that "stories have a great power to change," insisted on the demand for storytelling workshops in Birmingham in order to cultivate new storytellers. He said to the audience: "we need *you* to tell *your* stories." The Storytelling Café is a regular event that hosts one or more storytellers in an informal setting. The October 2008 event involves two main storytellers, Alma Simpson and Nell Phoenix, who each tell three stories, and two additional storytellers who both tell one very short story.

Common to all four storytellers is their personal, biographical identification for the audience: all four begin with an autobiographical statement so that their personal narrative connects them with the audience. The storytellers are: a motivational storyteller in education; a former teacher and now a professional storyteller; a formerly local non-professional storyteller visiting Birmingham from South Wales; and a professional storyteller who runs her own storytelling night at a London venue. However, this very limited biographical introduction in most cases has no firm connection with the stories told. The first speaker connects his story to his biography by telling a tale about his own school experience, and repeating for this audience a story told to students as an exercise in building self-esteem. The other storytellers tell myths, legends and stories from Italy, Pakistan, Africa, Hungary and the mythical "top of the world," but aside from some Italian language included in the story of Peronella, Lodovico and Giovanni, which implies that the storyteller has connections with Italy, the tellers make no explicit connection between the stories and themselves: they don't claim to have visited the locations or to have professional or family connections there. In this sense, the stories could have been told by any teller and the traditional expectation that the story is influenced by its teller is rendered uncertain. However, even if the storytellers seem at times to be performing character roles to tell their stories instead of revealing something of themselves through the telling, the audience is subject to its tellers' personalities and styles. The storytellers interact with their audience to ensure that the story is made real and not recited. Repetitive phrases, rhyme and rhythmical repetition characterize the way the narrative is performed, and the audience instinctively joins in with the refrains in Alma Simpson's stories. Storytellers ask questions requiring a yes or no answer from the audience, and they hold eye contact with members of the audience for extended periods in order to capture interest.

Unlike a conventional staged performance, the storytelling takes place within the current moment and is subject to what is going on specifically in the room: storytellers react to movements around them, note the gender and age bias of the audience and react to specific audience responses. Nell Phoenix gently encourages audience participation when she moves from one story to the next, asking everyone in the room to "blow" one element from the first story across the world to the location where the second story will take place, and again from the second story to the third. This sense of continuity and connectedness is another particular feature of the storytelling café: not only is the storyteller connected to the audience and dependent on the venue and audience members to enable this connectedness, but the stories and the storytellers are connected to each other, and are not perceived as separate speakers in succession. The stories are explicitly linked by theme, when storytellers refer to each other's stories, and to similarities between characters: there are a number of stories about powerful women tonight, countered by those that feature women who make bad decisions or who behave in ways perceived to be immoral yet are celebrated for their wiliness. They note common elements that recur, such as the barrel, considered a "very useful" prop in a story if a character needs to hide.

Though the Storytelling Café offers a direct example of ongoing oral storytelling in public places, there are other emerging storytellers. A culture of non-authorial storyteller figures is operating within digital culture and alongside published novels. Part of the effect of the Richard & Judy Book Club is to reinstate the storyteller figure, so that this figure re-emerges in public manifestations of literature from the more specialized storytelling cafes and poetry workshops and readings to other places where the story is retold. This kind of storytelling had an earlier, more hierarchical incarnation in the subscription book clubs, which offered cheaply available books and made recommendations based on members' stated preferences and editors' expert readings. Janice Radway's *A Feeling For Books* (1999), an examination of the Book-of-the-Month Club, observes the organization of this popular American book ordering club. In the process of carrying out research to find out how book club selections are made and promoted, she discovers that it isn't the book club members who become storytellers, but the editors. An editor's role is to write reports and reviews about the books chosen: while these serve a first purpose, which is to describe the book in a way that will make a potential reader or customer engage with the description and buy the book, the editors' reports are, Radway writes, at the same time an outlet for "their singular, highly accomplished presentation of self" (Radway, 1999: 43). This is very much a description that could be used to represent what any storyteller does while telling a story. Here the editors become storytellers who overlay the texts under discussion with their own narrative. Interestingly, the editors of the Book-of-the-Month Club refer to themselves as "readers"; they don't perceive those who buy the books to be "readers" – instead, these are "members." So it remains the "reader" who can become a storyteller, however that reader is figured.

The editors of the Book-of-the-Month Club see their members as consumers who will read specific books in accordance with the way that they have described those texts, in that traditional position as a solitary reader. This is a different kind of reader from those who join reading groups and meet to discuss books. Some of these groups of readers are so far removed from the notion of solitary reading that they specifically only use books that are meant to be read aloud. One group responded to Jenny Hartley's questions on the book selection process for her book, *Reading Groups* (2001), explaining that: "there is now a sort of rule that ... we read works intended to be read aloud" (Hartley, 2001: 51). Other groups simply enjoy the process of reading aloud together and so, irrespective of the text, "the group may decide that it wants to read aloud" (Hartley, 2001: 86). The reading group or book club is currently the most prevalent version of a context where storytelling takes place in a public space, permitting a constant renegotiation of a known and shared tale.

Though the Richard & Judy Book Club has caused an upsurge in reading groups in the UK, the current trend has a long history: "Reading in groups has been around for as long as there has been reading. … The Romans did it, emigrants on board ship to Australia did it … in fifteenth-century France a group of women who gathered to spin during the long winter evenings took turns to read aloud to each other" (Hartley, 2001: 1). This is, for Hartley, explained by an "impulse to share" books or the experience of reading, a need to share stories and an appreciation for readers' specific experiences related to the texts under discussion (Hartley, 2001: 2, 81). Like the traditional storyteller figure, these members with specific and relevant experience convey a particular engagement with and control over the story. When book club hosts become storytellers and impose the self on to the text, they resemble traditional storytellers, yet their democratic engagement with the texts invites their extended book club members to respond by contributing stories from their own experiences. Walter Benjamin has described the storyteller's role as democratic: "a great storyteller will always be rooted in the people, primarily in a milieu of craftsmen" (Benjamin, 1999: 100). Stories are mediated through their teller, whose personality resonates within the story told, in Benjamin's words: "traces of the storyteller cling to the story the way the handprints of the potter cling to the clay vessel" (Benjamin, 1999: 91). With passing generations, the story is told by new storytellers who adapt according to their style and experience. As a result, the story is subject to its storyteller, is dominated by its storyteller and creativity resides within the storyteller rather than the story.

Richard and Judy's presentation of the story is certainly democratic, and Oprah's is creative, if she becomes the narrative subject in her discussion of book club choices. Yet, there is resistance to book club hosts playing the role of storyteller. This resistance remains even when the book club hosts are fictional ones, as is apparent from suspicious online responses to the retelling of Austen's novels that takes place in the chapters of Karen Joy Fowler's novel, *The Jane Austen Book Club*. Benjamin suggested that in order to remain subject to the storyteller's power, the audience must maintain a particularly naive state of mind: "the more self-forgetful the listener is, the more deeply is what he listens to impressed upon his memory" (Benjamin, 1999: 91). So what happens when the audience member remembers himself or herself? That individual starts to question the story being told instead of memorizing it, and in filtering that story through memories of their own life, becomes a storyteller figure. Once the audience member can retell the story, the original storyteller figure – the author – has given authority to the reader to tell the story in their own way. In the reading group context, people tend to adopt personal ownership of the books that they suggest for the group. Jenny Hartley's research revealed that the story becomes somehow theirs because they suggest it to the group, and they can feel threatened and upset if their choice is not well received, as some of the members' comments revealed; when their choices were received badly, they report feeling "disappointed," "beleaguered," "threatened," even "under attack" (Hartley, 2001: 63–4). The story becomes theirs because they present it to the group, like a storyteller; the author doesn't come under criticism, but the reader who has suggested it does. Thus, the story, within the confines of the reading group meeting, is theirs and they are responsible for it.

If the book club forms a context where people can retell a story in a number of ways, to tell a story in the manner of traditional community storytelling, then equally, the book club often selects stories with a self-conscious and intrusive narrative voice, a character-narrator who performs that traditional storytelling role, which is consistent with Kreilkamp's theory. These texts are chosen instead of those featuring a more discreet impersonal narration. On a very simple analysis, almost two thirds of Richard and Judy Book Club and Summer Read fiction selections between 2004 and 2008 are narrated by character-narrators, immediately suggesting that there is a slight bias towards selecting these texts. Some of the selections that don't feature a character-narrator are texts that are written by established writers and fall within established genres such as crime (like Martina Cole's *The Know* and Michael Connelly's *The Lincoln Lawyer*), meaning that the texts adhere to the narrative features of the genre, and implying that the club is much more likely to select a story conveyed by an impersonal narrator if it comes from an established writer within a genre, where to exclude the text on the basis of its narration would be to misrepresent that genre. It is worth mentioning that other texts that don't have character-narrators do have a level of direct engagement with a character, though, such as the letters written by Hasina to her sister in Monica Ali's *Brick Lane*.

Some of the Richard & Judy Book Club selections employ a complicated and experimental form of character narration, such as *Then We Came to the End* (2007) by Joshua Ferris. Preceded by a quotation by Ralph Waldo Emerson on the value of being part of the group, of understanding people how they exist "in the gross, in the hundred, or the thousand, of the party, the section, to which we belong," the novel is narrated by a plural character-narrator who is always a "we" an "us," who talks of "our mornings," "our business," "our thanks," "our coffee mugs" (3,5,7). Though individual characters are named, they speak in direct speech, and their stories are told, they are contemplated by a nameless "we" that constitutes the employees of a typical advertising office. This isn't a collusive "we," though, or an intrusive author figure who demands authority. It is instead a plural character that the reader is expected to engage with in the same way as they would a more conventional character-narrator. Such an experimental form of storytelling is rendered more accessible by its thoroughly contemporary realist subject matter: office personality clashes, arguments and gossip, redundancies, family tragedies and furniture allocation. Telling a story collectively maintains the ethos of group storytelling, and allows reading groups to explicitly address the idea of understanding a story in the context of a group or retelling a story in the context of a reading group.

Reading The Jane Austen Book Club

The issue of authorial and competing storytellers is addressed in *The Jane Austen Book Club* by Karen Joy Fowler, which was a selection of the Richard & Judy Book Club in February 2005. *The Jane Austen Book Club* charts a book club's development over the six-month period in which they read each of Jane Austen's six major works. Structured like the minutes of book club meetings (if such formal procedures were a part of the intentionally informal book club meetings that Jenny Hartley, for example, has described), the novel also reveals the readers' stories including the past events and relationships that they recall privately, and their journeys taken while reading Austen's works. The novel is preceded by a quotation from Austen's *Emma*, which should prepare the reader for a non-straightforward narrative, especially when the novel is built on such an intertextual premise: "Seldom, very seldom does complete truth belong to any human disclosure; seldom can it happen that something is not a little disguised, or a little mistaken." The first indication that indeed, the novel will aim to question assumptions about authorship and reading is its bold assertion that "each of us has a private Austen" (1), and these "private" Austens are diverse – one reader's Austen "wrote wonderful novels about love and courtship, but never married" (1), while for another, she was "a comic genius" and for another reader, "a daughter, a sister, an aunt" (2). This engagement with a private, knowable, biographic Jane Austen has its rules, boundaries and limits for the book club members: when Prudie refers to Jane Austen as "Jane," the other book club members react strongly (but again, privately): "We exchanged secret looks. *Jane* … That was more intimate, surely, than Miss Austen would wish. None of the rest of us called her Jane, even though we were older and had been reading her years longer than Prudie" (21). While this is the deferential reaction of devoted readers to a prized author, Fowler presents their attitude towards authorship with quiet, Austen-esque disapproval – neither Prudie's affectionate use of "Jane" as a term of reference, nor the other book club members' distaste is seen as the correct way to engage with the text or its author: Fowler presents both, warmly, as flawed.

The question of authorial control and authority is again considered briefly when Jocelyn and Prudie discuss film adaptations of Austen's novels: the readers agree that adaptation is a dangerous thing, insisting on the contradictory position that: "The great thing about books was the solidity of the written word. You might change and your reading might change as a result, but the book remained whatever it had always been" (82). Surprises are only appropriate on reading the book "the first time" (82) and a film adaptation is understood as having the potential to be something akin to a second reading of the novel. This potential is seldom achieved because of film's dangerous habit of leaving the books "altered," even "reinvented" for the resistant Austen-reading viewer. The sense of legitimate authorship is not restricted to Austen's works, though: the notion of "poaching" is extended to the book club members' stories by the inclusion of Corinne, a creative writer who takes her partner Allegra's childhood stories and rewrites them as her own, to read at her creative writing class and to send to publishers. Allegra's reaction is comic, but at the same time, it addresses the notion of authorship to ask who the storyteller figure is and how they function, to consider the life of the story above the life of its first teller: "How dare Corinne write up Allegra's secret stories and send them off to magazines to be published? How dare Corinne write them so poorly that no one wished to take them?" (73). Nevertheless, there remains a question over how Austen functions in the book club members' lives: after they have read her six major novels together, where can they go? Contemplating retaining the book club by moving on to a new author, they wonder how this could be achieved, and collectively decide that "if we'd started with Patrick O'Brian, we could have then gone on to Austen. We couldn't possibly go the other direction. We'd let Austen into our lives, and now we were all either married or dating. Could O'Brian have done this? How? ... we'd just wait. In three or four years it would be time to read Austen again" (249).

Just like Austen's narratives, in *The Jane Austen Book Club*, the most fearfully dreaded things *don't* always happen: Prudie doesn't have an affair with her teenage student who makes her feel inappropriate desire, and her husband doesn't leave her in spite of her unspoken dissatisfaction. But when things do happen – things like marriages – they happen with just as much regretted lack of warning as they sometimes happen in Austen (such as Lucy Steele's hasty transference of affection to Robert Ferrars, leaving Edward Ferrars available for Elinor, in *Sense and Sensibility*): Bernadette goes on a bird-watching holiday to Costa Rica and decides to get married to her tour guide; Sylvia's marriage, broken at the opening of the novel, is healed quickly at the end with the unexpected (but desired) revelation that her husband David had made a mistake to leave her and had, unbeknownst to all, been living alone for two months instead of with the woman he had an affair with. Austen has an uncertain authority over *The Jane Austen Book Club*: Allegra's comments about occasional lapses in plot credibility are referred to as "Austen-bashing" (51). The book club thus expresses loyalty to Austen while it questions her narratives. There is an intentional communication between the novel and the body of work that it addresses, which is played out in more ways than general plot echoes, though.

Austen sometimes addresses her reader directly so at times she is an intrusive authorial narrator. At the same time, much of the meaning of the novels is gleaned from what is unsaid, and from plots left unfinished but implied. Similarly, there is much that is left unsaid in *The Jane Austen Book Club*, most notably the notion of textual and authorial boundaries. Karen Joy Fowler creates a text that is on first assessment a novel, replicating the structure of a book club and adding to it with stories about its members. However, the epilogue, the final part of the text that we might classify as decidedly fictional, is followed by 40 pages of additional materials, which hover uncertainly between fictionality and something else. The Richard & Judy Book Club selections have recently been published with reading guides: Carlos Ruiz Zafón's *The Shadow of the Wind*, for example, contains a plot summary, a brief author biography, a number of questions for discussion and a list of suggested further reading (Zafón, 2004: 507–10). Ostensibly, then, the reading guide forming part of *The Jane Austen Book Club*'s after-matter is performing this straightforward function. The first of these materials is a description of Austen's novels, including their dates of publication and composition, key character descriptions and a plot summary. This is likely to be useful for readers whether or not they will be taking this text to a reading group, and it isn't explicitly signed by Fowler so could be understood as something added by the publisher. However, the next item is titled "The Response," which almost suggests a response to this novel, but is in fact a collection of responses to Austen and her works, beginning with Austen's family and friends' comments on her works, and then moving on to a collection of comments on Austen made by other writers and critics, taken from reviews, letters and interviews rather than academic texts, and being of a largely personal style rather than an objective, critical one, as is exemplified by Mark Twain's poetic assessment: "Every time I read 'Pride and Prejudice' I want to dig her up and hit her over the skull with her own shin-bone" (266). This section is a little more difficult to categorize, as it is undoubtedly an edited, selected body of work instead of an exhaustive collection, provided to be read in conjunction with this novel and in that sense bearing some influence on it. This influence is conveyed too by the style of presentation: each separate selection of anecdotes and comments is gathered under a title beginning "In which…," to replicate the format in which each of the novel's chapters is presented – "Chapter Two in which we read Sense and Sensibility with Allegra" (43), for example.

Then comes a list of questions for discussion, a feature noted in Zafón's text. Very much unlike Zafón's questions, though, these questions aren't posed by a publisher – they are each of the characters' questions – Jocelyn, Allegra, Prudie, Grigg, Bernadette and Sylvia each ask three questions. It is possible that these are questions that a genuine reading group could answer, but the boundary between fictional character and the real world is difficult to find – the characters ask questions about their author, Karen Joy Fowler, and name the novel that they have been constructed for. Allegra relates her fictional events to the outside world to question Fowler's plot credibility in the same way as she has previously questioned Austen's when she asks: "In *The Jane Austen Book Club,* I take two falls and visit two hospitals. Did you stop to wonder how a woman who supports herself making jewellery gets health insurance? Do you think we will ever have universal coverage in this country?" All of the characters' questions maintain the character that has been constructed for them within the novel, yet suddenly by this act of questioning, they exist outside and beyond the novel. The positioning of these questions for discussion is significant in considering the relationship between the novel and additional material. If it had been positioned immediately after the epilogue, then the sense of fictional or textual boundary could, perhaps, have been more easily maintained.

The Acknowledgements section ends with a statement closely recalling the novel's opening, which insists: "Everyone has a private Austen" (288). It is only here that the voice that has acted as narrator and guide throughout the novel is represented in first person: "Mine," Fowler writes, "is the Austen who showed her work to her friends and family and took such obvious pleasure in their responses" (288). Throughout the novel there has been another person present – not a character-narrator who is identified, but not really an intrusive authorial narrator who we can associate as an implied author, either, because this is a person who sits reading with the other book club members, part of a "we" who "exchanged secret looks" (20), a "we" who sat in Jocelyn's porch watching the fog rising outside and the Rhodesian Ridgeback dog sleeping inside (28), a "we" who had mostly "also lost our mothers" (119). This silent narrator might be the author in unspoken presence, it might be a collective presence that characterizes the book club so much that it almost feels as if there is an additional sentient being when the book club members come together, or it might even be someone else never fully revealed, to match the other Austen works never read here (and seldom read elsewhere) – her juvenilia and epistolary novel, *Lady Susan*.

Perhaps most interestingly, though easy to miss and perhaps unintended, is the suggestion made by the inclusion of a standard Penguin order form encouraging readers to purchase more Penguin books: this particular "read more" order form is a Jane Austen order form, stating "if you enjoyed this book, there are several ways you can read more by the same author" and listing Austen's six novels along with their purchase price and order information. Does this imply that Jane Austen is that lingering additional reader who seems to be able to take part in the book club discussions but is never introduced, and who is able to access each of the other book club members' private thoughts and stories? The final item included in the after-matter is, appropriately, an advertisement for the Penguin Readers' Group with the URL of the reading group, a list of its key features (including reading choices, books and authors of the month, events, interviews and an annual prize to be awarded to an established book group) and the persuasive claim: "a whole community of book lovers is just a click away!."

Questions over where the author is actually positioned in this text, and what constitutes the boundary of the text (or the fiction) regarding *The Jane Austen Book Club* invite a consideration of the online book club and its function as (partial, perhaps) hypertext. As well as the book club series on television, and its replication and promotion in public libraries where Book Club books are ordered in bulk and held in special, short loan collections, the book club has a further forum: the online space. Here, the books are held in sequential lists and collections, along with summaries, pictures, reading notes and a message board, excerpts from the novels held digitally, author comments and also, reader and celebrity reader reviews.

The Richard & Judy Book Club website extends the reach of the books read on the television show further into the public domain. Readers can post their own reviews of the Book Club selections and the site contains resources intended for potential reading groups including tips on how to set up a reading group, and also reading notes. As well as links to a shopping area where readers can buy the Book Club selections in season sets or individually, the texts themselves each have a separate area of the site. Here, the text is situated within a multi-vocal space. Many texts include a note from the author, a reading guide, a digital extract from the book, which is often up to a chapter in length, a profile of the author and reviews. The reader isn't left to read the books on their own; instead, they are part of a network of readers supported by the book club resources presented in the same straightforward and non-threatening style as the broadcast program. And the sense of community enjoyed by the readers is evident from reading through the reviews, which are sometimes referential, meaning that they operate like a forum. One reader's review of *Then We Came to the End* wouldn't be recognized as a review traditionally, but is the kind of comment that readers make when they read texts in a community instead of alone: this reader writes, "I think I will have to be in the 'Mood' for this book, the first few pages I found quite irritating. I will reserve full judgement until I have attempted to read a few more, it may improve. If you have managed to read it then put your review down so I can see whether it is worth continuing with!" This reader is answered by some positive reviews, some of which emulate a more traditional style, but all of which privilege the notion of relevant experience, two reviews suggesting that this is a novel for "anyone who has ever worked in an office" and a further review placing the novel firmly in the realm of readers' experiences by reminding other website users that "not a lot happens in this but then sometimes not a lot happens in life" (*Then We Came to the End*: Book Reviews).

While the summaries, and celebrity and reader reviews offer further storytelling potential, simply by virtue of its online presence the book club is also a nod towards the hypertext. The digital book extracts mean that instead of reading the book in a bookshop or library before making the decision on whether to buy it, readers can engage with the text digitally and experience the first few pages before making the investment of time and money. However, while the website operates in a similar way to the conventional reading group by allowing readers to discuss the text together in a comfortable setting, there are some questions raised by the reactions to some of the texts. If the online space functions like a book club, then this leaves questions as to why the readers' reviews are so hostile to the one novel that seems to replicate the reading group most clearly, *The Jane Austen Book Club*. One review simply reads "Terrible! Do not buy this book" without explaining further why this is the case. A second review offers more detail, but similarly, this reader has been unable to engage with a novel that replicates the book club experience in a contemporary, realist style. This review reads: "I found this book really disappointing. I thought it was a good idea and had potential to be really interesting. As it was, none of the characters lives really had any link with any of the Jane Austen novels they discussed. It seemed like a [series] of unrelated and not particularly interesting short experiences about the characters, none of whom seemed especially likeable. Perhaps I just didn't get it!" (*The Jane Austen Book Club*: Book Reviews). These readers wanted Jane Austen's authority over her story to remain, and what they could not accept was the imposition of multiple layers of retelling, or metaphor.

Ultimately, the book club, while explicitly a celebration of authorship, forces a negotiation between the traditional status of the author, and the multi-authored space, digital or otherwise, where competing voices from non-standard, public sources renegotiate the text that they retell. Whose is the storyteller's voice, in this context: is it the voice of the author, the reader, the editor or publisher or printer who restructures the text for presumed market? Is the storyteller's voice a changing, public one, as heard in storytelling cafes? Is it a sometimes-anonymous, digital, multiple one as found in the hypertext? The online reviews of *The Jane Austen Book Club* ask this question by considering the purpose of the book. Who is permitted to be the storyteller of Jane Austen's (or Jane's) stories, her authorship, her textual life? Fowler can't tell the stories of people who read Austen's novels unless she does so by connecting each character to one of the novels in a very explicit way, according to the reader's review. Prudie can't talk about Jane Austen as "Jane," as if she knows the author intimately and can understand why she has made the textual choices that she has, and Grigg, a science fiction lover who had never even read *Pride and Prejudice* before its scheduled book club discussion can't say anything at all about the novels without being told by the others, "I'm afraid you've missed the whole point" (15). Corinne can't tell Allegra's stories – or can she? Fowler promotes the retelling of other people's stories in her acknowledgements, where she thanks those who have provided "a stolen image," "a stolen anecdote" and who did the "skydiving" for her (288, 287). The institution that is the Richard & Judy Book Club, as well as its online presence and many of the texts that it selects, operates in the mainstream in the same way as the storytelling café and the literary festival has operated in the (somewhat elite) margin to maintain and to reinstate the storyteller figure. And the digital text renders the storyteller figure's interpretation more important than the fixity of the printed text, while it is a democratic medium that privileges multiple voices over a dominating authority.

Reference List

Ashcroft, Bill, Gareth Griffiths, and Helen Tiffin. 2002 [1989]. *The Empire Writes Back: Theory and Practice in Post-colonial Literatures*. London: Routledge.

Ashcroft, Bill, Gareth Griffiths, and Helen Tiffin. 1990. Post-Colonial Reconstructions: Literature, Meaning, Value. In *Literature in the Modern World*, ed. Dennis Walder, 298–303. Oxford: Oxford University Press.

Benjamin, Walter. 1999 [1968]. Translated by Harry Zohn. *Illuminations*. London: Pimlico.

Bird, Charles S. 1999. The Production and Reproduction of Sunjata. In *In Search of Sunjata – The Mande Oral Epic as History, Literature and Performance*, ed. Ralph A. Austen. 275–96. Bloomington: Indiana University Press.

Bohannan, Laura. 1956. Miching Mallecho. In *From the Third Programme: a ten-years' anthology of imagination, argument, experience, exposition*, ed. John Morris. 174–89. London: Nonesuch Press.

Clarke, Gillian. 2008. Poetry workshop: Inner and outer landscapes. http://www.guardian.co.uk/books/2008/may/30/poetry.hayfestival2008 (accessed 3 November 2008).

Farr, Cecilia Konchar. 2005. *Reading Oprah: How Oprah's Book Club Changed the Way America Reads*. Albany: State University of New York Press.

Ferris, Joshua. 2007. *Then We Came to the End*. London: Penguin.

Fowler, Karen Joy. 2004. *The Jane Austen Book Club*. London: Penguin.

Hartley, Jenny. 2001. *Reading Groups*. Oxford: Oxford University Press.

Hay festival: Poetry in motion. 2008. http://www.guardian.co.uk/books/video/2008/may/30/poemhay (accessed 3 November 2008).

The Jane Austen Book Club: Book Reviews. 2008. http://www.richardandjudybookclub.co.uk (accessed 29 October 2008).

Kreilkamp, Ivan. 2005. *Voice and the Victorian Storyteller*. Cambridge: Cambridge University Press.

National Storytelling Network. 2009. What is Storytelling? http://www.storynet.org/resources/knowledgebank/whatisstorytelling.html (accessed 29 June 2009).

Radway, Janice. 1999. *A Feeling For Books – The Book-of-the-Month Club, Literary Taste, and Middle-Class Desire*. Chapel Hill: University of North Carolina Press.

Rooney, Kathleen. 2005. *Reading with Oprah – The Book Club that Changed America*. Fayetteville: The University of Arkansas Press.

Ross, Catherine Sheldrick, Lynne McKechnie, and Paulette M Rothbauer. 2006. *Reading Matters: What the Research Reveals About Reading, Libraries & Community*. Westport, Connecticut: Libraries Unlimited.

Storytelling Café. 2009. Events in Birmingham and the Midlands. http://www.tradartsteam.co.uk/diary/date_list.html (accessed 29 June 2009).

Then We Came to the End: Book Reviews. 2008. http://www.richardandjudybookclub.co.uk (accessed 29 October 2008).

Zafón, Carlos Ruiz. 2004. *The Shadow of the Wind*. London: Phoenix.

Chapter 8
A Good Authentic Read:
Exoticism in the Postcolonial Novels
of the Richard & Judy Book Club.

Helen Cousins

Of the 81 books included in the Richard & Judy Book Club and Summer Reads from 2004–2008 (after which the couple moved from Channel 4 to a new TV station "Watch"), only 16 have a setting outside of Europe and the North American continent. Similarly, American and British authors are in a majority having penned 71 of the texts – a proportion expected where only two of the texts listed are in translation (*The Shadow of the Wind* translated from Spanish and *The Bookseller of Kabul* translated from Norwegian). A further three texts are written by Australians; one is by a New Zealand writer. We might define all these authors as inhabiting the "developed world" or, in postcolonial parlance, as "Western" in cultural positioning if not geographically. This leaves only four books written by "other" authors: *Half of a Yellow Sun*, chosen for the Book Club in 2007, and written by Chimamanda Ngozi Adichie, a young Nigerian novelist; *The Pirate's Daughter* (Summer Read 2008) by the Jamaican author Margaret Cezair-Thompson; the Afghan writer, Khaled Hosseini's *A Thousand Splendid Suns* (Book Club 2008); and *Empress Orchid* (a Book Club choice for 2006) by the Chinese author, Anchee Min. These texts can be grouped under the category postcolonial literature, sharing the features of being set in previously colonized countries, and written by authors of that country.

Of course, like all statistics and categorizations, those above contain a wealth of hidden and mis-information. Various assumptions have been made in compiling them particularly regarding the nationality of authors. While various facts can be assembled from reviews, biographical material, images available on the internet and from their own official websites, if they have them, this tends to complicate an author's heritage and individual history rather than clarify it. So, for example, is a white author now resident in England but born and raised in Uganda "British"; what about a writer of Chinese and Welsh heritage who currently lives in America but was born and raised in England; and should a writer born and raised in Barcelona, writing in Spanish but living in America be defined as "Spanish"? However, it is just these complexities that drive the books' popularity and their inclusion in the Richard & Judy Book Club lists. The nebulous boundaries of belonging engendered by a colonial past and a nomadic present position the writers in a place labeled the "postcolonial exotic" by Graham Huggan. What is interesting, and the focus of this chapter, is not grappling with the precise nationality of these authors – a question probably impossible to answer – but to consider the nature of this space in relation to how the Book Club's readers perceived an "authentic" voice (or a non-authentic one) as expressed by the authors through their novels, and which, in the readers' views, made them "bona fide cultural *representatives*" (Huggan 2001, 26) of the countries about which they wrote. All four of these novels could be considered through the notion of authenticity however, it can be linked in most similar ways in relation to *Half of a Yellow Sun* and *A Thousand Splendid Suns*. Both of these novels are based in real wars arising, at least in part, from those countries' colonial legacies; and are wars that hold a place in the British imagination as both have attracted major coverage in the British media. By comparison, in *The Pirate's Daughter*, the fact that "Jamaica that steals the show" (Stuart 2007) tends to focus the exotic in those postcolonial notions of an authentic tropical paradise, and authenticity in *Empress Orchid* is made more complex by its claim to be based on the true story of the Chinese Empress Tzu-Hsi. Thus, the focus here will be on *Half of a Yellow Sun* and *A Thousand Splendid Suns* in order to hone in on what Graham Huggan labels the "anthropological exotic" (Huggan 2001, p. 37). This is a specific manifestation of the "postcolonial exotic," which is the subject of Huggan's book:

> like other contemporary forms of exoticist discourse, [the anthropological exotic] describes a mode of both perception and consumption; it invokes the familiar aura of the other, incommensurably "foreign" cultures while appearing to provide a modicum of information that gives the uninitiated reader access to the text and, by extension, the "foreign culture" itself. (Huggan 2001, p. 37)

It will use the reader reviews available on the Richard & Judy Book Club website to explore patterns in readers' reactions to the book in relation to authentic experience, as well as analyzing the novels themselves for evidence of how they reinforce and/or undercut notions of authenticity.

Little research has been done on exactly who these readers might be. Typically, Richard and Judy's show predominantly attracts ABC1 viewers, that is middle-class viewers as described by the National Readership Survey. More specific research has been carried out by DeNel Rehberg Sedo in her comparison of readers' attitudes to two specific book clubs. In her article "Richard & Judy's Book Club and 'Canada Reads': Readers, books and cultural programming in a digital era," she notes that the majority of respondents to her research were middle-class, female, educated to at least a further education level and white. Therefore, this essay will assume a "typical" reader who is certainly middle-class but also what Huggan describes as "uninitiated" (2001, 37) in terms of their experiences of "foreign" cultures and their understandings of any debates surrounding postcolonial theory. In *The Postcolonial Exotic*, Huggan notes that his reading of a particular text relies on the "construction of a Western model reader who views African literature, Africa itself, through the distorting filter of the anthropological exotic. Yet this, it goes without saying, is not the only type of reader these works are addressing" (2001, 41). In the following discussions, the model reader will be one for whom, authenticity is probably based in "common sense" and assumptions based on edited biographies of authors. Through the use of the reader reviews on the Richard & Judy Book Club website, the particular reader will be those who are motivated to post a response to the novels in a public forum.

To explore the idea of authenticity, we can start by considering the example of Khaled Hosseini: born in Afghanistan in 1965, he moved to Paris with his family in 1976 where his father had a four-year diplomatic posting. Although the family intended to return to Afghanistan after this, hostilities began in 1979 and the family was granted asylum in America where Hosseini has lived ever since. Although he visited Afghanistan in 2003 (for the first time since 1976) and 2007, he speaks of it being "impractical" to return citing his young children but also his ability to be more effective in aiding his country outside of it (Hosseini 2007–2008). Both the author information at the back of the book and on the Book Club website, emphasize Hosseini's Afghanistani roots and his current connections to Afghanistan through the United Nations Refugee Agency thus emphasizing his Afghani credentials and minimizing his rootedness in US culture.

Reader reviews on the Richard and Judy Book Club website suggested that many of these readers understood Hosseini's book as an authentic representation of Afghanistan from the 1960s to the present, despite his absence from the country for 36 years. Most prevalent in these reviews was the word "insight": from reading this book, three reviewers felt that they had been given "an insight into life as a woman in Afghanistan"; four others found insight "into the lives of people in Afghanistan." More broadly, reviewers commented about the "real insight into a culture" and were shocked that "these characters and tales really exist" in our world finding it "hard to believe how some people live"; all of which indicates that they were, at least partially, reading this text as non-fictional information that could move a reader from a position where they "knew very little about Afghanistan ... [but] now feel a greater interest." Furthermore, the book provided historical and political insight for several readers, one of whom felt that they "could not understand why our troops still stayed in that country, but now I do understand" and, from another, that the book "explained so much to me about the history" of Afghanistan (*A Thousand Splendid Suns*: Book Reviews).

The readers' recognition of authenticity can be contrasted with the reception, more generally of the other Richard & Judy Book Club choice set in Afghanistan. *The Bookseller of Kabul* by Anse Seierstad is a non-fictional account from a Norwegian journalist of her time living with a family in Kabul; like Hosseini's book it focuses primarily on the women's experiences emphasizing their lack of freedom and choice, imposed as much by the men and senior women in the family as by the exterior political circumscriptions of the Taliban. Unlike *A Thousand Splendid Suns*, this book only attracted two reviews on the Book Club site, albeit of a positive nature. Initially, *The Bookseller of Kabul* attracted good reviews in the British Press, although reservation was expressed that while it purported to be a non-fictional account of the family, it read most often as fictional. For example,

Tim Judah in his review for *The Observer* noted that "it is written as though it is work of fiction" (Judah 2003a); Caroline Moorhead in *The Guardian* thought, too, that it was "written sometimes more like fiction than fact, borrowing generously from speculation" (Moorhead 2003); and in *The Guardian*, Veronica Horwell suggested that writing chapters from different characters' perspectives, was:

> a difficult technique, since it ventures beyond fly-on-the-floor documentary into a risky exploration of inner lives. She is honest about the language problem – she did not speak the Persian dialect of the family, and relied on the English of Sultan Khan, his rebellious 17-year-old son, and Leila – although it means that the passages in which she delves into the motives of those with whom she can't converse directly are nearly impertinent in their assertions. (Horwell 2003)

Soon after publication, the already questionable position of the book as an authentic representation of women in Kabul, was further shaken by Mohammed Shah Rais' (the real Bookseller of the title) angry denunciation of Seierstad's misrepresentation of his family.

Rais published a personal statement expressing his grievances, entitled "A Matter of Honor and Truth" (Rais, 2003) and his own version of Seierstad's stay with his family entitled *Once Upon a Time There Was a Bookseller in Kabul* (2007). The press were equally interested in this story; in a *Guardian* article subsequent to his review, Judah suggested that the "case has opened serious questions about the ethics of journalists and authors from rich countries writing about people from poor countries with very different cultures" and he quoted:

> Norwegian anthropologist and Middle East specialist Professor Unni Wikan, who doubts the authenticity of much of the book – "especially some of those bits [Seierstad] gives in quotation marks." He said: "There is no way she could have possibly had such access to people's hearts and minds." (Judah 2003b)

It is perhaps less important to a Western audience that Rais objected to the book (as pointed out by Spivak, "there is no unrepresentable subaltern subject that can know and speak itself" (Spivak 1988, 285) and ironically, even while the book was being criticized for its lack of authenticity, Seierstad's representation of Rais as the stereotypical misogynistic patriarch a western reader might expect, allowed his objections to be ignored); and more significant that the authoritative western voice of the Norwegian anthropologist rejects its claims to authenticity. While the purported non-fictional account of real women's lives is rejected by readers, the fictional account in *A Thousand Splendid Suns* is embraced as standing for a genuine reality by the readers of the Richard & Judy Book Club.

One way in which Seierstad's book might be unattractive to readers is that it fails to deliver a message of hope: the first wife is never reconciled to the young second wife who ousts her from the family home, and all of the Bookseller's sister's plans to escape her life as the family's drudge and to become independent are thwarted. This is in contrast to *A Thousand Splendid Suns* appreciated by the

Richard & Judy Book Club reviewers for the heightened emotions encapsulated in the love story between Laila and Tariq, its positive resolution that affirms that "love can triumph" even in the most desperate conflict and also the moving account of the companionship between the wives that left one reader with a "sense of pride in womankind." While the novel is appreciated as "an education," it is also valued as a work of fiction, particularly in terms of being "a really great story … about the human spirit" played out, not by "people" but by "characters" (*A Thousand Splendid Suns*: Book Reviews). It appears that, to be recognized as authentic, the popular postcolonial novel must lend itself to being read as fictional romance and educational non-fiction, the latter tempered in the light of the romance that delivers an optimistic closure.

This is not to suggest that no authority pertains where authors write books set outside of their native countries (however we are defining that). *White Mughals*, written by the historian William Dalrymple, explores the story of James Achilles Kirkpatrick, the British representative at the Hyderabad court, and the Mughal princess Kahir un-Nissa, who first met in 1798 and subsequently married. Before this story begins, Dalrymple provides an account of the process of researching the events of Kirkpatrick's life and the court at Hyderabad. He describes his searches in various archives, his travels in India to the locations of the book, his purposes in developing this episode of colonial encounter in India, his ideas about the differences in Anglo-Indian relationships between this period and the height of British imperialism in India. In this way, his authority is established through grounding in scholarship that readers will recognize even if this does not provide a "good read."

A closer investigation of the text, however, suggests Dalrymple has a more complex relationship with his material than a simple scholarly and cultural authority. The story, he suggests, is both terribly familiar and mystically different for a modern reader:

> Parts of the story that unfold … are so strikingly modern that it is sometimes hard to believe it was written two hundred years ago. There is much talk of the embarrassing pregnancy, the family's desperate attempts to procure an abortion … and the girl's mother's heartfelt cry that if only the sectarian religious divisions which had plagued the whole affair did not exist, this man could have had her daughter … The remoteness of history evaporates: there are immediately recognisable and familiar human situations.

> But, equally, … there are other moments when the sensation of familiarity dissolves and it is as if we are back in some semi-mythical world of Scheherazade and the *Arabian Nights*: we read of discreet interviews taking place through bamboo harem screens, of hunting expeditions where cheetahs are let slip at grazing gazelles, of spies following palanquins through the bazaars, and of a threat by the girl's grandfather "to turn fakeer" … as the only recourse to save the family honour. (Dalrymple 2002, 9)

The distance of time and space that could potentially alienate a modern reader can be transcended as the story presents universally "recognizable ... familiar human situations." Yet "we" – a modern British audience – also encounter the exotic and thus, the unfamiliar, through the "semi-mythical world of Scherezade," a cultural touchstone of "otherness" within mainstream British culture.

This ambivalence marks the reviewers' readings of *A Thousand Splendid Suns*, where the "woman's perspective" and the love story is interpreted through a lens of universality but the war and the cultural misogyny is clearly separate from the readers' experience: "It made me feel glad for my own circumstances" noted one, and another, sweeping over the many cultural differences that exist in England, thought "how lucky we are to live in a country that allows women the freedom to marry whom they wish to, and wear what they want to" (*A Thousand Splendid Suns*: Book Reviews). Similar ambivalence marks the reviews of *Half of a Yellow Sun*; while it is a book about "'people' just like you and I," it differentiates those people by the use of quotation marks and, in another review, by remarking on the unfamiliar names. Partly this impedes as there are "lots of African names to remember" but one reader suggested a "glossary of soundings for the Nigerian names which [she] found difficult to understand fully" would have been helpful (*Half of a Yellow Sun*: Book Reviews) as if somehow the inability to pronounce the names, prevented an understanding of the characters, positioning them as very much not "like you and I" but somehow strange.

Such responses to the texts are examples of Huggan's "anthropological exotic" (Huggan 2001, p. 37). In terms of literature, the anthropological exotic is distinguished from the postcolonial exotic in that it focuses on those texts (like Chinua Achebe's *Things Fall Apart* (1958) in Huggan's example) that have been used as windows onto another culture. It is clear from the reviews of *Half of a Yellow Sun* and *A Thousand Splendid Suns* that readers do feel that in reading these books they are learning about other cultures, and while they are undeniably exotic and "foreign" there are those aspects that are familiar. While the familiar is frequently expressed in terms of the universal, often it is a familiarity of those (post)colonial recognitions whereby a sense of "us" as different from "them" is evoked; where the "insight" is not empathy for people like "us" but a sympathy based on reader's assumptions about that other culture and its people, mediated through difference.

This can be illustrated by considering veiled women in *A Thousand Splendid Suns*. Natasha Walter, in her review of the novel in *The Guardian*, notes that by switching the narrative from Rasheed's wife Mariam (with whom the book begins) to:

> the young Laila, who is growing up in a liberal family with a father who believes in her education ... we suddenly see Mariam from the outside: Laila never speaks to her, but one day she 'passed Rasheed, the shoemaker, with his burqa-clad wife, Mariam, in tow'. In a flash we see, as Hosseini clearly intends us to, how behind every silent burka in Afghanistan is an individual with a hidden history. (Walter 2007)

This might be the case, and it is laudable to personalize such hidden lives, but it is also true that Mariam as an individual merely fulfils an expectation of a veiled woman's life in Afghanistan. Mariam is a woman who:

> lived in fear of [Rasheed's] shifting moods, his volatile temperament, his insistence on steering even mundane exchanges down a confrontational path that, on occasion, he would resolve with punches, slaps, kicks. (Hosseini 2007, 97–8)

Thus, it could be argued that, for the reader, this individual is metonymic for womanhood in Afghanistan, rather than noticeably different through acknowledgement of her individuality providing proof of the assumed stereotype. As the Western reader might anticipate, Rasheed's increasingly brutal treatment of his two wives escalates until the lives of the women are in danger. Such behavior is not exceptional, as the text makes clear; minor characters are also subject to violent male control such as Leila's friend whose father "was an ill-tempered taxi driver who in two or three years would almost certainly give her away" (Hosseini 2007, 114); and the friend Mariam makes during her short stay in prison who has tried to elope and expresses relief at being in prison as her "father had sworn that the day she was released he would take a knife to her throat" (Hosseini 2007, 354). Mariam's final sacrifice – being executed for the murder of Rasheed and, by taking full responsibility allowing Laila to escape Kabul – confirms her status as a victim.

Walter recognizes more generally that "Hosseini does not challenge the usual western view of Afghanistan" (Walter 2007) and it is hard not to read the episode where Laila has to have a caesarean section without anesthetic with a certain ghoulish fascination; it is undeniably horrific but accepted as a realistic event based on preconceptions of women's lives during the Afghanistan war; but perhaps it evokes less sympathy than relief of the absolute foreignness of such an event that could not and would not happen "here." This is Huggan's "familiar aura of the other" operating through a paradigm of horror. So the text operates in a two-handed way: one pulling sympathetically towards; the other repelling what is thankfully other.

This is neatly demonstrated in Hosseini's description of Mariam's birth. Mariam and her mother live in a hut on the outskirts of Herat supported by one of the town's prominent citizens. Mariam's mother had become pregnant by this man when she was a servant in his household; his wives demanded her dismissal but, for the sake of the child, Jalil housed and maintained her and Mariam, his *harami* (bastard) child. According to Mariam's mother, she gave birth alone on the floor of the hut:

> Jalil hadn't bothered to summon a doctor, or even a midwife … She lay all alone on the *kolba*'s floor, a knife by her side, sweat drenching her body.

> 'When the pain got bad, I'd bite on a pillow and scream into it … And still no one came to wipe my face or give me a drink of water … Almost two days … [I] lay on that cold hard floor …

> 'I cut the cord between us myself. That's why I had a knife.' (Hosseini 2007, 11)

However, Jalil tells Mariam a different version, that:

> he'd arranged for Nana to be taken to a hospital in Herat where she had been
> tended to by a doctor. She has lain on a clean proper bed in a well-lit room ...
> 'They told me it was all over within under an hour,' said Jalil. (Hosseini 2007,
> 11–12)

As Mariam gets older she starts believing Jalil's account, but which version do readers prefer to believe in?

Ania Loomba notes that "one of the most striking contradictions about colonialism is that it both needs to 'civilise' its 'others,' and to fix them into perpetual 'otherness'" (Loomba 1998, 173) thus the reader may vacillate between these two versions. However, the text does little to resist a reading that privileges the latter. Readers, alongside Mariam, discover Nana's hanging body, after Mariam has run away to find her adored father and been sent home; Jalil's version of the birth can be rejected as sympathy for Nana, Mariam and for Laila swells. Such sympathy is predicated on a notion of cultural difference as part of the dominant discourses of postcolonial relationships. While for Huggan, exoticism is "bound up ... not just in the perception of cultural difference but in the sympathetic identification with supposedly marginal cultural groups" (2001, 17), it could be suggested that such a sympathetic identification is part of this perceived difference. Homi Bhabha suggests that:

> cultural difference is the process of enunciation of culture as 'knowledge*able*',
> authoritative, adequate to the construction of systems of cultural identification
> ... [it] is a process of signification through which statements *of* culture or *on*
> culture differentiate, discriminate, and authorize the production of fields of
> force, reference, applicability, and capacity. (Bhabha 1995, 206)

To insist upon a sympathetic stance is to control the signification of veiled women in a reading that ignores or dismisses evidence from the text that is in contradiction to this manifestation of otherness. Early in the novel several female characters are not veiled, are independent and encouraged to pursue education and this state of affairs is clearly recognized as desirable and normal by their husbands and fathers. Further, a brief recognition of Rasheed as also subject to cultural forces is made: "I'm a different breed of man ... Where I come from, one wrong look, one improper word, and blood is spilled. Where I come from, a woman's face is her husband's business only" (Hosseini 2007, 69), he states. His own acknowledgement of himself as one type in comparison to other Afghan men who do not insist on veiling, who do not subjugate women through violence, acknowledges a diversity in male/female relationships. It is the incursion of the Taliban that enables one type of behavior to predominate.

Yet, the "imagined access to the cultural other through the processes of consumption" (Huggan 2001, 19) of a national book club enables a "*cultural translation*" (Huggan 2001, 24). In exoticist discourses, this means that cultural difference is "channelled into areas where it can be attractively packaged and

... safely contained"; translation in this context means the "superimposition of a dominant way of seeing, speaking and thinking onto marginalised peoples" (Huggan 2001, 24). Readers expect the female Afghani women to be violently oppressed and the text makes it relatively easy for them to read this cultural difference. The unresisting nature of the narrative might be explained in reference to Hosseini's particular experience of migration manifested as a:

> desire to believe in the eventual redemption of Afghanistan [which] means that the ending verges on the schmaltzy ... in the last chapter, ... the reader cannot help but feel that Hosseini's understandable longing for a beautiful return to life for the oppressed peoples of Afghanistan has made for an ending that is just a little flimsy. (Walter 2007)

Stuart Hall suggested that the reconstruction of a cultural identity is a process of "imposing an imaginary coherence on the experience of dispersal and fragmentation" (1990, 224), recreating a past "through memory, fantasy, narrative and myth" (1990, 226); Walter's assessment of Hosseini's novel implies that *A Thousand Splendid Suns* is such a construction, which charts a movement through adversity to a positive cultural outcome for the Afghanistan people. However, this is entangled with the resolution of the love stories of the novel – that of Laila and Tariq's reunion, and the imminent birth of their child who will be called Mariam if female, which neatly concludes the sororal love between the two women. A reading through the lens of an authorizing discourse, such as one that equates veiling with oppression – a ideologically hegemonic idea in mainstream British culture – may interpret the closure as mainly part of the romance, and in no way contradicting a cultural truism, that veiled women are oppressed. Hosseini's need to rehabilitate his own cultural identity impedes the ability of the text to resist such a reading.

The capacity to resist is what distinguishes *Half of a Yellow Sun* from *A Thousand Splendid Suns*. Huggan suggests that:

> within this field [of the postcolonial exotic] ... exoticism may be understood conventionally as an aestheticising process through which the cultural other is translated, relayed back through the familiar. Yet in a postcolonial context, exoticism is effectively *repoliticised*, redeployed both to unsettle metropolitan expectations of cultural otherness and to effect a grounded critique of differential relations of power. (Huggan 2001, ix–x)

As suggested above, *A Thousand Splendid Suns* serves to shore up exoticism, meeting readers' expectations, which might explain its popularity; yet *Half of a Yellow Sun* also featured in the bestseller lists in 2007 (the year it was a Richard & Judy Book Club choice) even though it offers more resistance to interpretation through a postcolonial exotic filter.

When *Half of a Yellow Sun* was discussed on the Richard & Judy television show, the participants (for the discussion Richard Madeley and Judy Finnegan were joined by the BBC's Africa correspondent, Rageh Omaar and Brian Cox, the actor) identified in the novel, both the culturally particular and the universal, often vacillating between these two positions with stunning speed, as in this exchange:

> Finnegan: Bowling along in this wonderfully warm story of communities and sisters and lovers and all the rest of it … [to Omaar] You say that's very typical of African life.
>
> Madeley: It's also very much from a middle-class viewpoint … it's about intelligentsia, the university people and their tribal roots. This educated, intelligent, modern viewpoint which to me read totally British and I identified with everything about it and yet these great clashes between the very recent tribal cultures, for example one of the character's mother's arrives to see him in his relationship with another woman and she's furious and she genuinely believes that the other woman is a witch. (Richard & Judy 2007)

Generally, the universal aspects of the text were recognized as to do with the identifiably westernized setting of the university and war so the discussion began with Madeley explaining his anticipation that he would be:

> reading about a culture and a world that I'm not familiar with but actually within three pages I felt that I was reading about something that happened here in Britain … the parallels between all of our lives are just so identical.

Omaar agreed that "all themes and characters are universal" and, making links with Gaza, India, Pakistan, the Blitz, Northern Ireland, that it was "essentially a book about human beings"; Cox noted that it "rings a universal bell." The discussion avoided the paradigm of Africa as intrinsically violent and tribal, despite this still being commonly used in the western media to explain outbreaks of violence on the African continent. As Melissa Wall discusses in relation to the civil war in Rwanda, the news coverage "continued the adherence to old patterns such as interpreting conflicts in Africa as evidence of backwardness … and now the coverage seems to suggest that violence is simply tribal or inexplicable" (Wall 2007, 270–271). Instead, the Richard & Judy discussion panel drew parallels with British and European conflicts and Madeley, in a surfeit of sympathy, even suggested that the violence in Europe during the Second World War, was worse than it was in Biafra. It is difficult to know how to read this one-upmanship of violence; suffice it to say that it suggests an intention to convey understanding of a common experience that unites people in Europe, Africa, India and the Middle-East.

Yet references to "tribal roots" and a character who "genuinely believes that the other woman is a witch" imply that these readers are drawing on deep-rooted understandings of how Africa is "culturally different" in discussing the book. Drawing on a familiar vein of representation – of the ignorant, wide-eyed African amazed at the (western) culture he encounters – occasions hilarity to break out over the discussion of Ugwu's reaction on arriving at the University campus after a life spent in the village: "Never seen a tap … the fridge … takes chicken from the fridge and puts it in his pocket" (Richard & Judy 2007). However, Adichie is a writer, it appears, who knows her audience well; thus, she balances her character on a point between caricature and the "well-rounded" holding the audience in the anthropologically exotic moment. It is true that the text sets up oppositions between the "mud walls of his mother's hut ... the thatch roof" (Adichie 2006, 4) and Odneigbo's glass and cement home; and Ugwu is certainly overwhelmed by the excess of food – "Ugwu did not believe that anybody ... ate meat *everyday*" (Adichie 2006, 3). He describes the refrigerator as "the white thing, almost as tall as he was" and he stands helplessly by the sink "trying to remember what his aunty had told him about opening it to have water gush out" (Adichie 2006, 6).

In this way, perhaps we are reminded of Olaudah Equiano's first encounter with "civilisation" as described in his 1789 autobiography. Equiano was taken into slavery as a child and, although he acquired an education and eventually bought his freedom, in an early chapter, he recounts his experience as a child, on a plantation in Virginia, when he is required to fan one of the masters while he sleeps:

> I indulged myself a great deal in looking about the room, which to me appeared very fine and curious. The first object that engaged my attention was a watch which hung on the chimney, and was going. I was quite surprised at the noise it made, and was afraid it would tell the gentleman any thing I might do amiss: and when I immediately after observed a picture hanging in the room, which appeared constantly to look at me, I was still more affrighted, having never seen such things as these before (Equiano 2005, 91)

However, Ugwu is not naïve as Equiano: he knows the white object in the kitchen is a fridge and that it is used for storing food; he easily names the sofa, side tables, shelves, books, armchairs and vase of plastic flowers that he sees in the sitting room. It is not that he does not understand but that he finds it hard to reimagine these things when they are not in front of him. Ultimately, Ugwu (of course, in very different circumstances than Equiano) recognizes what this new job represents: he is "choked with expectation ... busy imagining his new life away from the village" (Adichie 2006, 3). It is this less stereotypical sense of Ugwu as a character, and the fact that chapters are told from his point of view, which allows the reading of Ugwu to develop into the deep sympathy for his plight after being conscripted into the army when he gives in to peer pressure and rapes a girl in a bar, expressed by those participating in the Richard & Judy discussion panel. Cox suggests Adiche's handling of this episode is "devastating" and that it is "totally understandable, the pressure that the kid was under and that character ... was the character I identified most with" (Richard & Judy 2007). For them, Ugwu – full of "self-loathing" even as he gives in to that pressure to show he is "a man" (Adichie 2007, 365) – represents how "good, loving people turn to casual violence" in war (Richard & Judy 2007) putting the events at fault not the character. Still, even as it resists reading Ugwu as a metonym for the typical village African boy, the sympathy occasioned – specifically not an empathy – could still be that directed to the other, as discussed in relation to *A Thousand Splendid Suns*. The character of Richard, the white Englishman who integrates himself into Igbo culture, appears to provide more opportunity for empathy.

In an interview with Stephen Moss in *The Guardian*, Adichie was asked about the character of Richard:

> When I ask her why a white character plays a central part in the book, she says it was with an eye on the film rights. Hollywood insists on it; in fact, she now wishes she'd had more. "That's a joke, by the way," she adds hurriedly. Except it's a joke which contains a truth: Hollywood does demand troubled, transformative white characters to make Africa accessible to a predominantly white audience. (Moss 2007)

Richard acts as a mediator for the British readers of the text and is set in opposition to those commonplace expatriate attitudes that might have been found in Nigeria in the early 1960s (when the first part of the book is set):

> he minded the all-expatriate parties where Susan would nudge him to 'join the men' ... He felt awkward with the men. They were mostly English, ex-colonial administrators and business people ... They were reddened from sun and alcohol. They chuckled about how tribal Nigerian politics was, and perhaps, those chaps were not quite so ready to rule themselves after all. (Adichie 2006, 53)

So, from early on, Richard is separated from those attitudes of colonial whites, whose attitudes are generally viewed today as racist and obnoxious. He represents a modern voice in the historical setting; one that respects and values the different culture in which he finds himself. His acceptability is endorsed from the Nigerian point of view through Olanna's perspective – another main character in the novel and twin sister to Richard's lover, Kainene. When Olanna meets Richard for the first time she notes that:

> She had never liked any of Kainene's boyfriends [but] ... Richard ... did not have that familiar superiority of English people who thought that they understood Africans better than Africans understood themselves and, instead had an endearing uncertainty about him – almost a shyness. (Adichie 2006, 36)

Far from being a superior white man, Richard's humility and deference marks him as attractive to the Black Nigerians in the text but also to the modern reader attuned to the nature of travel to Africa as a discovery of difference rather than as colonial exploitations and subjugation, which are assumed to be in the past. In the sections of the book set in the late 1960s, Richard has become a fluent Igbo speaker and integrated with the Igbo society through his involvement with Kainene thus finding that "it was the first time in his life he felt as if he could belong somewhere" (Adichie 2006, 82). Therefore readers can align themselves with him against those British who patronize Nigerians at their parties; the "British academics at the university in Zaria [who] encouraged the massacres" (Adichie 2006, 157) at the beginning of the war; and those in Kenya who Olanna urges Richard to write about – "write about the horrible things the British did ... Didn't they cut off testicles?" (Adichie 2006, 233).

However, Adichie has not merely inserted Richard into her novel for the simple purposes of providing an empathetic figure for her American and British readers. She recognizes that the search for an authentic exotic experience invests Richard with a different authority illustrated by Adichie through Richard's admiration of the Igbo-Ukwu art (metal-worked artifacts possibly from the ninth century), which inspired his move to Nigeria. At parties "when Richard mentioned his interest in Igbo-Ukwu art, [the expatriates] said it didn't have much of a market yet, so he did not bother to explain that he wasn't at all interested in the money, it was the aesthetics that drew him" (Adichie 2006, 53). However, this positions Richard as a purveyor of the exotic precisely in the ways that Huggan suggests, through the "reification of people and places into exchangeable aesthetic objects" (2001, 19). Kainene calls Richard "a modern-day explorer of the Dark Continent" (Adichie 2006, 62) but what he seeks is not rivers or lakes but an exotic and authentic cultural experience. So, stopping at Igbo-Ukwu, he notes with some disappointment that "a few cement houses dotted the village; they marred the picturesque quality of the mud huts that were crowded on either side of the dirt paths" (Adichie 2006, 70). Although this is written from Richard's point of view, it is hard to believe that a perceptive writer like Adichie has not deliberately voiced this very touristic attitude to a primitive African life.

A further discussion of Igbo-Ukwu art between Richard and Okeoma, a Nigerian poet who frequents the political discussions held each evening at Olanna's home in the University compound, reinforces this suspicion. Richard expresses his enthusiasm for to the artwork telling Okeoma that it is "quite incredible that these people [of Igbo-Ukwu] had perfected the complicated art of lost-wax casting during the time of the Viking raids [in Britain]" (Adichie 2006, 111). Okeoma responds: "'You sound surprised ... as if you never imagined *these people* capable of such things.' Richard stared at Okeoma; there was a new and quiet distain in the way Okeoma stared back" (Adichie 2006, 111). Later Richard justifies this to himself:

> It was wrong of Okeoma to assume that he was one of those Englishmen who did not give the African the benefit of equal intelligence. Perhaps he had sounded surprised, now that he thought of it, but it was the same surprise he would express if a similar discovery were made in England or anywhere in the world. (Adichie 2006, 112)

So, while Richard is clearly not in the mode of the colonial type, Africa still signifies as other in a discourse that insists on a western representation of the continent. As Huggan notes this "renders people, objects and places strange even as it domesticates them, and which effectively manufactures otherness even as it claims to surrender to its immanent mystery" (2001, 13). Richard would not be surprised at equivalent discoveries "at home" because they would not be perceived as enigmatic. A reader who has sympathetically identified with Richard would potentially find this uncomfortable to read. It undermines Richard's apparently good intentions, questions his position as part of the Igbo community and his justification based on Okeoma being "wrong" exposes Richard's actual understanding of himself as superior and as someone who does think that he "understood Africans better than Africans understood themselves," an assumption that has grown in direct relation to his knowledge of Igbo culture.

In the discussion on the Richard & Judy television program, while Judy starts by suggesting that: "[Richard]'s such a nice guy," Omaar turns this to a potentially more politicized viewpoint: "Richard was like Britain's involvement – you know carefree and stewardship under colonial rule ... in this kind of insipid character who's well meaning ... utterly, utterly ineffectual" and Cox adds "and the fact is he never writes the book he's going to write" (Richard & Judy 2007). Interspersed through the novel, are extracts from a book called "The World Was Silent When We Died"; the implication is that this is the book Richard is struggling to write through much of the novel but the final sentence of the novel reveals that it is Ugwu who has written the book. The "We" of the book, in the light of the rift between Okeoma and Richard, should have alerted readers that it could not have been Richard's work.

However, the novel does not easily fall into simple binary oppositions between Black and white. In the interview with Moss, Adichie expresses her frustration that too often the western world sees Africa as "one huge refugee camp." She continues: "People forget that Africa is a place in which class exists ... It's as if Africans are not allowed to have class, that somehow authenticity is synonymous with poverty and demands your pity and your sympathy" (Moss 2007). Further, she recognizes that "Americans think African writers will write about the exotic, about wildlife, poverty, maybe Aids. They come to Africa and African books with certain expectations" (Moss 2007). Through Olanna, Adichie expresses a middle-class, Nigerian view when encountering communities outside of the Westernized, elite life enjoyed by rich city-dwellers. When Olanna visits her relatives outside the city, she finds their poverty difficult. Sitting in the shared cooking space at their house with her aunt and cousin, Olanna "carefully avoided looking at the cockroach eggs, smooth black capsules, lodged in all corners of the table" (Adichie 2006, 41). As they cook:

> Olanna wished she could shift her stool closer to the door, to fresh air. But she didn't want Aunty Ifeka, or Arize, or even the neighbour to know that the smoke irritated her eyes and throat or that the sight of the cockroach eggs nauseated her. She wanted to seem used to it, to this life. (Adichie 2006, 42)

Equally, it is Olanna, and Ugwu – aspirant to an intellectually and materially better life – who are increasingly distressed by the deprivations brought on by the war. Even when the family is close to starving to death in a crowded refugee area, Olanna worries that her adopted daughter will "pick up [other children's] bush ... accent or some disease from the liquid-looking boils on [their] arms or fleas from [their] scrawny dog" (Adichie 2006, 327). Olanna – along with those builders of concrete houses in Igbo-Ugwu – desire access to those accoutrements of Western life, the acquisition of which is viewed in terms of progress and improvement not as a corruption of some idyllic past as Richard interprets it through his Western definition of authentic experience.

Juxtaposing these discursive practices suggests Adichie writes with a "postcolonial imperative to demystify 'foreign' cultures and, ultimately, to show the constructed nature of discourses about culture itself" (Huggan 2001, 19). But for the Richard & Judy Book Club readers, Adichie shares with Hosseini the authenticity that leads those readers who posted reviews to understand *Half of a Yellow Sun* as educative. It had allowed one reader to "learn more about the country," another felt it was a "must read to hear recent history from and African perspective" and, a different reviewer, noted that "it taught [her] something about a war [she] knew nothing about" (*Half of a Yellow Sun*: Book Reviews). Information about Adichie from the Richard & Judy Book Club website and the author profile in the novel established that she was born and bought up in Nigeria and the novel certainly contains enough poverty and war to satisfy the expectations of the postcolonially uninitiated reader identified by Huggan, or those expectations of Adichie's "Americans."

Adichie has expressed her hope that the novel contributes to a Nigerian understanding of the Biafran war (Moss 2007) yet this novel has to be understood as an example of "postcolonial writing bound up in a system of cultural translation operating under the sign of the *exotic* ... marketed for predominantly metropolitan readers" (Huggan 2001, viii). Amanda Ross, the executive producer of the Richard & Judy show, creator of the Richard & Judy Book Club and the person who selected the Club reads, rationalized those choices in this way: "Our choices each year are based on instinct, but we try to include something we know our viewers will enjoy reading and discussing" (Jury 2007). It is likely that Ross' instinct is, in fact, a response to the palatable translations of the Third World, discussed by Huggan who asks, in relation to the notion of authenticity: "Is this representativeness a function of their inscription in the margins, of the mainstream demand for an 'authentic', but readily translatable, marginal voice?" (2001, 26). In the case of these two novels, an affirmative response is justified both in terms of the authors' authenticity but also the authenticity of the novels' content, which fulfils readers' preconceived ideas regarding the two countries.

A less definitive response can be offered to another question: "Could it be that ... the Third World is marketable only insofar as it can be translated?" (Huggan 2001, 25). The analysis of these novels suggests that some popular postcolonial novels can evade an unambiguous translation and it can be suggested further that it is this evasion – rather than settings or an authors' nationality – which constitutes postcolonial writing. As Huggan notes:

> Postcolonial writers/thinkers ... are both aware of and resistant to their interpellations as marginal spokespersons ... What is more, they make their *readers* aware of the constructedness of such cultural categories; their texts are metacommentaries on the politics of translation, on the power relations that inform cross-cultural perception and representation. (Huggan 2001, 19)

While *A Thousand Splendid Sun* fails to raise such awareness, and while to claim that *Half of a Yellow Sun* is a metacommentary would be an exaggeration, this latter text does draw attention to the signifying practices of neo-colonialism, which still control representations of Africa. Richard characterizes all those experts on African whom Adichie complains about in relation to news coverage of African events: "They go to the Congo, for example, line the Congolese people up in the background, and then have a Belgian, who they say is a Congo expert, tell us about the Congo" (Moss 2007). Through even a small resistance to western cultural translations, *Half of a Yellow Sun* raises the specter of the red, sweating face of colonial power lurking behind the benign, sympathetic white presence.

Reference List

Adichie, Chimamanda Ngozi. 2006. *Half of a Yellow Sun*. London: Harper Perennial.

Bhabha, Homi K. 1995. Cultural Diversity and Cultural Differences. In *The Postcolonial Studies Reader*. Eds Bill Ashcroft, Gareth Griffiths, and Helen Tiffin, 206–9. London and New York: Routledge.

Dalrymple, William. 2003. *White Mughals: Love and Betrayal in Eighteenth-century India*. London: Harper Perennial.

Equiano, Olaudah. 2005 [1789]. *The Interesting Narrative of the Life of Olaudah Equiano, or Gustavus Vassa, the African*. http://www.gutenberg.org/files/15399/15399-8.txt (accessed 16 February 2009).

Half of a Yellow Sun: Book Reviews. 2009. http://www.richardandjudybookclub.co.uk/webapp/wcs/stores/servlet/ProductDisplay?catalogId=15201&storeId=10101&productId=51042&langId=100&catEntrySection=review&reviewTypeRef=review.type_user&reviewStatusRef=review.status_live (accessed 25 November 2009).

Hall, Stuart. 1990. Cultural Identity and Diaspora. In *Identity: Community, Culture, Difference*. Ed. Jonathan Rutherford, 222–37. London: Lawrence & Wishart.

Horwell, Veronica. 2003. At home with the Khans. *The Guardian*, 13 September. http://www.guardian.co.uk/books/2003/sep/13/featuresreviews.guardianreview (accessed 2 February 2009).

Hosseini, Khaled. 2007. *A Thousand Splendid Suns*. London: Bloomsbury.

Hosseini, Khaled. 2008. www.khaledhosseini.com (accessed 12 January 2009).

Huggan, Graham. 2001. *The Postcolonial Exotic: Marketing the Margins*. London and New York: Routledge.

Judah, Tim. 2003a. Family at war – with itself. Book review of *The Bookseller of Kabul*. *The Observer*, 31 August. http://www.guardian.co.uk/books/2003/aug/31/travel.features (accessed 2 February 2009).

Judah, Tim. 2003b. The Kabul bookseller, the famous reporter, and a "defamation" of a nation. *The Guardian*, 21 September. http://www.guardian.co.uk/world/2003/sep/21/books.afghanistan (accessed 26 January 2009).

Jury, Louise. 2007. Richard and Judy select Britain's next best-sellers. *The Independent*, 5 January. http://www.independent.co.uk/arts-entertainment/books/news/richard-and-judy-select-britains-next-bestsellers-430856.html (accessed 2 December 2009).

Loomba, Ania. 1998. *Colonialism/Postcolonialism*. London and New York: Routledge.

Moorehead, Caroline. 2003. Review: *The Storyteller's Daughter* by Saira Shah; *The Bookseller of Kabul* by Asne Seierstad, trans. Ingrid Christopherson. *The Independent on Saturday*, 16 August. http://www.independent.co.uk/arts-entertainment/books/reviews/the-storytellers-daughter-by-saira-shahbrthe-bookseller-of-kabul-by-asne-seierstad-trans-ingrid-christopherson-535995.html (accessed 2 February 2009).

Moss, Stephen. 2007. Madonna's not our saviour. *The Guardian*, 8 June. http://www.guardian.co.uk/books/2007/jun/08/orangeprizeforfiction2007.orangeprizeforfiction (accessed 2 December 2009).

Rais, Mohammed Shah. 2003. A Matter of Honor and Truth. In *The Survival Guide to Kabul* September 2. http://www.kabulguide.net/kbl-bookseller.htm (accessed 26 January 2009).

Richard & Judy. 2007. Channel 4. 14 March.

Sedo, DeNel Rehberg. 2008. Richard & Judy's Book Club and Canada Reads: Readers, books and cultural programming in a digital era. *Information, Communication & Society* 11(2): 188–206.

Seierstad, Asne. 2003. *The Bookseller of Kabul*. Trans. Ingrid Christopherson. London: Virago.

Spivak, Gayatri Chakravorty. 1988. Can the Subaltern Speak. In *Marxism and the Interpretation of Culture*, eds Cary Nelson and Lawrence Grossberg, 271–313. London: Macmillan.

Stuart, Andrea. 2007. Review: *The Pirate's Daughter*, by Margaret Cezair-Thompson. *The Independent*, 23 November. http://www.independent.co.uk/arts-entertainment/books/reviews/the-pirates-daughter-by-margaret-cezairthompson-760016.html (accessed 29 January 2009).

A Thousand Splendid Suns: Book Reviews. 2009. http://www.richardandjudybookclub.co.uk/webapp/wcs/stores/servlet/ProductDisplay?catalogId=15201&storeId=10101&productId=108257&langId=100&catEntrySection=review&reviewTypeRef=review.type_user&reviewStatusRef=review.status_live (accessed 25 November 2009).

Wall, Melissa. 2007. An Analysis of News Magazine Coverage of the Rwanda Crisis in the United States. In *The Media and the Rwanda Genocide*, ed. Allen Thompson, 261–71. London: Pluto Press.

Walter, Natasha. 2007. Behind the Veil. *The Guardian* 19 May. http://www.guardian.co.uk/books/2007/may/19/featuresreviews.guardianreview21 (accessed 24 November 2009).

Chapter 9
The Delicious Side of the Story: Culinary Writing, Cultural Contexts and the Club

Lorna Piatti-Farnell

Food represents an anchorage in the past, its strength deriving in part from the familial relationship in which the serving and preparing of the foods are located … Food serves as one of the links between historical time, individual time and household time. (Morgan 1996, 116)

Food books are flourishing. A variety of books centered on food consumption and preparation – ranging from romantic novels to inspiring volumes containing mouth-watering recipes – populate the shelves in bookstores. Recent "food works" could not fail to capture the attention of the Richard & Judy Book Club, soliciting the readers' interests in food, eating and recipes. The list is rich in titles, including Anthony Capella's *The Food of Love* (2004), Nigel Slater's *Toast: The Story of a Boy's Hunger* (2004), Toni Jordan's *Addition* (2008) and A.M. Homes's *This Book Will Save Your Life* (2006). One cannot help but wonder how the food book engages its readership. Questions concerning the readers' social interest – and the importance of culinary authorship – are particularly relevant to the analysis of food books, which often rely on cultural juxtapositions between the domestic and the exotic, the new and the old, the familiar and the experimental. The food books promoted by the Book Club, although all focusing on eating and cooking, offer different perspectives on culinary experience. *Addition*, for instance, presents an approach to food in terms of obsession and anxiety; eating habits are expressed through circles of phobias and mania in which arachibutyrophobia – "the fear of peanut butter sticking to your mouth" (Jordan 2008, 21) – deserves particular notice. *The Food of Love*, on the other hand, offers a romanticized vision of eating, which joins food consumption with the erotic dimensions of love and desire, as the lavishly presented "carciofini" (Capella 2004, 105), "chestnut mousse" (168) and "spaghetti carbonara" (226) are said to be a special brand of Italian "aphrodisiac" (226). Food acts as a cultural symbol, but in its representations it moulds into an expression of maternal love, sexual seduction, social ambivalence and health philosophy. It would seem that in its many incarnations the food book caters for a variety of literary appetites, attracting readers from different lifestyles and backgrounds.

In response to this growing national interest in culinary writing and experience, this chapter addresses the "food book" as a literary genre and how its variations engage the national readership of the Richard & Judy Book Club. I will particularly give attention to the way in which the food book interacts with the cultural context. Taking Slater's memoir *Toast* as a seminal example, my discussion focuses on how the food book tantalizes the readers through evoking food memories of family and childhood. Looking at the interdependency of sensorial phenomena and social experience, I will analyze how Slater maps the ways in which the experience of the senses is framed by cultural memory. I will explore how the culinary memoir functions not only as a representation of someone's culinary past, but also as a public historical archive. This chapter will also consider the development of "food books" as a popular genre and the importance of the "culinary text" as part of a system of consumerist consumption. Paying attention to key modes of national memory and nostalgia, I will go on to discuss the way in which the idea of "authentic culinary memory" might be exploited and commodified. I will finally unveil how the Richard & Judy Book Club acts as instrumental in the establishment of a national readership that values a sense of British tradition – as embellished or fabricated as it might be – as the most attractive element of culinary storytelling.

Toast narrates the childhood and teenage events in the life of its author; a fictionalized version of Nigel himself deals with the joys and heartbreaks of everyday experience, from being forced to drink milk at school and visiting the exciting local butcher's shop, to his mother's death and father's second marriage to a less than maternal woman. As the events in the life of young Nigel unfold, food functions as the principal connecting thread in the narrative. *Toast* is subdivided into chapters, each focusing on a particular episode – or particular moment in time – and named after a specific foodstuff. While the daily vicissitudes in the life of a young boy unfold, the readers learn as much about as Slater's career as a young, promising chef as they do of the socio-cultural value carried by foods such as "Christmas Cake" (Slater 2004, 1), "Crumpets" (85), "Boiled Ham" (147) and "Prawn Cocktail" (198). As a succession of dishes, treats and recipes build the framework for childhood memories, Slater dramatizes eating, adding dimensions of nostalgia and sentimentality to both everyday dishes and occasional treats. Culinary experiences in the memoir are proposed as symptomatic of a particular cultural situation, engaging with matters of national identity, displacement and interpersonal relationships (particularly through the concept of recipe, food products and brand). In addressing such concerns, my analysis offers a critical framework that highlights the material conditions – historical, political and socio-cultural – that encouraged the rise and popularity of the food book within an expanding national readership.

In terms of consumer accessibility, it is important to remember the format in which the Club's evaluation of *Toast* was originally presented to the viewers and, of course, potential readers; carefully targeted celebrities chat to Richard and Judy about their impressions of the literature in question. In the case of *Toast*, the celebrity reviewer who discussed the memoir's literary qualities was no other than Nigella Lawson, "domestic goddess" and culinary guru whose final word on anything to do with food is authenticated by her success as a published author of many cookbooks and gastronomic manuals. Needless to say, Nigella's review of *Toast* was an extremely positive one: as she praised the author's ability to recollect food memories so accurately and distinctly, she also praised the book's stylistic ability to contextualize the foods in question and allow the readers relate to Slater's experience. Nigella Lawson's involvement with the Richard & Judy Book Club undoubtedly had a definitive impact in the way *Toast* was perceived by the readers. The book's popularity was confirmed by the sales figures, which Oliver Bennett defines as "astounding" (Bennett 2004, 2). That popularity, one must remember, was also mirrored in the many awards that Slater received for his memoir, including the publically voted WH Smith People's Choice Awards in 2004. Nigella's appraisal of the book was of great impact on the audience for a number of reasons. Firstly, her constructive perspective of *Toast* came from a fellow "food writer," therefore bestowing on the memoir an aura of reliable respectability in terms of subject matter. Secondly, and perhaps most importantly, the impact of a celebrity culinary reviewer allowed *Toast* to be seen as not only an accessible book, but as a "fashionable read," confirming food as part of the world of show-business. In this light, Nigella was a truly apt choice for promoting the culinary and literary qualities of *Toast*. Her calm, and likeable manner – joined with her own personal success in the culinary publishing department – allowed her perspective on *Toast* to emerge as believable and dependable. Clearly, no unwelcome question was raised (at least within the Club itself) regarding her suitability as a reviewer. Nigella's "expert" review of Slater's book on the Richard & Judy Book Club was, as Bennett puts it, an "intelligent" move, since she did not "talk down to people" and that was "precisely the reason" for the review's success (Bennett 2004, 3). The culinary appraisal offered by Nigella did not make the viewer uncomfortable with intellectual critiques and her already iconic status removed any claim that by judging the memoir she was "trying to score points" (Bennett 2004, 4). The result was a celebrity-approved, mouth-watering and nostalgia-filled evaluation of Slater's *Toast*. The Book Club took to it enthusiastically and so did the future readers.

A Page of Culinary History

With its frequently domestic settings, its familiar routines and its convivial atmosphere, eating is liable to join other everyday activities mapped in texts that are often overlooked and taken for granted within contemporary Western society. Nonetheless, the consumption of food in literature appears to be charged with implications that elevate it beyond the trivial and the mundane. Attitudes to food, eating and cooking can be located here within larger patterns of individual and cultural behavior. As Terry Eagleton argues in "Edible Ecriture," food "makes up our bodies, just as words make up our mind," and "eating and speaking … continuously cross over in metaphorical exchange" (Eagleton 1998, 207).

One of the principal characteristics of *Toast* – and the most advertised "selling point" on the Richard & Judy Book Club – is its status as a "culinary memoir." In terms of written format, the autobiographical cookbook is *a genre* now conspicuously represented on the shelves of most bookstores. Think, for instance, of James Martin's *Great British Dinners* (2003), containing a number of traditional British recipes accompanied by short anecdotes from the author's life; or *"Feast: Food that Celebrates Life"* (2006), in which Nigella Lawson comments on the recipes with autobiographical tales and expresses her passion for food and cooking. On the American front, in particular, the market has seen an abundance of culinary autobiographies, biographical cookbooks and culinary memoirs. From the gastronomic journeys of M.K. Fisher to the nostalgic family meals in Diana Abu-Jaber's *The Language of Baklava* (2005), food and autobiography have been become interlaced in the international reading spectrum. European writers, for their part, have offered readers a number of varied interpretations of the biographically based food book, ranging from the nostalgic food recollections, which include Colette Rossant's culinary memoir *Return to Paris* (2003), to the technically orientated food discussions in Jacques Pepin's culinary autobiography *The Apprentice* (2003).

Responding to the commercial popularity with which food books have been received in recent years, *Toast* aptly contributes to the tradition that has made the culinary memoir a well-established and fashionable literary genre. Discussing the personal nature of cookbooks, Janet Theophano points out that culinary memoirs "are one of a variety of written forms, such as diaries and journals, that [people] have adapted to recount and enrich their lives ... blending raw ingredients into a new configuration" (Theophano 2002, 122). Food, it would seem, can often function perfectly as an idiom of the past. Tracie Marie Kelly describes "culinary autobiographies" as "a complex pastiche of recipes, personal anecdotes, family history, public history, photographs, even family trees" (Kelly 2001, 252). Kelly goes on to divide this type of autobiography into three principal sub-genres: the culinary memoir, the autobiographical cookbook and the autoethnographic cookbook. In the culinary memoir, of which Slater's *Toast* is a good example, one can find a life story interlaced with memories of food and eating. This category presents what Kelly calls "autobiographical gestures" and "may or may not provide recipes" (Kelly 2001, 255). In the autobiographical cookbook, on the other hand, "recipes play an integral part in the revelation of the personal history" (Kelly 2001, 258). This is the style in which Alice B. Toklas wrote her famous *Cook Book* (1954). Here, Toklas offers a detailed chronicle of the years she spent travelling with Gertrude Stein; the food recipes are fully intertwined with the memories, so that the two things, as Kelly argues, "could not be separated" (Kelly 2001, 58). Toklas moves directly from description of an event to the food recipe with which the moment is associated:

> Señora B. made a simple Spanish sweet of which *Panoche* is the coarse Mexican version. She made it like this and unpretentiously called it DULCE. In a huge copper pan put quantities of granulated sugar, moisten with cream, turn constantly with a copper spoon until it is done. Then pour into glasses (Toklas 1984, 132–3).

The recipes become part of the story-telling, so that Toklas's reaction to the dish and the way she describes it are as important as the biographical events themselves. It is this interaction between event and recipe that characterizes the autobiographical cookbook; as Jeanne Schinto points out, "the author's own idiosyncratic way of writing about food may well be the book's unique ingredient" (Schinto 1990, 491).

Finally, Kelly's third category, the autoethnographic cookbook, "present[s] information intended to educate an outside audience about personal or group activities" (Kelly 2001, 255). This particular culinary publication, which includes Jean and Carole Darden's *Spoon Bread and Strawberry Wine* (1994) and Carrie Young's *Prairie Cooks* (1997), includes details on other everyday activities – like sleeping and working – or particular events – such as birthdays and funerals – which validate the presence of eating scenes. The descriptions function as a catalyst for documenting the history of a particular group. In exposing regional culinary preferences, the autoethnographic cookbook involves, in the words of Mary Louise Pratt, "indigenous idioms to create self-representation" (Pratt 1993, 445). Despite their ostensible differences, each category of cookbook displays an integral interdependence between memories and food/recipe writing. In a culinary autobiography, Kelly concludes, "the divisions between functions of cooking, history and storytelling blur" and "the reader may wonder ... whether the recipes are the primary texts and the other devices incidental, or the reverse" (Kelly 2001, 253). The answer to this conundrum can be difficult to pin down.

However, in its peculiar report of British life in the Sixties, Slater's *Toast* is somewhat different. The writer's idea of "autobiography" – or even memoir – is perhaps not quite what a lot of readers might customarily expect. Slater offers us no dates, virtually no place indication and barely any information on the many people that drift in and out of the young boy's life. *Toast* does not have the descriptive sophistication of Fisher's memoirs; nor does it provide the detailed accounts of culinary history indulged in by writers such as Calvin Trillin and Ruth Reichl. In fact, as culinary autobiographies and memoirs go, Slater's lack of chronological clarity makes it (perhaps) a very poor attempt at historical recollection. And yet, the book is compelling to read, delicious, sweet and sour with every turn of the page. Food, it would seem, is the real protagonist in the memoir, a faithful coordinate that allows Slater to recall and reconnect with events, people and circumstances. The everyday outside the house – which includes meeting other people and formulating opinions of them – is joined with the "everyday" in the household, which for young Nigel revolves around eating and cooking. The portrayal of Slater's everyday life is conveyed by every recipe, every event, every piece of culinary information included in his recollections. This element confirms how the culinary memoir, as Floyd and Forster put it, interacts with personal "spheres of daily experience" (Floyd and Forster 2003, 1). In an openly Proustian turn of events, the look, smell and taste of food provide a strong travelling ticket into a clear exploration of the past, as the experiences of eating and drinking turn everyday events into history. Food truly is the connective thread of Slater's recollections.

In drawing attention to how the experience of food is connected to individual and cultural memories, the Richard & Judy Book Club highlighted how culinary recollections are dependent upon not only sensorial stimuli – such as taste and smell – but also familiar dishes and recipes. The club's praise of food memories in *Toast* – and how beautifully and sharply Slater records them – becomes not only the expression of familiar and cultural affiliation, but also the embodiment of personal and public history.

Reading Food, Memory and the Senses

Any episode of consumption is characterized by specific socio-cultural and economic conditions that construct it as a distinct temporal event. Blended with their cultural significance, commensal artifacts – or, put more simply, food and drink – have the ability to evoke a particular legacy of mnemonic experience. With their material connotations, consumables function, in Nadia Seremetakis's words, as "passageways" into the "entanglements of everyday ... experience" (Seremetakis 1996, 14).

The representation of memory in *Toast* seems to validate Paul Fieldhouse's claim that food maintains "continuity" by a set of "culture-specific" protocols, which include "characteristic flavourings and preparation methods" (Fieldhouse 1995, 76). The memory of food is also interconnected with sensorial stimuli. Certain foods and drinks automatically conjure up images and sounds, but arguably the most important sense in conjunction with taste is smell. Writing on the senses, Constance Classen observes that olfactory ability "is not simply a biological and physiological phenomenon ... smell is cultural, hence a social and historical phenomenon" (Classen, Howes and Synnott 1994, 3). The experience of the senses in *Toast* is not detached from sociality, so that matters of taste (and smell and touch) become matters of culture as well. The sensorial experience of food is uncovered as an amalgamation of personal and cultural memory. Any analysis of eating as a social experience must include, as social anthropologist David Sutton reminds us, a "consideration of cross-cultural, cognitive aspects of sensory memory, but without neglecting how such cognitive potentials are culturally elaborated" (Sutton 2005, 305). One could say that at the intersection of eating with cognitive processes of mnemonic recognition, food acts as a symbolic representation of location, people and structures of feeling.

Following the perception of meal as "ritual," the idea of "favorite food" is particularly significant, if one considers the psychological, behavioral and cultural notions with which it is associated. The mere thought of a "favorite" food – especially if complemented by seeing and smelling – can trigger hunger. That hunger, one might venture to say, is related to physiological stimuli – on most occasions – and mnemonic associations with a whole culinary culture. The same culture, in turn, might bring with it memories of family, friends and location, which are of value to the individual. Arjun Appadurai argues that "food may generally possess a special semiotic because of certain universal properties ... but this special force must always remain tacit until it is animated by particular cultural concepts and mobilised by particular social contexts" (Appadurai 1981, 509). Significantly, therefore, the sight, smell and thought of a known or favorite food will trigger different memories, thoughts and feelings that change according to each individual in question. The impact of sensorial experience in *Toast* – and its clear connection to culinary memories – did not leave the collaborators of the Club uninterested. In both Nigella Lawson's review and Richard & Judy's comments about the food and drink recollections in *Toast*, attention is given to how Slater merges the experience of the senses with cultural contexts, so that a certain smell – or a certain taste – becomes associated with a particular moment in the young Nigel's life. In general, the assertion that the experience of food is connected to remembrance is long-standing. Deborah Lupton argues that "the effects of memory are inscribed upon the body" in the form of "appetite for certain foods" (Lupton 1996, 32). The sensorial experience of food – particularly taste and smell – can trigger memories of previous culinary knowledge, so that memory can shape food preferences in the future. In pursuing the emotional and cultural connections between food and experience, Colette Rossant even goes so far as saying that "food is memory" (Rossant 2003, 100).

It is essential to point out that the part played by the senses in the recognition of a particular taste is, initially, anatomically based. The tasting process begins with simple sniffing, or "orthonasal olfaction," which is complemented by "retronasal olfaction" as odorants released by food and drink reach the nasal mucosa through the mouth (Bartoshuk and Duffy 2005, 27). A blend of stimuli originating from the tongue – also referred to as "true taste" – is therefore joined with a series of retronasal stimuli in order to create a "flavor" (a term that is often overlooked in favor of its equivalent, "taste"). Linda Bartoshuk and Valerie Duffy argue that "flavours are made up of taste sensations, which genuinely originate in the mouth, and olfactory sensations, which do not" (Bartoshuk and Duffy 2005, 27). In separating the origin of taste and smell Bartoshuk and Duffy's assertion seems to contradict the concept of retronasal stimuli. Nevertheless, the idea that taste and smell become conjoined in constructing the general idea of "flavor" remains important. The involvement of olfactory stimuli in the tasting process has been subjected to scrutiny for centuries. For example, in his treatise on food, taste and eating, *The Physiology of Taste* (1825), Jean-Anthelme Brillat-Savarin asserts that taste and smell "form but one sense, of which the mouth is the laboratory and the nose the chimney ... one sense serves to taste tactile substances and the other to apprehend their vapours" (Brillat-Savarin 2005, 19). According to Brillat-Savarin, when eating or drinking, a "flavour" or "taste" arouses three different orders of sensation: *direct*, *complete* and *reflective* (Brillat-Savarin 2005, 20). A "direct" sensation is, in Brillat-Savarin's words, the "first perception," carried by the immediate action of gustatory papillae on the tongue and preliminary olfactory stimuli from the nose (Brillat-Savarin 2005, 20). A "complete" sensation, on the other hand, is composed of these first, direct impressions, now joined with "the sensation aroused when the food abandons the first position, passes into the back of the mouth, and impresses the entire organ with both its taste and its aroma"

(Brillat-Savarin 2005, 20). Finally, the process of recognition is completed by a "reflective" sensation, which Brillat-Savarin understands as the judgment formed by the mouth in relation to the oral impressions originally generated (Brillat-Savarin 2005, 20).

There is evidence in Slater's text of this careful re-elaboration of sensual stimuli. It becomes quite clear (even from Nigella Lawson's evaluation) that one of *Toast*'s most laudable strengths is its ability to describe sensorial stimuli and render the experience of food in an authentic manner: "every home should smell of baking Christmas cake" (3); "Mother would make flapjacks ... it was their chewy, salty sweetness I loved" (22); "Warm sweet milk was what a mother should smell of" (30). As Slater describes the ins and outs of culinary experience – and how that is closely connected, conceptually and metaphorically, with the idea of home – *Toast* is flooded by memories triggered by the smell, taste and texture of food. According to Dan Sperber, the senses rely on the construction of "mental images" (1975, 117). The production of these images cannot be seen as a conscious process, but the connection between smell, taste and visual representation remains significant. There is a definite involuntary quality to the images brought to mind by taste and smell, which must be viewed differently from the mental images inspired by viewing, for instance, a photograph. Marcel Proust defined the former as *mémoire involontaire*: a richer, more "authentic" mnemonic experience that cannot be controlled. Proust placed this type of recollection in opposition to the *mémoire volontaire*, which he saw as a conscious, willed, artificial archive (and which included examples from photography and holiday souvenirs). Associations between consumption, memory and perception are of course articulated and explored by Proust in the famous instance of culinary time-travel in *Remembrance of Things Past*. After tasting a madeleine soaked in tea, offered to him by his aunt, Proust's narrator is instantly swept back to the happier times of his childhood:

> I raised to my lips a spoonful of the tea in which I soaked a morsel of the cake. An exquisite pleasure had invaded my sense ... and at once the vicissitudes of life had become indifferent to me ... what is palpitating in the depths of my being must be the image, the visual memory which, being linked to that taste, has tried to follow it into my conscious mind (Proust 1982, 49).

Proust perceives the memories of his childhood – inspired by the food – as untainted by the mind and thus "genuine." Walter Benjamin develops the Proustian idea of "involuntary memory" by saying that the memories inspired by taste and smell are from "the realm of the unwilled, unmediated ... recollection," occupying a space that is not controlled by the intellect (Benjamin 1999, 158). Echoing the idea of memory elaborated by Proust and Benjamin, it would seem that Slater intends to employ the involuntary nature of taste and smell memories in *Toast* to construct an idea of sensorial experience that is authentic and evokes feelings that remain largely unaltered across time. It is this distinctive emotional take on culinary memory that allows *Toast* to be rendered by the Club as an unmissable example of how food books can reach the readers on a personal, almost visceral level.

A Taste for Nostalgia

Memory in *Toast* functions as an essential part of cultural affiliation and in that framework food becomes a medium through which attachment to a particular geographical area becomes possible. Theodule Ribot reminds us that the "identity of the self rests entirely on memory" (Ribot cited in Ritivoi 2002, 83). Slater paints a heart-warming picture of childhood memories that are based on "properly British" dishes such as "Bread-and-Butter Pudding" (6), "Sherry Trifle" (9), "Jam Tarts" (14), "Pancakes" (21), "Arctic Roll" (20) and even the seemingly unexciting "Mashed Potato" (31). Slater's recollections of home food are accompanied by evocative renditions of corporate food products, such as "Butterscotch Flavour Angel Delight" (30), "Space Dust" (34), "Fry's Chocolate Creams" (26) and "Milky Bars" (27). Nigel's young years are filtered through a romanticized culinary imagination, as the foods are said to have "contained mysteries" (21) and essentially be "magic" (30). Nostalgically describing the food products of his childhood embellishes the dimension of Nigel's mnemonic experience. As recipes, brands and home-cooked dishes paint an entertainingly idealized vision of Sixties Britain, Slater humorously declares that some of these peculiar foods were "considered to be something of status symbol" in his native Wolverhampton (21). Romanticized culinary experiences in *Toast* are proposed as symptomatic of a particular cultural situation, as the food products and brands subtly engage with matters of national identity, displacement and interpersonal relationships. The reader can arguably feel emotionally attached to Slater's memories – as the food, recipes and procedures create a communicative bond between the writer, the reader and the social context – while a system of shared culinary experience establishes a common ground of cultural understanding. Culinary nostalgia, one might argue, functions on several levels. Here we need to remember the etymological origins of the word "nostalgia" itself. In Greek, the verb "*nostalgho*" is a composite of *nostó* and *algho*, the first meaning "to return" and the latter "to feel pain" (Seremetakis 1996, 7). In this manner, the Greek word *nostalghia* comes to signify a longing with pain to return, to journey back. As a result, one can view the nostalgic culinary memories in *Toast* as part of an imagined group psychology, which encourage the individual's sense of self. The food recollections here are fuelled by an underlying desire to return to the world of childhood and its associations with parental comfort.

Slater, however, does more than provide the reader with a romanticized journey into the past. The recollection of culinary memories brings with it a desire to recreate the culinary atmospheres and dishes that the memories represent. As the events in *Toast* revolve around eating and cooking, one can identify a nostalgic desire to both restore a whole culinary system and reflect upon the elements that created it. In order to grasp this idea, it can be helpful to recall Svetlana Boym's alternative interpretation of the concept of nostalgia. According to Boym, through an etymological exercise we can read the word "nostalgia" by concentrating on either of its components, *nostos* and *alghia*. Nostalgia is a two-stage process involving both "restorative" and "reflective" states (Boym 2001, 41). In the case of *Toast*, Slater's culinary recollections are inspired by a desire to return to the times of his childhood in Wolverhampton. According to Boym, restorative nostalgia places emphasis on *nostos* (to return) and, in so doing, conveys a wish to "rebuild the lost home and patch up the memory gaps" (Boym 2001, 41). Simultaneously, however, the author's realization that "times have changed" – and their effect on culinary habits – represents an attempt to reflect upon the past and instigate an alternative, perhaps educational, way to understand culinary memories: "Few things could embarrass a would-be chef quite as much as having to hold out a whole grapefruit speared with cubes of Cheddar and tinned pineapple on cocktail sticks to men in cardigans" (43). The instructive nature of Slater's home food stories also allows us to see their re-telling as both a "restorative" and a "reflective" act. Slater's reflective memories of culinary exploits become the trigger for the restorative process – so that, in a rather circular manner, embellished memories generate more embellished memories.

Through different representations of culinary recollection, however, it becomes apparent that the concept of "food memory" is not straightforward. Although inevitably connected to the physiological aspect of taste, food memories seem to involve a variety of historicized experiences that touch on elements such as nostalgia and cultural knowledge. Consumption, preparation and memory become entangled into offering a precise picture of a definite cultural moment; this almost indicates that the intended readers can be instructed into proper ways of cooking. Perhaps, then, *Toast* itself acts as a highly publicized advert for Slater's other culinary books, the culinary manuals that pledge to provide the reader – and the amateur cook – with a collection of handy recipes. Those recipes promise to recreate culinary pasts and, simultaneously, create new culinary memories for the future. It is possible to argue, then, that in encouraging the reading of *Toast* on the national scale, the Richard & Judy Book Club seems to contribute to the formation and establishment of a new brand of "home literature," a new culinary genre that, in exposing the author's own nostalgic love for food and cooking, tantalizes and exploits the reader's desire for domestic comfort.

Family, Community and Tradition

The practice of cooking – with its rules, methods and structures – relies on the application of personal and cultural memories and is perhaps as important as food itself. In the recipe, particularly, one can find a sense of culinary preference that simultaneously shapes and is shaped by a sense of belonging and identity. Recipes and cook books are historical documents that can function as testaments to individual, familial and cultural development. Janet Theophano argues that "in displaying their cuisine," the compilers of cookbooks and culinary memoirs "portray and define an image of themselves, their cultural groups, and their own rendering of their groups' history and identity" (Theophano 2002, 83). Culinary books can be read as chronicles of everyday life as well as an archive of cultural memory, uses, customs and beliefs. Perhaps it is the ability of food and cooking narratives to render socio-cultural belonging that has made *Toast* a very praised addition to the Richard & Judy Book Club. Slater's accounts of collective eating and habitual food preferences appear to validate David Bell and Gill Valentine's claim regarding the central "role that food plays [in people's idea] of 'home'" (Bell and Valentine 1997, 65).

As a routine activity – which often revolves around issues of timing, measuring and location – cooking contributes to the identification of social roles in any given setting. In the majority of family economies – at least in Western cultures – feeding is still generally understood as "woman's work." It is through cooking and feeding the family that women, Marjorie DeVault argues, actually "do gender" (DeVault 1991, 118). Cooking and nurturing remain associated with the woman in her capacities as wife and mother, so that food itself becomes an important component in the distinction of gender roles and activities. A mother's cooking is often associated with notion of "goodness," so that the food itself can be interpreted as the epitome and embodiment of a woman's love for her family. Slater describes baking a cake for the family as "the ultimate symbol of a mother's love for her husband and kids" (5). Cooking and feeding contribute to the formation of a gendered idea of family performance, a process of identifying, in DeVault's words, "adequate women ... through concerted activities" (DeVault 1991, 118). It goes without saying, of course, that layers of prejudice and social expectation surround the gendered interpretation of cooking, so that women who decide not to adhere to the proper model are often regarded as "bad" wives and mothers. In *Toast*, young Nigel openly regrets his mother's attitude to cooking as something that "simply has to be done" (5), almost equating the woman's dislike for food preparation with a lack of motherly love and affection.

As food in Slater's memoir is linked to ideas of maternal love and household adequacy, food and consumption also emerge as pivotal to the idea of community. Given that culinary practices impose behavioral rules, the control of food intake often appears in *Toast* as a way to regulate collective life. The concept of community, however, is a multifaceted one. Attitudes towards food and the consumption of specific dishes become emblematic for national identity, cultural affiliation and community prejudice. Taste and the desire for any individual commodity – in particular food here – are important elements in the process of cultural formation and reproduction. In the words of Alan Warde: cultural groups "can be identified by their consumption patterns ... and consumer behaviour can be explained in terms of the role of display and social judgement in the formation" of social identities (Warde 1997, 9). Consuming – or not consuming – the same foods creates a bond between members of this colonial community, validating Fieldhouse's assertion that "individuals who observe ... food rules make a public demonstration of belonging to a group" and "every day provide themselves with a private affirmation" of that belonging (Fieldhouse 1995, 122).

In contemporary Western society there appears to be a constant need to resurrect the idea of traditional food. Warde claims in this context that tradition is being "invented anew" (Warde 1997, 64). It could be suggested that, in an age dominated by technological advances, the idea of traditional food offers a compensatory surrogate. This would seem to validate Warde's claim that "in the face of the cult of the new, some people seek out ... shared sets of customs that can be reproduced" (Warde 1997, 61). The same interpretation of a need for tradition is directly connected to the cognitive experience of eating which, as noted above, is connected to a social validation of sensorial experience. A sense of reliability surrounds the idea of culinary tradition, promoting social ideals of uniformity and endurance. Tradition, when it comes to food preparation, is often understood as synonymous with "goodness," relying, as Alan Warde points out, on the use of "established conventions, proven procedures and well-tied practices" (Warde 1997, 61).

There are a number of examples in *Toast* that valorize the importance of authentic preparation methods and traditional foods. Slater decants the perfection of traditionally prepared mashed potato: "There was no moment so perfect as when you squished her [mother's] mashed potato into warm parsley sauce or hot gravy with your fork" (31); properly prepared treacle tarts – prepared in the unforgettable "aluminium tray" – are described as having "the most sublime texture" (85) young Nigel ever experienced. The clearest example, however, of how Slater is valorizing the importance of traditional food is the much-loved Christmas cake. The reader is assured that whenever the traditionally assembled Christmas cake appears on the table, young Nigel feels as if "all" is "well" (4); the old-fashioned Christmas cake – prepared according to an old recipe "written in green biro on a piece of blue Basildon Bond" (2) – is praised as making its consumers feel "safe," "secure" and "unshakable" (4). As Nigella Lawson – together with Richard and Judy themselves – continued to praise Slater's rendition of authentic memories and traditional foods, Nigel's memories became an integral part in the consumption of the dishes he wishes to prepare so that "tradition" ceases to be a static list of qualities and becomes instead a dynamic element in the cultural experience of eating.

Social anthropology, however, has pointed out the dangers of automatically associating culinary practices with the concept of tradition. Warde reminds us of the need to appreciate how "the term 'tradition' may serve as a rhetorical device for the legitimisation of a particular set of preferences" (Warde 1997, 62). Faced with the possible breaking down of cultural boundaries, "tradition" may be employed to valorize – whether positively or negatively – the foods and culinary habits of a nation or of any particular ethnic group. This becomes evident in *Toast* when young Nigel is confronted for the first time with the unfamiliar food served in an Indian restaurant, which, it is clear, fails miserably to impress the boy – especially when compared to mum's "traditional" British food. The experience is revelatory:

> The restaurant is almost empty and smells of armpits ... The menu is terrifying ... We get a pile of giant crisps as big as a plate and some spicy gunk to dip them in ... The Bombay duck arrives – a wizened bit of grey smelling like something that has been dead a very long time. Putrid. (35–6)

A number of significant elements emerge from this short episode. Firstly, the fact that Nigel describes the restaurant as "smelling of armpits" and the Bombay duck as "putrid" immediately identifies his distaste for different smells. In his mind, the Indian dishes are clearly completely disconnected from the comforting nature of traditional bread-and-butter pudding, which the reader is told smells like "a hug" (7). Furthermore, in his dislike of Indian foods he emphasizes a rejection of "the new" – what he calls the "exotic" (35); young Nigel's lack of interest in another cuisine marks a clear cultural split between his social background and the Eastern culinary framework into which he is forced. Eventually, the experience of eating Indian food is confirmed as uncomfortable, "sinister" and "grubby" (37). In valorizing the wholesomeness of authentic British food – and openly criticizing the unreliable and untrustworthy nature of unknown dishes – *Toast* appears to be acting as free validation for the British culinary model. The act of remembering traditional food here is exposed as a technique through which, in Bell and Valentine's words, social groups reproduce "their identities over time" (Bell and Valentine 1997, 66). Although one must consider the possibility that Slater may be mocking a properly British resistance to "foreign cuisine" in the Sixties, the negative impact of his cultural considerations is difficult to miss. Eating, as Fieldhouse maintains, sums up "the attitudes, beliefs and customs and taboos affecting" the life "of a given group" (Fieldhouse 1995, 30). *Toast* establishes the culinary superiority of traditional foods by emphasizing the inferiority of Eastern cuisine; disgust is employed as tool for ethnocentricity. It is that same emphasis on disgust and the dubious nature of Indian food that solicits the readers' cultural solidarity by "indirectly encouraging them to agree with certain statements" (Montgomery et al. 1992, 223). "Tradition" here functions as an implicit term that validates the familiar, the known and, to put it simply, the exceptionally British.

The appeal of culinary "traditions," however, does not stop at the authentication of socio-cultural conduct. The justification of culinary "tradition," Warde claims, is inspired by the "commercial gains" that derive from "enacting or displaying" familiar food practices (Warde 1997, 64). The possible exploitation of culinary tradition – especially in literary form – has to be confronted if one wishes to explore the relationship between food, consumption, community and cultural groups. Perhaps, then, one is ultimately faced with the source of the culinary memoir's appeal: in painting a picture of common life in Sixties, *Toast* joins history with the everyday, the cultural dimension of place that the reader is encouraged to find, explore and appreciate.

Conclusion

The memory of culinary practices, as Carolyn Korsmeyer puts it, surfaces as "subjective but measurable, relative to culture and individual and yet shared"; culinary memories are revealed as "transient experiences freighted by the weight of history" (Korsmeyer 2005, 8). In Slater's *Toast*, culinary knowledge emerges as both influenced by and influencing memory. Individual experience and cultural history are synthesized in the idiom of food. Nonetheless, one must bear in mind the capitalist forces in advanced Western societies feeding over-consumption and what Fredric Jameson aptly calls "commodity bulimia" (Jameson 2005, 390).

Food literature itself, as a result, runs the risk of becoming incorporated in a list of consumer desirables. The reader can learn to digest its culture and the "way of life" with which the culinary book is associated. Roger Haden remarks that:

> the culinary legacy of knowledge gained through the sense of taste has been one related to all practices, technologies and experiences that have affected taste … this represents our present-day archive of taste. (Haden 2005, 349)

In any archive of taste, favorite foods, along with their modes of preparation and consumption, are part of a network of socio-cultural influences that intersect on the body and help to shape subjectivity. In this context, Susan Bordo argues that culture has a "direct grip" on our bodily activities and it is through "routine" and "habitual activities" that social knowledge is generated (Bordo 1993, 16).

The interest in culinary autobiographies and memoirs – clearly shown by the Richard & Judy Book Club – allows us to see how the culinary texts have evolved as symbols of class and social importance, so that the cultural "language of food" was mediated by the written form. During the late twentieth and early twenty-first centuries the publication of recipe books became increasingly popular. This draws attention to the possibility that, over time, readers have become increasingly more interested in reading about "home food" and what it may represent on a personal, cultural and national level. In the first part of the twentieth century, examples such Margaret Compton's *Great Union Cookbook* (1902), Isabel Lord's *Everybody's Cookbook* (1924), Belle Lowe's *Experimental Cookery* (1932), *Kate Smith's Favorite Recipes* (1940), Edith Barber's *Silver Jubilee Super Market Cookbook* (1955) and James Beard's *Menus for Entertaining* (1961) were amongst some of the best-selling and celebrated books. As the century moved along – and gave way to a new one – publications such as James Beard's *American Cooking* (1972), Sharon Stumpf's *British Festival Cookbook* (1985), Thomas Keller's *The French Laundry Cookbook* (1999) and Jane Fearnley-Whittingstall's *The Good Granny Cookbook* (2007) formed but a few examples of the myriad of gastronomic texts available to readers. The culinary-orientated book, it would seem, has gained an importance in excess of any simple interest in cooking. This could be because the "traditional" foods and "authentic" recipes themselves hide an encoded meaning: they suggest the importance of people or of a social occasion. Culinary books – whether in the form of memoirs autobiographies or recipe collections – show affection or dislike for culinary trends and can provide, among the list of ingredients, profitable pieces of social history.

The food book – interpreted here in view of its relationship to the "club" – might sometimes be bracketed with other technologies of "gastro-porn" bringing food representations and gratifications to the reader – the culinary traveler who prefers to stay at home (Bell and Valentine 1997, 203). Here one must bear in mind all those television shows and lavishly illustrated cookbooks that render representations of food into highly consumable products. In providing the reader with "consumable" descriptions of regional, ethnic and traditional dishes, *Toast* makes culinary experiences and histories attractive to the would-be purchaser. This "appetising text" exposes how food literature itself forms, in Bell and Valentine's words, an "inherent part of consumer culture" (Bell and Valentine 1997, 202–3). A scholarly interpretation of the impact of food books on the Richard & Judy Book Club, therefore, must maintain a critical awareness of the modes of nostalgia and commodity fetishism that often underpin representations of food in culinary memoirs. The literary food industry, in contemporary Western society, capitalizes on consumer desire for the "healthy" and the "authentic" within a broad context of simulation and excess. Although Slater – together with Nigella, Richard and Judy –proposes the culinary recollections in *Toast* as truly "genuine" and "authentic" mnemonic embodiments of time and place, the published fate of the book as anti-commodity appears slightly less unadulterated. Through the nostalgic acculturation of the senses, culinary memories are transformed into a commodity that can be sold in exchange for money. The historical return to the "senses" associated with the culinary memories in *Toast* is eventually exploited for profit. This denouement poses questions regarding the validity of the sensorial memories that Slater is apparently attempting to legitimize. It remains difficult to decide whether the author is aware of the possible dangers of commodification or whether, perhaps, he is embracing and developing his own special brand of "consumable literature." In any case, the final treatment of the authentic memories in *Toast* suggests that when it comes to food and drink the idea of "memory" can be sold as a product – this is, after all, what the book itself is trying to do. The intellect is tantalized before the taste buds, and historical associations are constructed, as Proust and Benjamin would have put it, through instances of *mémoire volontaire*. Memories of consumption, therefore, are treated as a possession, and are commercially dealt with "as though they are objects" (Hallam and Hockey 2001, 3).

Nonetheless, it would be unwise to conclude with a uniformly bleak assessment of the politics of food writing within the Richard & Judy Book Club. The interest of the "literature of food" lies precisely in its ability to adapt to changing cultural and historical contexts and its refusal to be tied to a single discursive or representational form. Food emerges as inextricably linked to communication. Slater's *Toast* recovers food as a communicative apparatus that detaches eating from simple nourishment and actively constructs a path into cultural customs, anxieties and pleasures. This underlines the extent to which, in Warde's words, memories of food and drink "are principal channels for the communication of self-identity ... people define themselves through the messages they transmit to others by the goods and practices they process and display" (Warde 1997, 10).

Reference List

Appadurai, Arjun. 1981. Gastro-Politics in Hindu South Asia. *American Ethnologist* 8: 494–511.

Bartoshuk, Linda and Valerie Duffy. 2005. Chemical Senses: Taste and Smell. In *The Taste Culture Reader: Experiencing Food and Drink,* ed. Carolyn Korsmeyer, 25–33. Oxford: Berg.

Beard, James. 1972. *American Cooking*. Boston: Little, Brown and Company.

Bell, David and Gill Valentine. 1997. *Consuming Geographies: We Are Where We Eat*. London: Routledge.

Benjamin, Walter. 1999. *Illuminations*. London: Pimlico.

Bennett, Oliver. 2004. Never Judge a Book by Its Clubbers. *The Independent*, Book Section, 28 June: 1– 4.

Bordo, Susan. 1993. *Unbearable Weight: Feminism, Western Culture, and the Body*. Berkeley: University of California Press.

Boym, Svetlana. 2001. *The Future of Nostalgia*. New York: Basic Books.

Brillat-Savarin, Jean-Anthelme. 2005. On Taste. In *The Taste Culture Reader: Experiencing Food and Drink,* ed. Carolyn Korsmeyer, 15–24. Oxford: Berg.

Capella, Anthony. 2004. *The Food of Love*. London: Time Warner.

Classen, Constance, David Howes and Anthony Synnott. 1994. *Aroma: The Cultural History of Smell*. London: Routledge.

DeVault, Marjorie. 1991. *Feeding the Family: The Social Organization of Caring as Gendered Work*. Chicago and London: University of Chicago Press.

Eagleton, Terry. 1998. Edible Ecriture. In *Consuming Passions: Food in the Age of Anxiety*, ed. Sian Griffiths and Jennifer Wallace, 203–8. Manchester: Manchester University Press.

Fearnley-Whittingstall, Jane. 2007. *The Good Granny Cookbook*. London: Short Books.

Fieldhouse, Paul. 1995. *Food and Nutrition: Customs and Culture*. London: Chapman & Hall.

Floyd, Janet and Laurel Foster. 2003. *The Recipe Reader: Narratives – Contexts – Traditions*. Aldershot: Ashgate.

Haden, Roger. 2005. Taste in an Age of Convenience: From Frozen Food to Meals in *The Matrix*. In *The Taste Culture Reader: Experiencing Food and Drink*, ed. Carolyn Korsmeyer, 344–58. Oxford: Berg.

Hallam, Elizabeth and Jenny Hockey. 2001. *Death, Memory and Material Culture*. Oxford: Berg.

Homes, A.M. 2006. *This Book Will Save Your Life*. London: Granta.

Jameson, Fredric. 2005. *Archaeologies of the Future: The Desire Called Utopia and Other Science Fictions*. London: Verso.

Jordan, Toni. 2008. *Addition*. London: Hodder and Stoughton.

Keller, Thomas. 1999. *The French Laundry Cookbook*. New York: Artisan.

Kelly, Traci Marie. 2001. "If I Were a Voodoo Priestess": Women's Culinary Autobiographies. In *Kitchen Culture in America: Popular Representations of Food, Gender and Race*, ed. Sherrie A. Inness, 251–70. Philadelphia: University of Pennsylvania Press.

Korsmeyer, Carolyn. 2005. Introduction: Perspectives on Taste. In *The Taste Culture Reader: Experiencing Food and Drink*, ed. Carolyn Korsmeyer, 1–9. Oxford: Berg.

Lawson, Nigella. 2006. *Feast: Food that Celebrates Life*. London: Chatto & Windus.

Lupton, Deborah. 1996. *Food, the Body and the Self*. London: SAGE.

Martin, James. 2003. *Great British Dinners*. London: Mitchell Beazley.

Montgomery, Martin, Alan Durant, Nigel Fabb, Tom Furniss and Sara Mills. 1992. *Ways of Reading: Advanced Reading Skills for Students of English Literature*. London: Routledge.

Morgan, David. 1996. *Family Connections: An Introduction to Family Studies*. Cambridge: Polity.

Pratt, Mary Louise. 1993. Arts of the Contact Zone. In *Ways of Reading: An Anthology for Writers*, ed. David Bartholomae and Anthony Petrosky, 582–96. Boston: Bedford.

Proust, Marcel. 1982. *Remembrance of Things Past*, Vol. 1. New York: Vintage.

Ritivoi, Andreea Deciu. 2002. *Yesterday's Self: Nostalgia and the Immigrant Identity*. Oxford: Rowman & Littlefield.

Rossant, Colette. 2003. *Return to Paris*. London: Bloomsbury.

Seremetakis, Nadia. 1996. *The Senses Still: Perception and Memory as Material Culture in Modernity*. Chicago: University of Chicago Press.

Schinto, Janet. 1990. The Art of Eating Words. *Yale Review* 72: 489–502.

Slater, Nigel. 2004. *Toast: The Story of a Boy's Hunger*. London: Harper Perennial.

Sperber, Dan. 1975. *Rethinking Symbolism*. Cambridge: Cambridge University Press.

Stumpf, Sharon. 1985. *British Festival Cookbook*. North Wankato: Walter.

Sutton, David. 2005. Synaesthesia, Memory, and the Taste of Home. In *The Taste Culture Reader: Experiencing Food and Drink*, ed. Carolyn Korsmeyer, 304–16. Oxford: Berg.

Theophano, Janet. 2002. *Eat My Words: Reading Women's Lives Through The Cookbooks They Wrote*. New York: Palgrave.

Toklas, Alice B. 1984. *The Alice B. Toklas Cook Book*. New York: Perennial.

Warde, Alan. 1997. *Consumption, Food and Taste: Culinary Antinomies and Commodity Culture*. London: SAGE.

PART 3
After The Richard & Judy
Book Club

Chapter 10
"What really counts is the story": Interview with Andrew Smith, Author of *Moondust*, (February 10, 2010)

Jenni Ramone

Andrew Smith's *Moondust* is an account of the author's journey to meet all of the remaining astronauts who had undertaken missions to the moon. The book was a Richard & Judy Book Club selection in 2006. The title, reminiscent of science fiction, is an indication of the mood of this work. Not a science book, as Smith points out, the story instead explores the mystique of the moon landings and of the astronauts as they are positioned by the public gaze. The moondust itself gets everywhere – although a government decree bans anyone from owning pure moondust, still it remains clinging to the fabric of the space suits that the astronauts keep in their homes, and is even used by former astronaut, now full-time artist, Alan Bean to improve the sense of connection between his hypothetical realist lunar landscapes, a style that involves producing "photorealistic renderings of places and things you can't get photos of" (Smith, 149), and the moon: he has decided to cut up his mission patches and to use small pieces impregnated with moondust in each painting: "I really was devoting the rest of my life to doing this, so that was a good place to put them" (Smith, 160).

Unusual not only because it's one of very few non-fiction titles selected by the Richard & Judy Book Club, *Moondust* is also a very unusual kind of book: part narrative journalism, part American road trip, it is also in many ways a biographical portrait of the astronauts, which is at the same time autobiographical. For both of these reasons, Andrew Smith was very surprised when his book was chosen for the book club. For Smith, it was when Nick Hornby wrote about *Moondust* in *The Polysyllabic Spree* that he realized why the book was an unusual choice for a mass broadcast book club, which generally selected novels from established genres such as historical fiction, crime, and "chick-lit." Smith describes how, having read Hornby's piece, he realized that: "It's not a particularly mainstream book. Its terms of reference are not particularly mainstream, and even its sensibility is not mainstream. It speaks a lot of ideas as well, which some people might have thought would be off-putting and yet they chose it – I got one letter complaining about the swearing in the book, which is up on my wall now, but other than that, its style didn't seem to put people off. Any way you look at it, it's an unlikely choice, but I thought it was really nice that they chose it anyway." So, this being the case, in many ways the choice of a non-mainstream book for a mainstream discussion format like the Richard & Judy Book Club could be worrying for the author. Its selection could raise concern that the book would reach an unlikely audience, and perhaps not reach its ideal audience. However, it is in terms of style that the text fits in to a more mainstream category: it engages readers because of its discursive, questioning, personal narrative tone, and this means it overcomes any issues that might arise because the ideas aren't mainstream, or because the approach to the story is somewhat unorthodox or at least unexpected. In terms of style and expression, Smith says that what he writes is "more mainstream than what a lot of the publishing industry puts out and thinks of as mainstream. My biggest fear is boring people – if people don't engage with something they'll stop reading. The traditional view in literature is that if a book is boring it's your own fault, that as a writer you're not trying hard enough. I would never, ever want somebody to put down my work because they don't understand it." With this in mind, his aim was to write a book that has "content and substance" without sacrificing readability. In this way, the book is more mainstream than some of the other books selected by the Richard & Judy Book Club. For example, *White Mughals* is a dense, 640-page account of an English man and an Indian princess in early colonial India, which addresses the politics of such an encounter. For Smith, the range of books selected is one of the strengths of the club, and this goes beyond the book club itself: "the Booker Prize list that year was full of books I liked but also books that were more arcane, and it's nice to have the two things existing in parallel." The interesting point here is that both mainstream and more esoteric books are brought together by prize lists and book clubs, which implies that perhaps the book club even opened up things like the Booker list to include more mainstream styles and genres – biographical and autobiographical writing being among this mainstream style that might not have been included in prestigious literary prize selections before the book club.

For, Smith, to keep the reader interested it is imperative to "write clearly, as clearly and simply as possible. I try never to complicate things unnecessarily. I like music and it's like that too: most of the things I like are uncomplicated." This comes across particularly in the first chapter, which seems like a gentle way in, while afterwards the text employs more complex language. For Smith, though not a deliberate strategy, this gentle introduction is part of his established writing style: "I think that's in part due to my journalistic background. When you're competing for attention in a newspaper where there's so much going on, essentially if you don't give people a reason to carry on and read it straight away they'll turn the page. I'm the worst reader – if something doesn't grab me I'll put it down. With novels, I do try to give them a good go but beyond about 100 pages, if the book doesn't grab me I'll put it down as a poor job. The one exception to that was *The Corrections* which people had warned me would take a lot of time, and so I did stay with it."

The Corrections is Jonathan Franzen's (2001) novel, perhaps the most controversial text associated with Oprah's Book Club, or even the most controversial event associated with the club. As Kathleen Rooney has described in detail in her book *Reading with Oprah: The Book Club That Changed America* (2005, 26), Franzen sparked debate over the impact of selection for Oprah's Book Club and the function of the book club itself when he expressed some uncertainty over the choice of his novel as one of Oprah's selections. Widely reported as refusing permission for Oprah to discuss his book, Franzen has since claimed that in fact he only refused to have Oprah's logo on his book, and as a result of this it was announced by Oprah that he had chosen not to be part of the book club, the incorporation of the logo perhaps being a demand of the publishers or booksellers if not of Oprah herself. Smith considers the two book clubs to be built with fairly contrasting agendas, based on the hosts themselves: "Oprah represents something very different to Americans than Richard and Judy ever represented here. Most people thought of them as a charming odd couple." This may account for the more ambiguous response received by the Richard & Judy Book Club in Britain, in comparison with the more clearly divided public opinion on Oprah's Book Club in America. As a writer with a generally positive attitude towards the Richard & Judy Book Club (RJBC), Smith expresses some ambivalence as well, sympathizing with Franzen's wariness of the mass broadcast book club: "I think Franzen's view was completely reasonable – he was in a nice position of knowing the book was already out there, and it had received very good reviews in hardback. As his book was already very popular and well-received, why should he carry advertising on its cover? I remember we laughed about the use of the logo on my book; in previous years they'd had stickers on the books and some of the booksellers had taken the stickers off the covers after the book club series to sell them in shops without the logo. As a result, they started to actually print the RJBC logo on the cover, as part of the cover. No way was I happy about doing that with my book, not at all. It's a trade off I would have preferred not to have made, but a lot of people came across the book who wouldn't have done otherwise so I think it was probably worth it. It got irksome after a while, though. In fact, they published the new edition this year which didn't have the logo on and in reviews and articles where people have discussed the book two or three years later they say it's embarrassing sitting on the bus with a book with the RJBC logo and I'd probably feel the same."

It is the televised studio discussion of his book that caused the most apprehension for the author. In his article on the impact of the Richard & Judy Book Club written for the Sunday Times, Smith mentions that he didn't originally see the broadcast discussion of *Moondust*, which involved invited celebrities, musician Myleene Klass and astronomer Colin Pillinger, and he was anticipating some controversial debate: "I was happy that Myleene Klass had been invited to participate in the discussion, because I knew she was bright and had studied astronomy, that she was a fairly fun but serious person. I wasn't as comfortable with Professor Colin Pillinger's invitation because in the book I do very gently but affectionately make fun of him. However, they said they needed a popular scientist and he was the one chosen. It was absolutely hilarious to watch because he wanted to come on the programme and be sour about the book but couldn't. To be fair, I can understand why; some people from the scientific world want more science in the book – and, of course, there is science in the book but it's not a science book. It's more about asking what the moon landings meant to the rest of us watching, and it's not about what they found on the moon." This is certainly the way that the book comes across to the reader: though there are sustained descriptions of technical feats, there is at the same time a constant reference to the emotional content of the voyages. This is particularly memorable in Smith's meeting with John Young. Smith describes listening back to Young's recorded the interview, and claims that when Young talks about the abrupt end of the missions to the moon, his tone of voice "sounds like that of someone who's *in love*" (191). The emotional content of the moon missions is something that Smith and many others point out, claiming that the scientific value of sending humans to the moon was minimal, when robots could collect data and samples just as effectively without risking human lives. The moon missions are, Smith insists, emotional events and not just scientific ones, meaning that to write a book that was purely a science book would be to write an incomplete story, even if some members of the science community would have preferred to read a new scientific analysis of the space program. "It was really funny watching Colin Pillinger try to make that point and to complain about the book from his perspective, but Richard just steamrollered him – it was like watching a real pro at work. They also sent a team over to film me in Norfolk and they were really nice, I had a really good time doing that. They were telling me about the other films they'd made for the programme and marvelling at the other novelists, and in particular they mentioned filming Julian Barnes at Hampstead Heath, who, following the filming accused them of taking their 'pound of flesh'."

Smith refers to the difficult process of selecting book club choices, noting that if there is a choice of just 10 books per series, it's so difficult to choose that to an extent, "it's just pot luck," and can only be based on instinct: "Amanda Ross and her team seem to work in the same way that I do; if something interests me, the assumption is that it will interest a good number of other people as well. If something sparks my curiosity and I want to learn more about it when I'm writing, then I find that most of the time people respond to that. I work in the same way in journalism – as a journalist you're trying that week in week out. It's a question of feeling it rather than trying to second-guess. Second-guessing is rife in the publishing industry. Publishers never really know what they're looking for as they're knocked around from pillar to post by booksellers; they're looking for something they can sell but when confronted with an idea they always ask, how can you be sure this will sell? You can't. The only way to respond to that position is to ask, what did it do for me? How did I respond to it when I was reading it? If I responded well, probably others will."

Jonathan Franzen's misgivings about his book club selection were not shared by Andrew Smith, who was very pleased that his book was chosen, partly, he says, "because everyone around me, including my publishers and my editor, were so excited about it – for them it was a big deal. And although it had had quite a lot of interest already, this meant that it was suddenly out there and in everyone's faces so more people could make that choice and ask themselves if the book was something that they were interested in or not. My publishers don't think it sold any more in paperback than it would have done anyway because of the book club, but they think but it sold a lot quicker so that in six or nine months it had sold what it would have done in two years. Obviously that was helpful – it's hard to make a living as a writer and anything that can help you to pay back your advance more quickly is helpful. I spent all my savings on *Moondust* and at one point I was presented with a choice: I thought, I can stop here and produce something that's OK or I can carry on and write something that I'm really proud of for the rest of my life and on my deathbed I can say I've done something that I'm happy with. So I carried on, even though the two years while I was finishing writing the book were the hardest years of my life materially and financially. When I was first working as a writer I lived in a squat in Camberwell so I'm used to roughing it, but these years were very difficult indeed and this made the book club experience very strange: reports of the millions of pounds earned by authors were all over the papers that year, and that was completely ill-informed actually. The publishers make millions but the author makes about 50p a book. I was still paying off the loans and overdrafts from writing *Moondust*. And all the money I earned from *Moondust* is going towards research for my new book – if I can continue to do that, I'll be very pleased."

Authors who have been selected for the Richard & Judy Book Club receive automatic nomination for the British Book Awards. For Smith, this was another strange experience. He recalls arriving at the same time as Anchee Min, author of *Empress Orchid*, who he describes as looking very striking in blue satin dress: "We walked down the red carpet and turned around a corner where all the press photographers were waiting in the same place and there was a sudden explosion of bright flashbulbs all going at once. I actually jumped back and then moved along very quickly. All that stuff was strange. Odder, though, for some – J.K. Rowling was at our table and she came in after everyone else had been seated so there were just two places reserved for her and her partner. As she came in the director of the ceremony and the other officials were all genuflecting, even though she's not the kind of person who demands that kind of reaction. Then suddenly a load of paparazzi came up to her and started taking photos until they were led away by security. That level of attention must be bizarre."

After the book, and after the book club, the text has been reproduced in a number of ways and the opportunities for retelling the story in different media are ongoing. Smith read an audiobook version of *Moondust*, which he describes as "the hardest job, ever, in the world! Harder than writing it, seriously! It was truly exhausting. It was interesting and fun but they asked me to do the unabridged version and I said I'd rather jump in the channel and not come back!" It wasn't an emotionally draining process, though: "You're concentrating so much on the delivery so the content doesn't affect you emotionally. The only time I do feel emotionally drained is when I do readings sometimes and I often include evocative music written by Brian Eno and the visual footage from the camera behind Buzz Aldrin's head. I always feel quite moved by that, as if they might not make it this time, and I'm always surprised when they do. But I don't think that reading the audiobook was a revelatory thing except that I would not rush to do it again." Smith was not involved in the abridging process: "I thought they abridged the book very well, but it's still unsatisfying for me because that book seemed more like a jigsaw puzzle, and some of the things that you'd naturally pull out when abridging seemed to me more important than the more obvious things that they left in. When they serialised the book in *The Guardian* they more or less rewrote it and that did rankle with me."

More unusually, there is a *Moondust* album, a musical soundtrack to the book. "That was a dream come true and a nightmare at the same time. I'd always thought that there was so much music in the book because of the time – the space race and its contemporary music were very much parallel in my imagination if not in the real word. The rock and roll years and the height of space travel both ran from 1956/1957 to the end of 1972. EMI went through a complete meltdown shortly after we had planned to make the *Moondust* album so we had the track list and everything ready to burn and then almost everyone got sacked when EMI were bought by a venture capital firm, and the album ended up being delayed for two years. So it was nightmarish in that way, and again everyone involved in making the album was made redundant straight away after it had come out." The album is also accompanied by special sleeve notes written by Smith in order to tell the musical story that accompanies the book, meaning that this is in many ways a new story, and also meaning that the book is remarkable in attracting this kind of side-project.

In addition, Smith has received numerous invitations to produce a documentary based on the book, but insists that any documentary would be impossible unless it did something quite different, had something new to say. To simply recreate the book in documentary form would, for Smith, "be a lie. The book conveys the meetings and the journey as they were; they were happening for the first time. If you simply retraced it, it would be a lie. So much of the book is just about me putting myself in situations and at those moments you feel very alive. I think probably every TV company in the country came to me and asked if they could create a documentary but I felt uncomfortable with the idea. If I was going to repeat it, I'd have to be upfront about the fact that I was repeating something and showing something I'd already seen, retracing the journey. There wouldn't be any point doing the same thing so soon afterwards but I can imagine that doing it again in five or ten years time might have merit. To put yourself in the same situation again won't necessarily create the same experience. The only way anyone could do that – and a few people have suggested this – would be to dramatise it."

Since writing *Moondust*, Andrew Smith has become firmly associated with space travel and the moon landings, and is often considered an expert on space: "I always try to be upfront about the fact that I'm not! I know more than I did before, more than I ever intended or even wanted to know. And I must admit I do enjoy being able to go and talk about it – whenever there's anything to do with space, people like the Today Show on Radio 4 tend to call me, which is nice." More a science-fiction reader than a science expert, perhaps, Smith writes that "sci-fi never did catch up with Apollo" (294). This, he says, is because, viewed 40 years after the first moon landing, the feat seems somehow "like a sci-fi event because it's so impossible and ridiculous." Smith was a science fiction fan and read novels by Asimov and Phillip K Dick, but he wasn't aware that *Moondust* is reminiscent of sci-fi at times, in terms of its style and structure. The text employs the sci-fi convention of shifting conspicuously between scientific or technical information and character development, although in this case, the character "developed" is the author's or the astronauts' rather than a fictional one. At the same time, the book describes the way that the astronauts and the space program seem to have a place in the American, or, perhaps, in global consciousness, which is not clearly made distinct from sci-fi; for example, the astronauts make appearances at sci-fi conventions. It is rare that other genres of literature create such close connections with their real-world equivalents. *Moondust* does not offer a position of certainty regarding the position of sci-fi in relation to the moon landings. It both reflects the genre because the public may not clearly distinguish between real space travel and sci-fi, while at the same time permits the audience to share the view that there is a connection while understanding the difference.

The fickleness of public attention to the space program was part of Smith's inspiration for the book, as he has reflected upon in the new edition of the book: "They asked me to write a foreword for the new edition and I decided to base it on something that someone said to me at the BBC – this person said, 'how clever of you to have anticipated the anniversary of the first landing' which I hadn't done at all. The reason I found the subject so interesting when I decided to write the book in 2002 was the *lack* of interest in the astronauts; it seemed like they were a forgotten part of history. The thirtieth anniversary was barely remembered at all, unlike the recent fortieth anniversary in 2009. That was what I thought was so interesting, that they'd been forgotten about. And in terms of the sci-fi, the further we get from the time of the moon landings the more bizarre it seems. To people in 1972 it seemed pretty mundane and they stopped watching space travel on television, but as more time elapsed the more it seemed like science fiction. Thirty or forty years later you start looking at it and asking, why did they do that? *Did* they do that? In 2002 there wasn't a nation on earth that had the capability to go to the moon, and yet they'd done it more than thirty years earlier when the lunar module had something like a 56k memory, which is a fraction of what you've got in a mobile phone. Because of that, by the time I started working on the book, I wasn't surprised to find one of the astronauts signing autographs at a sci-fi convention because it seemed a little bit like sci-fi to me, like a weird forgotten future." Perhaps, too, popular taste dictates a sci-fi element in a non-fictional text about the space program and its astronauts.

Another element shared by the non-fiction titles selected by the Richard & Judy Book Club is the biographical or autobiographical genre. Smith's interest in the astronauts isn't primarily to do with their careers and their experiences in space. It's as much an exploration of their lives before and afterwards, their personalities and values. The book is anything but a frozen snapshot of the astronauts at the moment they went to the moon. It is an account of their lives before and after that period, gained through interviews usually conducted at their homes, with their families. Because of that, the photographs of the 12 men reproduced at the front of the book produce an odd contrast, shown in their space suits very much in the way that they are still cast in the public gaze. Like the moon landings themselves, which, for Smith, seem almost like sci-fi 40 years afterwards, these images create a piercing echo when glimpsed while reading the stories about the astronauts' lives today. The book offers a presentation of these sometimes publicly worshipped (in the case of Neil Armstrong, especially) and sometimes forgotten figures in new ways. One of the most interesting and unexpected portraits is perhaps the presentation of Buzz Aldrin. "Astonishingly fit" (89) and active for his age he is a contradictory figure, at times demonstrating extraordinary confidence and at other times distinct humility. This is conveyed by Smith's description of his speech style: "His syntax can be disorientating when you're with him and takes a while to tune into, but once on the page you see that he speaks a private creole of tiny sentences with no predicate. They capture the essence of a thought and are often very direct in themselves, yet circle like moons around something that Buzz can't quite bring himself to say, like the speech of a small child, or haiku" (90). Smith points out that throughout their meeting, Aldrin uses the register of technology in reference to the personal and the everyday: he describes overcoming depression as acquiring a "sufficiently healthy status" (97), and talks about the need to "network actions mutually between people" (106), or, in other words, to counteract the astronauts' intense personalities by working to create better relationships with each other with the help of other people. But two of the astronauts stand out as having a particular – and a particularly contradictory – significance for the author: Gene Cernan and Neil Armstrong.

Whilst Cernan intimates that some of the other astronauts "prostituted to some degree their celebrity status" (264) while others were perhaps even more mercenary and mediated this self-prostitution to make it serve their business interests, Smith places Cernan firmly within this group, and portrays him as a cold, business-minded individual. Smith seems almost hostile towards Gene Cernan, while the other astronauts are in general presented very warmly. To the reader, it feels as if a clash of values has made this particular encounter difficult, even to the extent that at times the atmosphere of tension is tangible on the page. "This was something that I was aware of at the time. In a way, Cernan represented everything I'd expected from more of the astronauts: he was a straight-laced military man, ultra-Republican, a Texan, a Bush supporter, quite self-aggrandizing and certainly not modest; in fact, he embodied the cocky stereotypical cliché of the military pilot when in reality I haven't found any American military pilots to be like that, and certainly not the astronauts, who were all very modest and self-effacing, which was quite unexpected. Cernan says in the British documentary *In the Shadow of the Moon* (2007) that it bothered him that he didn't go to Vietnam; he says: 'that was my war'. That attitude doesn't endear you to someone. At the same time, though, I was aware that that was a generational thing; I was judging him on the basis of my values and that's not what the book was for. So what I did there was to try to be truthful. When he rubbed me up the wrong way, or said something that I found really objectionable, I just decided to be honest about it and let the reader know what he had said, but at the same time I also tried to get into his head and understand what he was feeling. Although I'm less sympathetic towards him than the other astronauts, I did try to understand his perspective. When he was talking about the moon landing and what it meant to him I didn't really feel like he was talking openly. Later on he did relax and told me that when you've heard the same questions repeatedly – those questions like, 'what does it mean to you?' and 'how did it feel?' – you have nothing new that you can say. The same questions are repeated over and over again and people expect a sound bite response, so you can never satisfy people. You just can't do it and so people go away disappointed, and then you're perpetually working with this sense that you're disappointing people and needing to be profound when most of the time that's not possible. So when he started talking about that I could empathise with him. I did worry about the way I was presenting him, so because I didn't want to be unfair to him I tried to make it clear when what I conveyed was my viewpoint and my prejudice. I tried to make that explicit so that people could make their own minds up and perhaps decide to side with Cernan on some points. What I tried to do was to make sure that I didn't misjudge him or any of the astronauts – I hope I didn't and if I did, I've failed. Nevertheless, I would imagine that he wouldn't like the book, just because it's coming from a European liberal perspective that couldn't be further from his own. Cernan and I didn't particularly have any rapport but nor would one have been possible – but he was the only one. I went away from the meeting feeling slightly disappointed but when I listened to the interview again afterwards I was glad that it had happened in that way; it needed to happen because that was one side of the story."

The presentation of Neil Armstrong couldn't be more different. Renowned as an enigmatic figure, Smith never expected to be able to arrange an interview with Armstrong. It is in this sense that Smith writes "what really counts is the story" (274). The story is to do with the process rather than the product, and so, "unlike TV where you only have what you've got on camera," it is after the process of gathering information and material that the story can begin to take shape, and for Smith, that meant speaking as much about the process as about the things that the astronauts told him. "When I was planning the book, a friend said that unless I could 'get' Neil Armstrong, I couldn't write the book but I always felt that if Armstrong doesn't do interviews then that's part of the story." Unlike the other astronauts who generally appear in one sustained section of the text, Armstrong seems to haunt the text as a semi-godlike figure. Throughout, Smith almost constructs a myth of Neil Armstrong as separate and special: Smith's contact with him is constantly deferred as if it's always tantalizingly almost within reach of the reader. "I didn't make a conscious effort to present any of them in a particular way, I tried to just describe what happens. I have a lot of respect for Neil Armstrong. Very few people know that his withdrawal from the public was actually a thought-out strategy, a survival strategy which he developed partly after talking to the only other person who had gone through a similar experience, Charles Lindbergh, whose life had been destroyed by celebrity. He does set himself aside because of the status he has been given, and I don't think status was something that he particularly cared about. But in the way he interacts with the world, he is like that – always out of reach. There is a museum dedicated to the moon landing in his home town, Wapakoneta, which he visits once every ten years or so to surprise everyone, yet he's not around or visible in his home town. Even so, not long before I visited Wapakoneta he'd been to his High School reunion and after people had their pictures taken with him, he disappeared. He was always a private person and when you see him in public situations you can understand why he withdrew – it must just be a nightmare for someone. I couldn't cope with that and I'm a reasonably outgoing person."

One particularly telling image in *Moondust* is the moment when Smith compares Armstrong with Atticus Finch, the fictional Alabama lawyer in *To Kill a Mockingbird* who dares to defend a black man in the 1930s. This particularly reinforces Armstrong's heroic status because immediately after evoking Atticus Finch, Smith describes how he learns that Buzz Aldrin and Gene Cernan, present at the same event, have been seen at adjacent urinals. Smith imagines them competing to see who could "pee highest" (138); this, he says, is because they are two of the most competitive people that he has ever met, but still the image is mundane, human, and irreverent in comparison to the image of Atticus Finch, perhaps the most morally upstanding and ideal literary figure: wise, patient, and just. Reminded of this comparison and of the naïve narrative position in which Smith is placed in relation to a figure resembling Atticus Finch, he says "I had completely forgotten about that. He felt like that to me but I'm sure that's me projecting on to him – it was obviously something I was doing unconsciously." The later portrait of Cernan in this context almost seems to create a binary between Cernan the villain and Armstrong as hero of the piece. However, the presentation of the astronauts is not a simplistic one of uncritical admiration. Smith asserts constantly that many of the decisions about who would fly in each trip and about the delegation of roles were fairly arbitrary. Likewise, he acknowledges the astronauts' discomfort because of the public bias towards those who had walked on the moon and the pilots who had stayed in the command module, as well as the order in which they had made their journeys, as Buzz Aldrin confirms most clearly, making reference to a "very layered and defined" hierarchy: "there's a first group of astronauts and a second group, then the third group. And where you flew. And whether you were a commander" (94). The text also carefully conveys the distinctiveness of each astronaut in terms of experiences, personality, and outlook, and these objective aspects of telling the story seem to contrast with the way in which Armstrong haunts the text as a revered figure. The question of objectivity in a narrative like this one is complicated. "I'm not trying to produce any great objectivity beyond the kind of objectivity that I bring to my life generally. For example, in a relationship with a partner you are constantly struggling with having to maintain that sense of objectivity if they do something that really irritates you. And I try and do the same thing in my writing, which I think is more honest; to pretend to be objective is just a lie. Armstrong is a good figurehead for that in lots of ways: he was a real pilot and was chosen accidentally for the first moon landing. Yet I'm part of the world that accords him that very special status and, like it or not, he has a very emotional symbolism and it's not fair and it's not right. So you're probably getting that tension in the book."

For the reader, there is constant expectation that Neil Armstrong might agree to an interview: Andrew Smith manages to speak to him briefly at an Apollo Astronauts Reunion Dinner that he attends in Reno (108), where Armstrong, to the surprise of the other attendees, those autograph-hunters "with the fixed gaze of cobras on their prey" (134), writes down his email address (138). Towards the end of the book, having eventually sent an email, Smith receives a reply and a tentative invitation to continue the conversation: "He asked me to expand on what I wanted to talk about, to tell him who this thing was for and to provide a few sample questions so that he might decide whether he could 'make a meaningful contribution'" (290). Achieving this level of dialogue, Smith had managed to cross barriers where many others had failed, and there is a moment where he knows that, if he really wanted to, he could say the right thing and achieve a meeting. Knowing that Armstrong did not give interviews if he was asked to discuss his emotional response to the moon landing, and also that Armstrong's main interest was to do with the history of aviation, Smith is aware of how to use his media skills to get an interview: "if I wanted to sit down and speak with Neil Armstrong, the best bet would be to persuade him of my interest in the X-15's landing gear. I'd done this kind of thing many times before. It's understood in the modern media and the modern world that everyone has something to sell: you talk to them about whatever it is, then guide or drag them on to the things you really want to know" (291). However, Smith is in the end compelled to reply to Armstrong's email with honesty and emotion, to ask a series of questions based on "childish wonder" about the feeling of standing on the moon, having eventually concluded that this "childish wonder" was in fact "the whole point" of understanding Apollo (299): "was the feeling like any he'd had before? Like sex? Like swimming in the sea at night? Going out without your parents on Halloween for the first time? Like he'd imagined all along, with no surprises? Did he feel alone, like a representative of Earth, or closer to the stars? … And when he got back, did he feel longing? Relief? Irritation? Disappointment?" (298). At this point, his emotional connection with Armstrong and with space travel and the moon landings more generally, an emotional response that has punctuated the narrative throughout, exerts more power than his objective intention to achieve a complete record of the astronauts' experiences and responses. "I had a secret fear that he would say yes to an interview, that we'd sit down and he would be dull. I'd sooner leave him as this aloof, slightly mythic character on whom we could project. We've elected him and people like him to that role: they're effectively vehicles for us to project ourselves on to."

Smith was aware that, in responding to the email in this way, he was unlikely to receive a response, and he was correct in this supposition. This is a broader issue than simply the presentation of individual astronauts, though: "The book isn't as much about them going to the moon, it's about us watching them which is the thing that I think is interesting – it was obviously a very technical achievement, but the book is about that fascination. I was very pleased when they published the Dutch edition of the book, and the cover they chose was a picture of a TV with one of the space crafts inside it which I thought expressed that idea very well."

It is this engagement with the story from the position of the viewer that perhaps led Smith to write with such a personal and revelatory narrative voice, to write from a clearly defined autobiographical position rather than taking a more distant position. *Moondust* begins with an autobiographical section and there are – as well as brief personal memories and insertions throughout – other extended autobiographical sections. It is in part the very personal journey that made the book so popular, and perhaps made it accessible to the readers of a mass broadcast book club like Richard & Judy's. "I think that's one of the things that the people who do like the book like about it. The reason I wrote it in that way was purely because I tend not to know exactly where I'm going when I start out. If you saw the proposal, it could not look more different from the finished book. When I handed in the manuscript my editors and publishers were really surprised – I think they were expecting that chapter one would be about Neil Armstrong, chapter two about Buzz Aldrin, and so on. My American editor even said that to me. The reason it isn't written that way is purely because when I sat down, having gone on this journey and collected all this information, once started to process all of this material I started to wonder, how am I going to process that into something that I think is going to do the story justice, and tell the story best? In the end I thought the story of *telling* the story was the interesting thing. If I did it that way, it had the advantage that the reader could learn at the rate that I did. I started out not really knowing very much about this subject or about the astronauts themselves, but just being really curious. I started out by having a series of questions. I wasn't aware of the reader while I was doing this because the story was really for me, but I decided to write in a way that I thought would satisfy me, but that also someone picking it up later on would enjoy. It was probably one of the happiest periods in my life, actually, taking all this information and seeing where it would go, processing all this vast amount of information, only a small amount of which – about 1 per cent of it – is in the book."

It's also the kind of narrative voice that Smith feels most comfortable with: "I don't normally like books or TV programmes that lecture me from a great Olympian height. From my career in journalism I know how conditional and partial our knowledge is, so I don't want to pretend I know everything. To me, by telling the story in the order that it happened was important. Once I'd decided that I was going to present the story in the way I learned it, I was committed to it, although that did create some structural problems because in my ideal world chapter two would not be there at the start of the book as it's more difficult and a kind of odd way into the book."

Chapter Two is an account of the author's meeting with Edgar Mitchell, whose response to space travel was wholly intellectual. Soon after returning from the moon, Mitchell formed the IONS (Institute of Noetic Sciences) Research center, which has as its founding principles the need to negotiate the meaning of consciousness itself, and the call for a global change of consciousness. The research center is described as "more a state of mind than a place" (44), bringing together paranormal phenomena and physics, and so it is little wonder that the author feels this is not the most accessible of his encounters with the astronauts. Smith is somewhat dubious of the center, in part because of its "hippy" fundraisers who contradict his ideas about space travel, but also because Mitchell expounds a genuinely marginal and challenging intellectual position, in a four-hour lecture from which Smith leaves somewhat exhausted.

Though writing the book was a longer process, it did not differ significantly from Smith's career in journalism: "the voice that was in the book and the process of starting from the position of just having a few questions was exactly the same. I'd been working in that way for a long time, especially at *The Face* in the 1990s where I was really allowed to go and explore a question. I'd discuss it with the editor and in the end we'd decide that either we could answer the question already, or that there was a question that needed answering. And the same is true of *The Observer*: the editor would trust my instinct and say, 'just go and find out' and that was fantastic. That was great preparation for doing *Moondust* which was just a longer version of that process."

Moondust is also very clearly a book about America, though. In a recent Radio 4 interview, Smith noted that the event of the moon landing was the first time that we saw ourselves as one planet. In contrast, perhaps, the book seems like a particularly "American" one. There are lots of descriptions of travelling through America – driving in Arizona, and through the Mojave desert, for instance: "It's the end of the day and the sky's painting a singed rainbow of purple, gold, vermillion across the sand, while clouds flame and the jagged mountains point like spectators at a firework display towards a perfect sliver of silvery moon. It's majestic even from the road" (76). This style represents perhaps a conscious attempt to present America to a UK audience, or to situate the moon landings as an American project or experience rather than an international one. Smith understands this more as an impact of the strong autobiographical narrative position, rather than a considered statement of the way that the moon landings are perceived globally today. He says that the American feel of the book is: "no reflection on the moon landing, I think that's my doing. I have much more of a fondness for American literature and culture than I do Britain and British literature, maybe because I grew up there. I studied English here in the UK, but there's something about the openness and the space in American fiction and also the non-fiction, that had a very big influence on me. When I started off as a music journalist our heroes were from the 'new journalism' school, Thom Wolf, Hunter Thompson, Norman Mailer, writers who went in and got their hands dirty, who would get right inside a story and immerse themselves. That really appeals to me – music journalists of my generation and the one before me were really inspired by that, but it seems to me that the American novels are like that too, in scope and scale. I'm not saying I don't like British novels, there are many I love, but they often seem very claustrophobic, they're often very class-bound and I didn't grow up with that. My father migrated to America purposely because he wanted to be an advertiser and could never have done that in Britain. He was one of the 'Mad Men,' who worked on Madison Avenue."

His parents' background is portrayed evocatively in *Moondust*: "It was the New York street-life yarns of Damon Runyon that drew my father to the city, and my mother, a plasterer's daughter from Acton Town, London, with him. ... To my working-class father, New York felt like a frontier, a place in which the past had no purchase and there was nothing outside of himself to constrain him" (109).

Set against this dramatic backdrop of the American landscape is a sense of self-questioning and self-discovery also common to the American road trip genre: reflecting after one of the interviews, Smith writes: "some unvoiced expectation of mine hasn't been met and this unsettles me ... I can see that the problem is mine and am thus drawn back to a question I left lying like a discarded fag end in the Mojave desert sand. What do I want from these people? Why am I here?" (250). It is towards the end of the journey that the autobiographical narrator, like a true American road narrative protagonist, learns about himself and the question that has been plaguing him all along: "The Moonwalkers are interesting because of what we've invested in them ... just as they travelled to the Moon only to find the Earth, I've come to find them, but what I seem to be seeing is myself and everyone else reflected *in* them, finding that the thoughts and questions the Moonwalkers provoke when we look at them are more valuable than any answers they might attempt to provide; that our fascination is not about them, it's about us" (251).

Andrew Smith explains how the Union of Persian Storytellers had feared the moon landings would damage the livelihood of storytellers, that the moon would no longer represent "romance and unspoken feeling," and refers to Tom Stoppard who, in an interview in the *Sunday Times*, expressed his agreement with the Union, and conveyed as well the fear that humanity would appear petty and its moral questions insignificant when viewed from the vastness of space (147). Having placed himself in a naïve narrative position by casting Neil Armstrong as Atticus Finch, the benevolent, wise, father figure, Smith as protagonist of this story can in the end voice his own feelings and choose to end the story in a way that meets his needs and not the expectations of others. Choosing not to gain an interview with Neil Armstrong by means of persuasion, he instead tells a story of the moon that retains its mystique and its power, to construct a story of which the Union of Persian Storytellers would probably approve. After all, "What really counts is the story" (274).

Reference List

Rooney, Kathleen. 2005. *Reading with Oprah: The Book Club that Changed America.* Fayetteville: University of Arkansas Press.

Smith, Andrew. 2005. *Moondust.* London: Bloomsbury.

Smith, Andrew. 2008. The pleasure – and pain – of being a Richard and Judy choice. *The Sunday Times.* June 15, 2008, http://entertainment.timesonline. co.uk/tol/arts_and_entertainment/books/article4120331.ece (accessed 1 February 2010).

The Today Programme. 2010. BBC Radio 4, 1 February.

Chapter 11

Ten of Thousands:
The TV Book Club

Helen Cousins

In a recent edition of Radio 4's *You and Yours* program (17 February 2010), the presenter, Winifred Robinson, wondered how we choose a good book to read concluding that we used to leave it to Richard and Judy when their Book Club was running. This was by way of introducing her interview with Amanda Ross (whose Cactus production company was responsible for the Richard & Judy Book Club) who had been invited onto the program to talk about her new book discussion program, *The TV Book Club*, broadcast on Sunday evenings on digital channel More4. The TV Book Club is somewhat different from the Richard & Judy Book Club in that it is a dedicated book program of 30 minutes hosted by a group of regular presenters unlike the husband and wife team joined by two special guests as was the format for the Richard & Judy Book Club. The five core regular presenters for the first series were: Jo Brand, the comedian; Nathaniel Parker, the actor; actress, Laila Rouass; comedian, Dave Spikey; and Gok Wan, fashion stylist and television presenter, representing, according to Ross "a good mix, somebody for everybody" (*You and Yours* 2010). The presenters sit on three sofas arranged in a semi-circle around a coffee table and changes in the seating plan are used to create a democratic studio space. In a review of the first episode in *The Independent*, Gerard Gilbert suggested the first episode was "more like Jo and Dave's book club" (2010) as Jo Brand sat on a central sofa next to the invited guest and shared the presentation of each item with Dave Spikey. It was also noted by several critics that Laila Rouass had little to say. After episode one, however, it became clear that the lead role was being deliberately spread between the presenters, something that was probably planned from the start of the series. For example, in episode two, Nathaniel Parker and Gok Wan led on most items; in episode three, it was Laila Rouass and Dave Spikey. Additionally, in episode three changes to the arrangement of presenters on the sofas were made, something that seemed to be a natural consequence of Wan's absence. With Brand's absence the following week, places were changed again and this has continued in subsequent episodes. Such changes have established the group as more democratic and it has rapidly developed into something resembling a real book group where there is rarely a chair but where some members might predominate, or some will be more dominant in discussing particular types of books or themes.

As a dedicated book program, the TV Book Club presents more than a discussion of that week's book. Retained from the Richard & Judy Book Club is the author segment, which introduces that book but there are other book-related features. In the first series of the show, this included a discussion with an invited guest who is usually (although not always) promoting their own book; a pre-recorded segment based around another book (for example, in episode one, comedian Mark Watson took to the streets to ask people if they knew the meaning of words contained in *The Completely Superior Person's Book of Words* by Peter Bowler); and a section entitled the "Book Club Story," which showcases a writer from the Richard & Judy Book Club speaking about their past experience of being a Book Club choice, career developments that arose from this opportunity and more generally about their writing. This segment studiously avoids any mention of the Richard & Judy Book Club, only referring to "The Book Club" as if to merge both manifestations of the Cactus book campaigns (as Ross refers to her lists in the *You and Yours* interview) into a single entity.

What is clear from this final section, and from the interview with Ross in *You and Yours*, is that Ross conceives of the TV Book Club as a continuation of the Richard & Judy Book Club. In developing the new show, Ross explained that she had tried explicitly to replicate successful aspects of the Richard and Judy formula such as the celebrity endorsement and that "the team who are selecting the books are exactly the same as before ... we're still looking for the same kind of books and we won't repeat authors and we won't repeat subject matter" from the Richard and Judy Book Club. The second series also revives from the Richard & Judy Book Club, the segment where a real book group discusses and comments on the book – missing from the first series of the TV Book Club. The official website associated with the new show (www.tvbookclub.co.uk) reinforces connections through a "Vintage Book Club" link, which takes you to a limited list of books for purchase from the Richard & Judy Book Club lists. It is important that this link is established firmly as the TV Book Club is reliant on the previous reputation built by the Richard & Judy Book Club. In the introductory section of the first episode (January 17, 2010), Spikey announced that they would be discussing "one of this year's ten best reads," the term "best read" referring to the list of books for discussion put together by the team at Cactus. This is a shift in terminology from the Richard & Judy Book Club, which only labeled its lists descriptively by year as, for example, "The Book Club 2004" and "Summer Reads 2004." The more qualitative statement of "Best Read" is an assertion that can be made only in relation to the successes of the Richard & Judy Book Club lists, as measured by the high sales figures of books on these lists and by the subsequent success of the authors, which is expressed in the "Book Club Story" sections of the program. Spikey's statement, spoken in a program broadcast in January, is predictive in the same style as other arts programs and commentary where critics are asked to speculate on who or what will be the most significant people and events featured over the coming year. Here, though, Spikey does not take his authority from a specialist critical knowledge but from the proven success of the Book Club in its previous manifestation.

There are however, other changes that might be noted that do not work only at this material level. It is interesting to note, for example, that the first book chosen for discussion was Sarah Waters' *The Little Stranger* (2009). Although Waters is a popular author whose works have also been adapted for television, this is the first time one of her books has been chosen. This might be because it is the first book of hers considered a "safe" choice for a mass broadcast book club, as all her previous works include explicitly gay or lesbian characters or themes. Specific reference was made in relation to this in both Waters' piece and in the subsequent discussion; in fact, Jo Brand directed a question to Wan (an openly gay celebrity who markets his body image and fashion programs through his identity as a gay icon) asking if he had been trying to "spot the lesbian" in the book, something Waters suggested several readers had attempted on being faced by a new book by her that did not clearly include such a character. The opening up of the TV Book Club to more adult themes might have been enabled by the new format of the book club, which is a less "domestic" set up as it includes five adults rather than a husband-and-wife team and as it is programmed in an evening slot. The specific inclusion of Wan could be read as an attempt to reach a new demographic and several posts on the TV Book Club forum mention (although usually in irritable tones) his persistent flirtations with the male guests and his constant use of the word "gorgeous" to describe people and novels alike, which can be read as a playful foregrounding of "camp." That a different kind of list is being produced might also be suggested by the second choice of novel: *Blacklands* by Belinda Bauer centers on a series of pedophilic murders, which Brand in particular expressed some horror at as a mother. However, the Richard & Judy Book Club did not entirely avoid this theme on its lists with novels such as *The Lovely Bones* (2002) narrated *post mortem* by the victim of a brutal rape and murder and *A Quiet Belief in Angels* (2006), which also deals with serial assaults on young girls.

The establishment of a regular panel of presenters, with just one guest, also helps to establish the appeal of the range and variety of the books listed for every reader. This was important in the Richard & Judy Book Club: as Richard Madeley stated in one discussion, "that's the strength of our book club ... it makes you, if you're going to play a part in it, read books you wouldn't normally choose" (*Richard & Judy – Book Club My Best Friend's Girl* 2007). This is something reiterated by Spikey in the TV Book Club discussion of *Sacred Hearts* in episode three, series one, which he claimed he would never usually have picked up to read. The important issue here is that both men go on to say how much they have enjoyed the books. However, the celebrity guests on the Richard & Judy Book Club were often chosen to reflect a particular interest in the novels – such as Rageh Omar (Somali born, British journalist and writer) to discuss *Half of Yellow Sun* by the Nigerian writer, Chimamanda Adichie Ngozi – which implied that novels might attract specific, not general, readers. However, the visual manifestation of a something looking like a real book group in the TV Book Club emphasizes the intention to provide a list of books that each reader will want to read in its entirety. The range might imply a principle of trying to appeal widely providing something for every reader but in fact, the aim is not that readers will pick and choose books from the list according to their interest. In fact, the TV Book Club website – subtitled "the official TV Book Club Book Shop" – allows all the series books to be purchased *en bloc*; an Amazon search for TV Book Club also brings up all current titles while the show is on air.

This takes us back somewhat to the idea of a "good read," which transcends genre, setting or gender. What is important for Ross is that the books are:

> entertaining and also something that's going to sustain and stay with you a bit afterwards ... [and] make you want to have a proper conversation with your friends afterwards and ... that's the key to a good book club recommendation. (*You and Yours* 2010)

Ross states that an aim of the new TV Book Club remains to encourage the public to read collectively, to make reading a social event by identifying books that everyone can enjoy and discuss either as individuals or in book groups. Indeed, in many book groups the group members will take turns choosing a book for all members to read and discuss, and the opportunity to be exposed to different literature is part of the purpose of belonging to the group. What the TV Book Club does, through Ross and her team's efforts, is to remove the wider "graft of reading" required to choose the right books to read and Ross suggests that people do trust the recommendations of her book clubs as they "know that we've worked really hard on their behalf to ... take the work out of choosing a book" (*You and Yours* 2010). She makes the point that the thousands of books published means that "there's too many books ... there's so much choice that you need something to punch through to make you notice a book ... our endorsement is ... a quality stamp of control." Ross implies here that continuing some manifestation of the book club is an important social duty, bringing confidence to the reading public that they can read books that are already identified as appropriate in terms of quality and enjoyment as well as value for money "so they're not going to risk their £6.99" (*You and Yours* 2010). The risk is also expressed in terms of people's uncertainty about their critical ability (also hampered by the lack of time to read widely) to choose suitable books both in terms of enjoyment and peer acceptability.

Yet critics question Ross's social altruism, in insisting that her book clubs are merely a commercial venture and that in promoting particular titles she is less interested in creating social cohesion and more in maintaining her reputation as one of the most influential people in the British book trade able to pick and promote books that will all become bestsellers. In response to the TV Book Club, a group of book bloggers have set up their own blog-based reading group "inspired by last week's inaugural broadcasting of the TV Book Club on More 4 ... [but] in no way trying to denigrate that club or steal its thunder" (Reading Matters 2010). This venture is hosted between four well-established book blogging sites: Dovegreyreader, Reading Matters, Savidge Reads and Other Stories. The initial post on the Reading Matters blog, notes that "the choices... were decided by us and us alone. No publishers or booksellers have been approached about this venture, and all titles selected have been purchased or borrowed by us" implying that this is their particular distinction from Ross's book clubs. Lynne Hatwell (who blogs as Dovegreyreader), in an interview with Alison Flood of *The Guardian*, makes the point that one of their rules for choosing books is that "freebies" from publishers cannot be chosen: "We aren't interested in sales or marketing and have encouraged people to borrow from libraries if they can" (Flood 2010). This implies that somehow, even though not individually financially motivated, Ross's decisions are not as independent as she claims, relying on books being sent to her by publishers (much like the Mann Booker prize) and it is the case that while Ross makes much of her role in ensuring people don't waste their £6.99 on a book they don't enjoy, in the *You and Yours* interview, she never once mentions borrowing the books from a library. Being outside of a commercial mode is clearly linked in Hatwell's mind to the quality of the discussion; her full independence from the publisher means: "we'll be saying if we haven't liked [the books] but hopefully being constructive about that" (Flood 2010), which she clearly perceives as being less possible when publishers are involved as does Gerard Gilbert in his review for *The Independent*:

> this underlines an inherent problem with the Book Club format. If the selected tome is simply there to be puffed, what is the point of the critics? ... On the other hand, if there is going to be genuine dissent, and the possibility that their top authors will be slagged off on prime time, will publishers continue to be so enamoured. (Gilbert 2010)

He concludes with the comment that The TV Book Club may "actually have teeth" following the rather negative opinions the group expressed about *The Little Stranger* in episode one. He wonders if this will be allowed to continue in future episodes, which seems to imply an assumption that the program's success is measured by the book sales it generates and not by the viewing figures it attracts. Although Ross does rely on the submissions of publishers for her long-list, presumably she is not compelled to do so and although the success of the TV Book Club will inevitably be connected to book sales, the sanction of the publishers seems unlikely to be required. After all, the few authors who have subsequently expressed dissatisfaction with being chosen as Richard and Judy book choices have not reduced the power of that brand. To dismiss the TV Book Club as complicit in a marketing deal between Cactus and the publishers seems to overlook the point. Viewers who have chosen to watch the TV Book Club are not gullible or ignorant; they will not be convinced by continual and unanimously glowing reports of these books any more that they will be attracted by negativity posing as independence. What they require is a balanced discussion against which to match their own opinions, not just negative critique of books, which, after all, have already been judged as good reads through their inclusion on the TV Book Club list, and in which they may well have already invested their time and money.

Yet, the commercial aspects of the TV Book Club remain uncomfortably at the fore as can be illustrated through the very first episode. In the first show 10 minutes were taken up by discussion with Chris Evans, the invited guest, discussing (or promoting!) his recently published autobiography. As Gilbert notes: "the club predictably 'loved' [it] as he was sitting there" (2010). Viewers are clearly uncomfortable with blatant promotion; something suggested by the appreciation of Emilia Fox's appearance on the show in episode three, series one. The actress was introduced as substituting for Wan as well as to "discuss her favourite books." Having a guest who was manifestly not there to promote a product was well received; one of the forum posts had "praise for Emilia Fox – her obvious love of books came across and her interest and enthusiasm would inspire people to go out and buy books" (After episode three 2010). Fox mentioned books she was currently reading and those that had influenced her. She provided her definition of a good book: one that she had to keep rushing back to in between filming takes. Where the regular presenters were familiar with the books she mentioned the discussion became more general. In response to Dave Spikey's enquiry if she would like to write a book, Fox only conceded that she might consider an adaptation but not an autobiography as "no one would want to read it." In a program that prides itself on being independent of direct financial gain from the book choices, to have celebrities blatantly promoting their individual product sat uncomfortably so Fox's contribution that week signaled attempts to dilute commercialism. This section has continued into the subsequent episodes where guests have spoken about current projects – including, for example, Martine McCutcheon who had recently published her first novel – but the focus is on the guest as an enthusiastic reader and more general conversation about their own reading preferences is encouraged. This is not to say that promotion of their own books is off the agenda of the guest celebrities, nor that the buying of books becomes irrelevant. At the beginning and the end of each episode, one of the presenters draws attention to the TV Book Club website where comments can be made and where viewers can vote for their favorite book but also, most importantly, where the books can be bought.

A further problematic relates to more generally to celebrity endorsements as highlighted by Danielle Fuller and DeNel Rehberg Sedo in this volume. Ross identifies this as one of the key successful elements transferred from the Richard & Judy Book Club to the TV Book Club. Patrick Gale, an author whose *Notes from an Exhibition* (2007) appeared on the Richard & Judy Book Club list in 2008, was also interviewed in the same *You and Yours* edition as Ross; he suggested that the success of the Richard & Judy Book Club was "to do with the celebrity judgement. It's very odd that readers trust a celebrity endorsement far more than they trust a prestigious literary critic." However, for Ross, the celebrity endorsement makes perfect sense:

> not because … celebrity endorsement is necessarily a fabulous thing … all, I'm going to buy that book just because [of] that particular person … but I think that a lot of book critics can be quite intimidating … The beauty of Richard and Judy and now our new five presenters is that they speak like the rest of us and they're not known for their literary prowess on purpose … [viewers] feel that they can talk about books in the same way as the people that they are seeing on TV. (*You and Yours* 2010)

In her view it is not odd at all that general readers prefer their books mediated through the discussion of people who are recognizable as general readers rather than known as literary critics. This does beg the question of why celebrities are needed specifically; why not just rely on the discussions of real book group, which are aired as an associated part of the Book Club discussions? The fact that this has been reinstated in the second series of the TV Book Club suggests that viewers are interested in the opinions of people who are "like the rest of us." Yet, in a culture in which "celebrity" status confers value, readers perhaps require also the opinions of discussants different in that one significant way. Endorsement incorporates within its sense the notion of approbation, an official approval; therefore, it is important that the celebrity discussants are *not* us in terms of their celebrity status, which separates them from the ordinary reader, but in ways that maintain a trust. They differ from the critic who is not ordinary in terms of reading and whose specific expertise is intimidating. The celebrities are not choosing the books themselves (which would imply a "literary prowess") but mediating books recommended by another trustworthy source while still assuring viewers that they are enthusiastic, if amateur, readers. This trust for the TV Book Club builds on the foundation of the Richard & Judy Book Club, which Ross considers to have "a good reputation with the public ... [because] they know we don't get paid to make a selection ... we are completely independent" (*You and Yours* 2010). Her independence from the publishers in an environment where it is usually understood that people are paid to endorse, creates a sense of the books' genuine quality. However, as we have seen, the reputation of the lists may rest on a more circular notion that all the books chosen have been best sellers because they are "good reads" (rather than that they are bestsellers through being chosen). In this way, the lists retain their value for readers who might still maintain suspicion over the pure independence of the Book Clubs remains.

And what of these "good reads" and the celebrities' opinions of these? What seems most disappointing to viewers is the continual deferral of the discussion about the book. In the first episode in particular, the presenters continually stated that the program's purpose was to discuss the book of the week but this happened only after all of the other features, leaving a mere a few minutes at the end of the 30-minute program for an unsatisfactory discussion. Flood notes that "Jo Brand and other celebrities spent about two minutes discussing ... *The Little Stranger*" (Flood 2010) and on the official website there was much disappointment about the short time spent discussing the book. In the live chat with Sarah Waters, one of the posters even asks her if she was disappointed that so little time was spent discussing her work – a question that Waters diplomatically ignored (*The Little Stranger* by Sarah Waters 2010). One book blogger summed it up it in this way:

> The discussion ... felt rushed, unorganised and critical. It seemed to appear that all the panel members disliked the book, but without enough time it was impossible to decide whether they didn't enjoy any of it, or just certain sections. The rushed discussion failed to address any aspect of the book properly and just as it seemed to be getting going it was all over. (Farm Lane Books 2010)

The unsatisfactory nature of the discussion was not merely about time, but more about the narrow range of the discussion, which got stuck on one aspect of the novel (the narration) that many of the group had found problematic but that may not have been an issue for other readers. Gilbert commented on how the negative reception the group gave Sarah Waters' *The Little Stranger* compared oddly with Jo Brand "manufacturing positive unanimity for what had actually been an equivocal discussion" (2010) as she jumped into the discussion to sum up by asking "but are we all agreed it's a good read?" It was an uncomfortable moment where the mechanisms of a broadcast reading group were exposed, in the attempt to provide an acceptable conclusion with a formula clearly carried over from the Richard & Judy Book Club, which did not reflect the opinions expressed but blatantly did promote the worthiness of the choice. In the *You and Yours* interview, Ross also recognized the problems in that first discussion:

> the guys had forgotten that we're coming from the point of, we've got ten brilliant books and we want them to discuss them but we don't want them to completely get carried away with becoming critics and I think in the first show they did that … then they got the hang of it … and they realised that it's just about insight[ful] discussion. (*You and Yours* 2010)

Certainly terminology like "Dickensian" and "narrator" had cropped up plus a fairly complex explanation from Spikey about his frustration with the narrative point of view, which prevents the reader from "seeing" the strange occurrences at first hand. However, it would be patronizing and probably incorrect to suggest that the viewers, who are likely to be regular readers, would not be able to engage with a discussion at this level. Nor is the problem entirely temporal, although, in most real book groups discussion about the book would be longer. With pre-recorded segments and a standard format, it would be difficult to increase the time allocated to the book discussion yet, within the same time frame of around five minutes, the final book discussion is an aspect of the show that has improved rapidly. What has changed is the range of the discussion. In the later shows, all the presenters, and the guest(s), contribute, and they consider character, narrative structure, the use of history where relevant, the evocative nature of settings, the writing style and the presentation of feeling. Increasingly confident, the presenters are prepared to explore their own personal narratives in relation to the text, which is a common feature of book group discussion. For example, Wan linked the book *Brixton Beach* to his personal experiences, admitting that it had made him want to go and talk to his father about his experiences of being an immigrant to Britain. The discussion of *Brixton Beach* perhaps did not have intellectual depth (as defined by academic readers and critics) but it had breadth, a much more valuable commodity for the viewers who now might encounter different opinions on an aspect of the book they have thought about or discussed with friends or in their own book group, even if they had different views.

In the interview with Alison Flood, Hatwell makes the comment that the Not the TV Book Group "will perhaps feel more like a real book group" (Flood 2010) but it is difficult to know precisely what she means by this. In several ways their online book discussion is less like the book groups who meet in people's homes and libraries than is The TV Book Club. This is not to do with it taking place online – many jokes on the blogs regarding pulling up sofas, having another scone or even a claim that the group is being hosted in one member's grandmother's home, make reference to the equal value of a virtual space for discussion – but that the membership of the group and structure of the discussion is very different. Not the TV Book Group lacks a stable group whose discussions are shaped by the accruing knowledge of each other as readers. In their discussions, there is the core of four experienced book bloggers who choose the books and who are visible in the forum discussions; in addition anyone else who logs into the blog can participate and can drop in and out of the discussion at any time. This creates a much larger and more fluid group than would usually be found in a face-to-face group (if that is what Hatwell means by a "real book group"). In addition, the online discussion has no end point. People are encouraged to post later than the date designated for the group's meeting, particularly if they have not read or finished the book as the group allow plot "spoilers" as an acceptable part of the discussion. So unlike both the "real" groups and The TV Book Club there is no summing up, no opportunity to finalize that endorsement with a judgment about whether or not this is a "good read." The TV Book Group members may be a group who is paid to sit and discuss these books, and filmed while doing it, which is not the normal experience of a book group, but the members have all read the book and appear genuine in putting forward their views and in responding to the other group members; isn't this essentially what a book group is? It was particularly satisfying to see Alistair McGowan, a guest on the second series of the TV Book Club, brandishing his disintegrating copy of *Ellis Island* – a truly well-read book.

For book groups as well as individuals, what to read can be a pressing question. Whichever model a book group follows (for example two common ones are that all groups read the same title, or that each member brings a different title to recommend for reading outside the group) a popular method for making the choice of what to read is to look at the choices of various broadcast book discussions as well as reviews in newspapers and magazines. The TV Book Club is useful in providing a list for those reading groups who were previously reliant on, and enjoying, working their way through much of the Richard & Judy Book Club lists. Yet, promoters of such recommendation lists need to carefully balance commercialism against the needs and perceptions of those whom they rely on to make these reading "campaigns" successful – the readers. Through the debates and discussions around the Richard & Judy Book Club in particular, readers are more wary of how their consumption of books might be being manipulated. Ross appears to be very aware of this in her criticism of Richard and Judy's 2010 comeback. *The Bookseller* reports that apparently she has "complained to the Advertising Standards Agency that 'people need to be clear that this is not a continuation of the previous book club'" (Bookseller 2010) because what Richard and Judy are doing with WH Smith is entirely different as a "paid-for promotion." While it should not be lost from our sights the hard cash value the book club represents to the book industry and to the people involved in promoting this as a brand name, the democratic principles of communal reading remain a prominent feature of

Richard and Judy's new club. Taking a wholly online format, which incorporates blogs, reader reviews and videos in addition to the features established on earlier versions of the website seems a popular move for readers who continue to post lively and confident responses to the books they have read. The development from broadcast to digital spaces seems an enabling one for readers and an indication of the future shape of communal reading experience.

Reference List

After episode three. 2010. *The TV Book Club Forum*, 3 February. http://forum.tvbookclub.co.uk/showthread.php?t=3561 (accessed 5 March 2010).

Farm Lane Books. 2010. The First Episode of the TV Book Club. *Farm Lane Books Blog*, 17 Jan. http://www.farmlanebooks.co.uk/?p=4070 (accessed 5 March 2010).

Flood, Alison. 2010. Forget Richard and Judy, join the Not the TV Book club. *The Guardian Books Blog*, 5 February. http://www.guardian.co.uk/books/booksblog/2010/feb/05/richard-judy-not-tv-book-club (accessed 5 March 2010).

Gallagher, Victoria (2010) ASA to investigate complaint over WH Smith book ad. *The Bookseller* http://www.thebookseller.com/news/131845-asa-to-investigate-complaint-over-w-h-smith-book-club-ad.html (accessed 29 November 2010).

Gilbert, Gerard. 2010. Book Club begins new chapter without Richard and Judy. *The Independent*, 18 January. http://www.independent.co.uk/arts-entertainment/books/news/book-club-begins-new-chapter-without-richard-and-judy-1871108.html (accessed 5 March 2010).

Reading Matters. 2010. Not the TV Book Group. *Reading Matters*, 24 January. http://kimbofo.typepad.com/readingmatters/2010/01/not-the-tv-book-group.html (accessed 5 March 2010).

Richard & Judy: My Best Friend's Girl. Video clip [nd]. *www.Youtube.com* http://www.youtube.com/watch?v=iYZfARvUHyo (accessed 7 March 2010).

The Little Stranger by Sarah Waters. 2010 *Live author web chats: The TV Book Club forum*, 18 January. http://forum.tvbookclub.co.uk/showthread.php?t=3547 (accessed 7 March 2010).

The TV Book Club. 2010. http://www.tvbookclub.co.uk/webapp/wcs/stores/servlet/qs_home_tbp?storeId=351&catalogId=353&langId=100 (accessed 7 March 2010).

The TV Book Club. 2010a. More4, 17 January.

The TV Book Club. 2010b. More4, 24 January.

The TV Book Club. 2010c. More4, 31 January.

The TV Book Club. 2010d. More4, 28 February.

The TV Book Club Forum. 2010. http://forum.tvbookclub.co.uk (accessed 7 March 2010).

You and Yours. 2010. BBC Radio 4, 17 February.

Appendix
The Richard & Judy Book Club and Summer Reads Lists by Year

2004 Book Club

Monica Ali, *Brick Lane*
Martina Cole, *The Know*
William Dalrymple, *White Mughals*
Zoe Heller, *Notes on a Scandal*
David Nicholls, *Starter for Ten*
Joseph O'Connor, *The Star of the Sea*
Alice Sebold, *The Lovely Bones*
Asne Seierstad, *The Bookseller of Kabul*
Nigel Slater, *Toast*
Adriana Trigiani, *Lucia, Lucia*

Summer Reads

Cecelia Ahern, *P.S. I Love You*
Jennifer Donnelly, *A Gathering Light*
Maile Meloy, *Liars and Saints*
Bella Pollen, *Hunting Unicorns*
Ben Richards, *The Mermaid and the Drunks*
P.J. Tracy, *Want to Play?*

2005 Book Club

William Broderick, *The Sixth Lamentation*
Paula Byrne, *Perdita: The Life of Mary Robinson*
Justin Cartwright, *The Promise of Happiness*
Karen Joy Fowler, *The Jane Austen Book Club*
Chris Heath, *Feel: Robbie Williams*
David Mitchell, *Cloud Atlas*
Audrey Niffenegger, *The Time Traveller's Wife*
Jodi Picoult, *My Sister's Keeper*
Andrew Taylor, *The American Boy*
Carlos Ruiz Zafón, *The Shadow of the Wind*

Summer Reads

Karen Quinn, *The Ivy Chronicles*
George Hagen, *The Laments*
Anthony Capella, *The Food of Love*
Susan Fletcher, *Eve Green*
Ben Sherwood, *The Death and Life of Charlie St Cloud*
David Wolstencroft, *Good News, Bad News*

2006 Book Club

Julian Barnes, *Arthur and George*
Richard Benson, *The Farm*
Geraldine Brooks, *March*
Michael Connelly, *The Lincoln Lawyer*
Nichole Krauss, *The History of Love*
Anchee Min, *Empress Orchid*
Kate Mosse, *Labyrinth*
Eva Rice, *The Lost Art of Keeping Secrets*
Andrew Smith, *Moondust*

Summer Reads

Sam Bourne, *The Righteous Men*
Victoria Hislop, *The Island*
Elisabeth Hyde, *The Abortionist's Daughter*
Dorothy Koomson, *My Best Friend's Girl*
Elizabeth Kostova, *The Historian*
Jim Lynch, *The Highest Tide*

2007 Book Club

Chimamanda Ngozi Adichie, *Half of a Yellow Sun*
William Boyd, *Restless*
A.M. Homes, *This Book Will Save Your Life*
Catherine Ryan Hyde, *Love in the Present Tense*
Griff Rhys Jones, *Semi-Detached*
Lori Lansens, *The Girls*
James Robertson, *The Testament of Gideon Mack*
Jed Rubenfeld, *The Interpretation of Murder*

Summer Reads

Kim Edwards, *The Memory Keeper's Daughter*
Jane Fallon, *Getting Rid of Matthew*
Simon Kernick, *Relentless*
Mary Lawson, *The Other Side of the Bridge*
Mark Mills, *The Savage Garden*
Kate Morton, *The House at Riverton*
Paul Torday, *Salmon Fishing in the Yemen*
Jonathan Tropper, *How to Talk to a Widower*

2008 Book Club

Tim Butcher, *Blood River*
Peter Ho Davies, *The Welsh Girl*
R.J. Ellory, *A Quiet Belief in Angels*
Joshua Ferris, *Then We Came to the End*
Patrick Gale, *Notes from an Exhibition*
Khaled Hosseini, *A Thousand Splendid Suns*
Lloyd Jones, *Mister Pip*
Katherine McMahon, *The Rose of Sebastopol*
Danny Scheinmann, *Random Acts of Heroic Love*
Mark Slouka, *The Visible World*

Summer Reads

Linwood Barclay, *No Time for Goodbye*
James Bradley, *The Resurrectionist*
Margaret Cezair-Thompson, *The Pirate's Daughter*
Julia Gregson, *East of the Sun*
John Hart, *Down River*
Sadie Jones, *The Outcast*
Toni Jordan, *Addition*
Rebecca Miller, *The Private Lives of Pippa Lee*

2009 Book Club

Kate Atkinson, *When Will There Be Good News?*
Beatrice Colin, *The Luminous Life of Lilly Aphrodite*
Andrew Davidson, *The Gargoyle*

David Ebershoff, *The 19th Wife*
Steven Galloway, *The Cellist of Sarajevo*
Jesse Kellerman, *The Brutal Art*
Joseph O'Neill, *Netherland*
Frances Osborne, *The Bolter*
Kate Summerscale, *The Suspicions of Mr. Whicher*
Elizabeth H. Winthrop, *December*

Summer Reads

Bateman, *Mystery Man*
Dave Boling, *Guernica*
Stephen L. Carter, *Palace Council*
Jill Dawson, *The Great Lover*
Charles Elton, *Mr Toppit*
Julian Fellowes, *Past Imperfect*
Janice Y.K. Lee, *The Piano Teacher*
Sue Miller, *The Senator's Wife*

2010 The TV Book Club

Belinda Bauer, *Blacklands*
Sarah Dunant, *Sacred Hearts*
Nick Hornby, *Juliet, Naked*
Liz Jensen, *The Rapture*
Wendy Moore, *Wedlock*
George Pelecanos, *The Way Home*
Matthew Quick, *The Silver Linings Play Book*
Roma Tearne, *Brixton Beach*
Abraham Verghese, *Cutting for Stone*
Sarah Waters, *The Little Stranger*

Summer Reads

Heather Gudenkauf, *The Weight of Silence*
Kate Kerrigan, *Ellis Island*
Clare Morrall, *The Man Who Disappeared*
Iain Pears, *Stone's Fall*
Matthew Plampin, *The Devil's Acre*
Kathryn Stockett, *The Help*
Katherine Webb, *The Legacy*
Lucie Whitehouse, *The Bed I Made*

The Richard & Judy Book Club 2010

Rachel Hore, *A Place of Secrets*
Rosamund Lupton, *Sister*
Ben Macintyre, *Operation Mincemeat*
Maria McCann, *The Wilding*
Jo Nesbo, *The Snowman*
Naseem Rakha, *The Crying Tree*
Delphine de Vigan, *No & Me*
Thomas Trofimuk, *Waiting for Columbus*

TV Book Club 2011

Emma Donoghue, *Room*
Alan Furst, *Spies of the Balkans*
Daisy Goodwin, *My Last Duchess*
Patrick Hennessey, *The Junior Officers' Reading Club*
Andrea Levy, *The Long Song*
Sarita Mandanna, *Tiger Hills*
Jon McGregor, *Even The Dogs*
Catherine O'Flynn, *The News Where You Are*
Michael Robotham, *Bleed For Me*
Rebecca Skloot, *The Immortal Life Of Henrietta Lacks*

Richard & Judy Book Club Spring Reads 2011

Sarah Blake, *The Postmistress*
Suzanne Bugler, *This Perfect World*
Emma Donoghue, *Room*
Nigel Farndale, *The Blasphemer*
Gregg Hurrwitz, *You're Next*
Lucinda Riley, *Hothouse Flower*
Helen Simonson, *Major Pettigrew's Last Stand*
Rose Tremain, *Trespass*

Richard & Judy Book Club Summer Reads 2011

Suzanna Dunn, *The Confession of Katherine Howard*
Erin Kelly, *The Poison Tree*
Bella Pollen, *The Summer of the Bear*
Anna Quindlen, *Every Last One*
Jed Rubenfeld, *The Death Instinct*
Natasha Solomons, *The Novel in the Viola*
Elizabeth Speller, *The Return of Captain John Emmett*
Sarah Winman, When God Was a Rabbit

Index